How to Measure a World?

New Jewish Philosophy and Thought

Zachary J. Braiterman

MARTIN SHUSTER

How to Measure a World?

A PHILOSOPHY OF JUDAISM

INDIANA UNIVERSITY PRESS

This book is a publication of

Indiana University Press
Office of Scholarly Publishing
Herman B Wells Library 350
1320 East 10th Street
Bloomington, Indiana 47405 USA

iupress.org

© 2021 by Martin Shuster

All rights reserved
No part of this book may be reproduced or utilized in any form or by any means, electronic or mechanical, including photocopying and recording, or by any information storage and retrieval system, without permission in writing from the publisher. The paper used in this publication meets the minimum requirements of the American National Standard for Information Sciences—Permanence of Paper for Printed Library Materials, ANSI Z39.48-1992.

Manufactured in the United States of America
First printing 2021

Library of Congress Cataloging-in-Publication Data

Names: Shuster, Martin, author.
Title: How to measure a world? : a philosophy of Judaism / Martin Shuster.
Description: Bloomington : Indiana University Press, 2021. | Series: New Jewish philosophy and thought | Includes bibliographical references and index.
Identifiers: LCCN 2020027348 (print) | LCCN 2020027349 (ebook) | ISBN 9780253054531 (hardback) | ISBN 9780253054548 (paperback) | ISBN 9780253054555 (ebook)
Subjects: LCSH: Judaism—Philosophy. | Jewish philosophy—21st century.
Classification: LCC BM565 .S463 2021 (print) | LCC BM565 (ebook) | DDC 181/.06—dc23
LC record available at https://lccn.loc.gov/2020027348
LC ebook record available at https://lccn.loc.gov/2020027349

For Lev and Amilia—
May the world be worthy of you, and you of it.

מים רבים לא יוכלו לכבות את־האהבה

CONTENTS

Acknowledgments	ix
Introduction	1

I.
Having a World

§ 1. Wonder and World: Maimonides's Phenomenology	29
§ 2. Suffering and World: Adorno's Negativity	73

II.
Preconditions of Having a World

§ 3. History and World: Benjamin and Adorno on Ethical Depth	119
§ 4. Language and World: Levinas and Cavell on Ethical Foundations	158
Conclusion	202
Works Cited	209
Index	239

ACKNOWLEDGMENTS

The ideas that make up the argument of this book have evolved over the last decade, and there are a great many people to thank. Above all, I have benefited from being able to present this material at several colleges and universities, namely Furman University, the Johns Hopkins University, Worcester Polytechnic Institute, Lehigh University, Hamilton College, Avila University, Fordham University, Marlboro College, and the University of Nevada. I have also benefited from the opportunity to present this material at the American Academy of Religion, the Association for Jewish Studies, the Levinas Research Circle, the North American Levinas Society, and the Society for Continental Philosophy in a Jewish Context.

In addition to the various audience members in attendance at all these presentations, I have also benefited especially from encounters with Deborah Achtenberg, Steven Affeldt, David Armstrong, Jenny Astin, Wes Atkinson, Nancy Bauer, Gordon Bearn, Tahl Ben-Yehuda, Bettina Bergo, Jeffrey Bernstein, Zak Braiterman, Sharon Brous, Martijn Bujis, Emily-Jane Cohen, Mercy Corredor, Drew Dalton, Julia Kolchinsky Dasbach, Hent de Vries, Tarek Dika, Kathryn Doran, Oona Eisenstadt, Richard Eldridge, Lizzie Finnegan, Eckart Förster, Xandy Frisch, Samir Gandesha, Daniela Ginsburg, Lara Giordano, David Glickman, Peter Gordon, Tim Gould, Lisa Guenther, Luc Gutiérrez, Espen Hammer, Annabel Herzog, Dana Hollander, Alex Host, Aaron Hughes, Owen

Hulatt, Ada Jaarsma, Marianne Janack, Kelly Dean Jolley, Claire Katz, Kathy Kiloh, Alan Kim, Olga Knizhnik, Carly Lane, Sandra Laugier, Amos Levi, Ruth Leys, Iain Macdonald, Paola Marrati, Kelly Minerva, Edward Mooney, Ryan Nace, Anne O'Byrne, Michael Paradiso-Michau, Ken Parsons, Diane Perpich, Henry Pickford, Terry Pinkard, Robert Pippin, Shari Rabin, Kathryn Reklis, Kevin Schilbrack, Erin Seeba, Stuart Seltzer, Shayna Sheinfeld, Oshrat Silberbusch, Lissa Skitolsky, Santiago Slabodsky, Leslie Dorrough Smith, Joshua Snyder, James South, Jill Stauffer, Lauren Shizuko Stone, Mina Suk, Jonadas Techio, Yannik Thiem, Stephen Vicchio, Drew Walker, Debi Wechsler, Rick Werner, Elliot Wolfson, and Aaron Zaiman. My deepest and sincerest apologies to anyone I may have forgotten.

My friends, students, and colleagues (or former colleagues) at Goucher College—despite so many things going on—have made research and teaching a rewarding thing to continue doing. I am most grateful to everyone in the Center for Geographies of Justice and the Center for Humanities, my two "homes" here, and I especially want to thank La Jerne Cornish, Seble Dawit, Kelly Brown Douglas, Ann Duncan, Robin Herlands Cresiski, Ailish Hopper, Jas Levy, Lana Oweidat, Ellie Pelton, Phaye Poliakoff-Chen, Larisa Reznik, Zaidel Sanchez, Nyasha Grayman-Simpson, Charlee Sterling, and Isabelle Turner for discussions that contributed to my thinking in this book.

A large part of this book was supported by a subgrant from Stephen Grimm's "Varieties of Understanding" project, funded by the John Templeton Foundation. I am grateful to Stephen Grimm, and to J. Aaron Simmons for serving as my coprincipal investigator and also grateful to Sai Bhatawadekar, William Edelglass, and Amer Latif for their involvement in the project. I am grateful to all the students, colleagues, and members of the public who participated in the discussions that we organized on "religious understanding" by means of this grant; it has all greatly aided my understanding and my research.

I am equally grateful to Avila University and to Goucher College for providing environments and support that were conducive to working on a project that spanned so many figures and issues; the same is true of Beth Shalom and Chizuk Amuno, which aided the construction of this book in other, but no less academic and important, ways.

I also have to thank Dee Mortensen and Ashante Thomas for their work on this project. I am especially grateful to Martin Kavka and Aaron W. Hughes for penetrating and useful comments that greatly improved the manuscript. Martin Kavka has been so generous with his time and thoughts, and I am so grateful for his erudition and charity. Finally, I am also grateful to Carol McGillivray for managing the copyediting.

Earlier portions of the book appeared in several sources, notably the *Journal of Religion*, where a shorter and earlier version of chapter 1 appeared as Martin Shuster, "On the Importance of the World: Phenomenology in Maimonides's Guide of the Perplexed," *Journal of Religion* 99, no. 2 (April 2019): 194–218, copyright © 2019 by the University of Chicago (reproduced by permission); the *Graduate Faculty Philosophy Journal*, where a shorter and earlier version of chapter 2 appeared as Martin Shuster, "Adorno and Negative Theology," *Graduate Faculty Philosophy Journal* 37, no. 1 (2016): 97–130, copyright © 2016 by the *Graduate Faculty Philosophy Journal* (reproduced by permission); an earlier, shorter version of chapter 3 appeared as Martin Shuster, "Philosophy of History" in The Routledge Companion to the Frankfurt School. Copyright (©) 2018 From The Routledge Companion to the Frankfurt School by Peter Gordon, Espen Hammer, and Axel Honneth. Reproduced by permission of Taylor and Francis Group, LLC, a division of Informa plc; and, finally, the *Journal for Cultural and Religious Theory*, where a shorter and earlier version of chapter 4 appeared as

Martin Shuster, "On the Ethical Basis of Language: Some Themes in Davidson, Cavell, and Levinas," *Journal for Cultural and Religious Theory* 14, no. 2 (2015): 241–66 (reproduced by permission). Thank you to all of these venues for allowing me to reproduce this work here in updated and modified form.

I am grateful to my parents, family, and friends. My mother, Raisa "Lyalya" Shuster (zt"l), passed away during the writing of this book; this is not the book to dedicate to her (that's a book for the future), but she has certainly been in my mind throughout the writing, and she taught me much about how to measure a world.

Finally, I am thankful for Robin, Amilia, and Lev, who together form the innermost core of my world. This book, and its exploration of the notion of world, especially in the context of Judaism, is dedicated to Amilia and Lev, who daily teach me about what it means and can mean to love the world.

How to Measure a World?

INTRODUCTION

What animates this book is a suggestion by the philosopher Emmanuel Levinas that Judaism ought to be understood as a sort of anachronism. Here is how he describes the idea: Judaism, he writes, "is a non-coincidence with its time . . . an *anachronism* . . . the simultaneous presence of a youth that is attentive to reality and impatient to change it, and an old age that has seen it all and is returning to the origin of things."[1] The image is typical of Levinas—precise, puzzling, ultimately playful. He continues, suggesting that "the desire to conform to one's time is not the supreme imperative for a human . . . monotheism and its moral revelation constitute the concrete fulfilment, beyond all mythology, of the primordial anachronism of the human."[2] Later in the essay, he harnesses the same idea to suggest that Judaism "has always wished to be a simultaneous engagement and disengagement," noting that the "most committed [*engagé*] . . . [the] one who can never be silent, the prophet, is also the most separate being . . . the person least capable of becoming an institution."[3]

Such a gloss of Judaism is by no means clear; it also, at first glance, might make contemporary readers uncomfortable in at least two ways. First, Levinas appears to claim that

---

1. Emmanuel Levinas, "Judaism and the Present," in *Difficult Freedom: Essays on Judaism* (Baltimore, MD: Johns Hopkins University Press, 1960), 212–13.
2. Ibid.
3. Ibid., 213.

Judaism has an essence, an idea that many now find questionable. As the famous scholar of Jewish mysticism, Gershom Scholem, put it, "Judaism cannot be defined according to its essence, since it has no essence."[4] And this apart from the fact that even if they agree about there being an essence to Judaism, particular Jews are likely to disagree about what that essence is (cue here the joke about two Jews and three opinions). Second, Levinas also appears to conflate Judaism and monotheism, an idea that is open to debate in light of alternative origins for monotheism.[5]

One tempting way to read Levinas's remarks is as expressing the standard picture of Jewish difference and of the relationship between Judaism and the world: that the Jew stands apart from the world even as he or she is a part of that world (think of Judah Leib Gordon's Haskalah ideal of being a Jew "in your home" and "a man outside of it").[6] My suggestion—and the aim of this book—is to read Levinas's remarks as *philosophical* assertions. Doing so is to prioritize

---

4. Gershom Scholem, "What Is Judaism?," trans. Jonathan Shipman, in *On the Possibility of Jewish Mysticism in Our Time and Other Essays*, ed. Avraham Shapira (Philadelphia: Jewish Publication Society, 1997), 114.

5. See, for example, Jan Assmann, *Of God and Gods: Egypt, Israel, and the Rise of Monotheism* (Madison: University of Wisconsin Press, 2008). See also *Moses and Monotheism* in volume 23 of Sigmund Freud, *The Standard Edition of the Complete Psychological Works of Sigmund Freud*, trans. James Strachey, Anna Freud, and Alan Tyson, 24 vols. (London: Hogarth, 2001). More recently, see James Hoffmeier, *Akhenaten and the Origins of Monotheism* (Oxford: Oxford University Press, 2015). See also Gilad Sharvit and Karen S. Feldman, *Freud and Monotheism: Moses and the Violent Origins of Religion* (New York: Fordham University Press, 2018). One can make this point another way by noting the likely evolution of ancient Israelite religion, likely from polytheism to henotheism and only later to monotheism. On this point, see Fritz Stolz, *Einführung in den Biblischen Monotheismus* (Darmstadt, Ger.: Wissenschaftliche Buchgesellschaft, 1996).

6. For more on Gordon, see Michael Stanislawski, *For Whom Do I Toil?: Judah Leib Gordon and the Crisis of Russian Jewry* (Oxford: Oxford University Press, 1988). In this context, note how Stanislawski stresses that Gordon essentially had no sophisticated philosophy of Judaism.

the suggestion that Judaism or monotheism (or both) is a "concrete fulfilment" of the "*primordial* anachronism of the human" (my emphasis, and with Levinas's stress on *primordial* as exactly suggesting such a philosophical approach). These phrases suggest a distinct tenor to Levinas's claims: they are fundamentally philosophical claims—more specifically, they are *phenomenological* ones.

Phenomenology, a philosophical tradition chiefly developed in the nineteenth century by Edmund Husserl (but having precursors),[7] becomes a rich and variegated philosophical tradition, claiming figures as diverse as Martin Heidegger, Maurice Merleau-Ponty, Jan Patočka, and Jean-Paul Sartre (just to name a few).[8] From its beginning, it is also a "*radical* way of doing philosophy,"[9] and so the obviously nonconformist elements of Levinas's statements here should not be surprising. One early thought in this tradition is the idea that one can gain philosophical insight from a description of phenomena, and that what is real and objective is so only through particular forms of appearance. One commentator puts it well when he notes that "phenomenology is not a theory about the *merely* appearing, or to put it differently, appearances are not *mere* appearances. *For how things appear is an integral part of what they really are.*"[10] Any particular appearance cannot inherently or immediately be reduced to illusion and cannot simply be understood as

---

7. For an introduction to Husserl's phenomenology, see Dan Zahavi, *Husserl's Phenomenology* (Palo Alto, CA: Stanford University Press, 2003).

8. The most comprehensive introduction to this entire tradition is Dan Zahavi, *The Oxford Handbook of the History of Phenomenology* (Oxford: Oxford University Press, 2018). Levinas has long been recognized as a phenomenologist. For a succinct recent approach to this point, see James R. Mensch, *Levinas's Existential Analytic: A Commentary on "Totality and Infinity"* (Evanston, IL: Northwestern University Press, 2015).

9. Dermot Moran, *Introduction to Phenomenology* (London: Routledge, 2002), 4.

10. Zahavi, *Husserl's Phenomenology*, 55. Emphasis added.

subjective, for the distinction between objective and subjective is itself one that is decided within an earlier sphere of appearance. Phenomenology begins with the idea that there are philosophical insights to be had from figuring out how something can appear in the first place. Phenomenology may therefore be taken to be concerned with the modes by which things are given to us, the means by which they appear. For some basic examples, think for a moment about how a particular object can appear at all. Or how something can appear as illusory. How certain situations appear to be boring. Or how a particular object can come to appear as a work of art.

Phenomenologists sometimes address these types of puzzles by noting that our relationship with the world is fundamentally practical: that we are *in* a world. It is only later that we might take a theoretical stance toward the world: that we think *about* a world.[11] Since Husserl, phenomenology has

---

11. Although this will become apparent only at the conclusion of this book, I can note now that while the orientation of this book has certain overlaps with Fackenheim's invocation of "world," my orientation is fundamentally different from how "world" is taken in Emil L. Fackenheim, *To Mend the World* (Bloomington: Indiana University Press, 1994). Fackenheim also attempts a sort of phenomenological analysis, but it occurs a bit downstream from mine, instead orienting itself around the alleged phenomenological category of resistance (and thereby *tikun* or repair); it is in that way concerned with assessing a world, not with the very production of one. The category of תיקון (*tikun* or repair) does, however, raise broader and important questions about the relationship between this study and Jewish mysticism, exemplified chiefly but not exclusively by *The Zohar* and related works. Because this topic is so multifaceted and so extensive across time, it is simply impossible for me to offer a sustained account of how the argument here relates to Jewish mystical trends and approaches. I can note, however, that, fundamentally, at a very high altitude, it is my belief that the basic phenomenological (ontological) categories deployed here (world, negativity, positivity, history, and so forth) can be mapped onto various moves within this tradition. To my mind, this highlights again the importance of Maimonides to the story that I am telling (see the discussion that follows). While Maimonides and the kabbalists are generally taken to be opposed to each other, I think at this sort of high-altitude view, the oppositions fade from view. It is not by accident, then, for example, that one of the oldest Hebrew translations of Maimonides's *Guide for*

oriented itself around the idea that philosophy could explore not only this (derivative) theoretical stance toward the world, but also our (originary) practical stance toward it and within it. Cognitive relations—of the sort that identify, grasp, or abstract from the world in conceptual thought—are derivative of a more primordial relationship with the world. Reading Levinas's claims in a philosophical or phenomenological register would be to see them as suggesting that there is some basic element about human beings—an element that equally may be termed *Judaism* or *anachronism* or *monotheism*—that is somehow central to human experience being the way that it is, indeed for human experience seemingly being possible at all (and equally important here is the thought that this element is often overlooked or forgotten or possibly even somehow eroded). Levinas confirms this reading when he states that "to be Jewish is not a particularity; it is a modality. *Everyone is a little bit Jewish*, and if there are men on Mars, one will find Jews among them."[12] This hardly appears to relieve the concerns raised, for we've now moved from one set of worries about the historical tenor of Levinas's claims

---

the Perplexed was explicitly commissioned for Moses de Léon (the most likely author of *The Zohar*). On this point, see Gershom Scholem, *Major Trends in Jewish Mysticism* (New York: Schocken, 2011), 194. Moses de Léon and others were almost always in dialogue with Maimonides, and the basic orientation of Kabbalah as oriented around the אין סוף (*ein sof*) or infinity—no matter the way in which the various subsequent moves descending from infinity are glossed—also fundamentally suggests a basic negative theological viewpoint that has strong resonances with Maimonides's basic orientation. Again, though, this point requires significantly more elaboration, and a proper study of the topic would need to move from Maimonides down to Schelling (touching on an massive assortment of Jewish, Christian, and Muslim philosophers in between), and still remains a desideratum. (I can note that, in a series of interesting articles, Paul Franks has recently been pursuing work on Jewish mystical influences on German philosophy more broadly, and, of course, Elliot Wolfson's work covers this ground from kabbalistic sources.)

12. Emmanuel Levinas, "Reality Has Weight," in *Is It Righteous to Be?: Interviews with Emmanuel Levinas*, ed. Jill Robbins (Palo Alto, CA: Stanford University Press, 2001), 164. Emphasis added.

to even more vexing claims about their philosophical meaning. Even when and if "anachronism" could be given some more robust content in this philosophical register, it is hard to understand how such an element or aspect of human existence ought also to be understood as Judaism or monotheism.

One way to approach these questions is to make explicit a segment of Levinas's phenomenology. In *Totality and Infinity* (1961), Levinas speaks of a "true temporality," a term of art he uses to refer to a distinct sense of time that we might develop as humans. Using language quite similar to the language quoted earlier, he notes that "true temporality, that in which the definitive is not definitive, presupposes the possibility *not* of seizing all that we could have been, but of no longer regretting the lost occasions before the limitless infinity of the future."[13] A true temporality, if such a thing exists, means to exist in such a way that one can approach the potentially infinite possibilities presented by the future: it is as much avoiding falling prey to assumptions of whatever sort about what's possible (social, political, technological, or whatever else) as it is avoiding dwelling on the concrete particular possibilities that were missed. Levinas continues by noting that "it is not a question of reveling in some sort of romanticism of the possible, but of escaping the overwhelming responsibility of existence which veers into destiny, of getting back to the adventure of existence as the infinite."[14] Emerging here is one chief concern of *How to Measure a World?*: the possibilities for, importance of, and particular qualities inherent in human freedom. When Levinas asserts

---

13. Emmanuel Levinas, *Totality and Infinity* (Dordrecht, Neth.: Kluwer, 1961), 282, emphasis added and translation modified. The comparison between the passages I quoted earlier and this section of *Totality and Infinity* was suggested to me by Martin Kavka, "Is There a Warrant for Levinas's Talmudic Readings?," *Journal of Jewish Thought and Philosophy* 14, nos. 1–2 (2006): 172–73.

14. Levinas, *Totality and Infinity*, 282, translation modified.

that everyone is a little bit Jewish, he means that everyone is (a little bit) free (a point that Levinas already makes in some of his earliest philosophical remarks, as when he conceives of the "philosophy of Hitlerism" as a sort of closure of freedom, a conception of the human as fated to the limits of a narrow understanding of what it means to be human as a mere [racialized] body).[15]

Such a theme might strike certain readers as puzzling, for both the title of this book and a cursory glance at its contents should reveal topics ("world," "history," "language") that may not be taken to be central to any concern with freedom. After all, isn't it the case that we simply are free or are not? My guiding impulse, which is different from much of what is taken as central in contemporary discussions of freedom (especially of the sort found in "philosophy of action"),[16] is that these features are fundamental to any understanding of human freedom (much more so than, say, whether we *really can* initiate novel causal chains). This is the case because the most prominent feature of human freedom is its normative dimension: that we can always ask what we *ought* to do or to have done, regardless of how we ultimately—causally—explain what happened. One way to bring this point into focus is to highlight, say, that when a US Customs and Border Patrol agent is deciding whether to follow his orders to separate this nine-month-old child from her mother, it is of no help to that agent—unless he already takes it as relevant—for him to remind himself that we have evolved to avoid blatant acts of cruelty (if he were to try to

---

15. Emmanuel Levinas and Sean Hand, "Reflections on the Philosophy of Hitlerism," *Critical Inquiry* 17, no. 1 (1990): 63–71. I discuss this essay briefly in chapter 4.

16. For an overview of these various issues, see Laura Ekstrom, *Free Will: A Philosophical Study* (London: Routledge, 1999); Robert Kane, *The Significance of Free Will* (Oxford: Oxford University Press, 1996); Timothy O'Connor, *Persons and Causes: The Metaphysics of Free Will* (Oxford: Oxford University Press, 2002).

justify refusing the order), or that we have evolved to prefer organizing ourselves into tribal dynamics (if he were to try to justify obeying it).[17] As one commentator puts it, "Knowing something about the evolutionary benefits of altruistic behavior might give us an interesting perspective on some particular altruistic act, but for the agent, first-personally, the question I must decide is whether I ought to act altruistically and, if so, why. I cannot simply stand by, waiting to see what my highly and complexly evolved neurobiological system will do. The system doesn't make the decision, *I* do–and for reasons that *I* find compelling, or that, at least, outweigh countervailing considerations."[18] This normative dimension—associated with a first-person perspective on the world as a world for me—is fundamentally irreducible to any "sideways-on"[19] understanding of myself as a biological or mechanical entity that is "programmed" to act (in whatever way that such programming is understood).

Let me be clear about what this means: I am not suggesting that this normative dimension has a priority, that facts or states of affairs about what sort of entities we are as physical creatures are somehow unimportant, only that such facts are distinct from this normative dimension, which in words ascribed to the philosopher Wilfrid Sellars, is "fraught with ought." What's central is that a conflict between what is

---

17. This example is a modification of the sort of examples that Robert Pippin marshals in Robert B. Pippin, "Natural and Normative," *Daedalus* 138, no. 3 (2009): 38–39.

18. Ibid.

19. On this terminology, see John McDowell, *Mind and World* (Cambridge, MA: Harvard University Press, 1994), 35. There is an immense amount more to be said here, especially about what such a first-person authority amounts to. For a statement of such, see Richard Moran, *Authority and Estrangement: An Essay on Self-Knowledge* (Princeton, NJ: Princeton University Press, 2001). For a gloss on the phenomenological tradition in light of Moran's work, see Steven Crowell, *Normativity and Phenomenology in Husserl and Heidegger* (Cambridge: Cambridge University Press, 2013), 81–100.

and what ought to be can *always* emerge. Such a possibility, at a very high altitude, raises the most basic issue at the heart of this book: that a dissonance, a friction—a conflict, an *anachronism*—between self and world is always a possibility, and, at many times, a necessity. This is one way to understand and organize large swaths of Jewish tradition, from Noah or Abraham's initial moral questioning of God to the story of Exodus to the various prophetic calls for justice to rabbinic disputes with God to kabbalistic claims about the relationship between appearance and reality.[20] Putting things in this way, however, threatens to overshadow a basic phenomenological point: that while the distinction between self and world is a useful heuristic, it is not a fixed or ultimately fixable distinction. For example, the very norms that I use to assess my world and my possibilities for action are themselves affected by my world, in, say, what I take to be salient (or not) and what I take to be possible (or not). Merleau-Ponty puts this point well when he notes that "the world, which I distinguished from myself as the totality of things or of processes linked by causal relationships, I rediscover 'in me' as the permanent horizon of all my *cogitations* and as a dimension in relation to which I am constantly situating myself."[21]

A deep connection between self and world, but also the possibility of a deep rift between the two is a way to understand the structure of this book: it is one way to make sense of how a book about time (anachronism) fundamentally unfolds through an analysis of space (world). The notion of

---

20. Noah may be the most profitable example to the extent that the Noahide covenant is the most universal of all the divine covenants. On this point, see David Kishik, *The Book of Shem: On Genesis before Abraham* (Palo Alto, CA: Stanford University Press, 2018).

21. Maurice Merleau-Ponty, *Phenomenology of Perception*, trans. Colin Smith (London: Routledge, 2002), xiv. This point is not exclusive to phenomenology but is also found in Wittgenstein's understanding of the relationship between language, world, and self. On this point, see Cavell, *Claim of Reason*, 86–129.

measuring[22]—*of how to measure a world*—connects self and world, time and space, *is* and *ought*.[23] An irreducible feature of this connection is that there exists the possibility of what might be termed simply "beyond" or "the beyond" or more plainly "God" or "the divine"—taken as something that exceeds self and world as the two presently exist (the proper name, content, scope, and even possibility of this "beyond" is itself one of the topics of this book). When the aforementioned aspects of human freedom are stressed—aspects that prioritize the qualitative character of our world, of what appears and can appear for us, of what actions strike as possible and as not—then the worries that emerge as most salient are not worries about our biology or determinism (are we the sort of creatures who can do x or y—are we *truly* free?), but rather worries about who we presently are as humans (are we beholden to or have our imaginative capacities been warped by ideology, prejudice, ignorance, callousness, or apathy—what is the nature of our world and therefore us?).[24] Questions about what's beyond self and world are thereby

22. On this point, there are analogies to be drawn with the way in which measurement is linked to world in Martin Heidegger, "'... Poetically Man Dwells...,'" trans. Albert Hofstadter, in *Poetry, Language, Thought* (New York: Harper and Row, 1959).

23. The normative dimension of such measuring is disclosed well in Steven Crowell, "Measure-Taking: Meaning and Normativity in Heidegger's Philosophy," *Continental Philosophy Review* 41, no. 3 (2008): 261–76.

24. This is one way to understand how Heidegger—with his later stress on "earth" in a too narrow and distinct register—himself falls short of his own insights with respect to measurement and world. On this point, see Karsten Harries, *Art Matters: A Critical Commentary on Heidegger's "The Origin of the Work of Art"* (Dordrecht, Neth.: Springer, 2009), 106. Harries writes, "But any attempt to name the gods and thus to take the measure of human being-in-the-world, if only to return that measure to human beings and to let them dwell, is always a violation of the essentially elusive essence of divinity. We are thus always in danger of obscuring divinity with some golden calf, as Heidegger demonstrated when he turned to National Socialism in the hope of discovering there a new popular religion. To repeat: What are the gods to us moderns?"

themselves already ethical and political in nature, for they affect the qualitative nature of our world and its possibilities, and our assessment of the same.[25]

My aim in *How to Measure a World?*, without relying solely or exclusively on Levinas's thought, is to make a case for how Judaism might—philosophically—be understood as an anachronism. The aim is to understand what it would mean to conceive such an anachronism—with its suggestion that self and world do not exhaust each other, that there crucially remains more to each—as philosophically central to being human, being (a little bit) Jewish. What does it mean to see Judaism (as anachronism) as central (to being human)? The historical nature of Judaism is left aside unless it bears on this task (in this regard the approach here is in fact sympathetic to Scholem's position). Levinas therefore should not be understood as making a historical claim, or, if he is, it is a very peculiar one.[26] What the idea of Judaism as an anachronism suggests is a claim about the *form* of any such a religious orientation—this is what Levinas means when he calls it a modality as opposed to a particularity.[27] Such a form

---

25. This is one way to parse the deep connection but also the difference in focus between this book and Elliot Wolfson's excellent work around the topic. See Elliot R. Wolfson, *Giving Beyond the Gift: Apophasis and Overcoming Theomania* (New York: Fordham University Press, 2014).

26. Scholars have generally taken Levinas to be an antihistoricist thinker, but as Sarah Hammerschlag shows, Levinas's antihistoricism is itself couched in a historical moment (as a response to the Nazi genocide) (Sarah Hammerschlag, "'A Splinter in the Flesh': Levinas and the Resignification of Jewish Suffering, 1928–1947," *International Journal of Philosophical Studies* 20, no. 3 [2012]: 405–11). For an argument about Levinas's historicism, see Samuel Moyn, "Emmanuel Levinas's Talmudic Readings: Between Tradition and Invention," *Prooftexts* 23, no. 3 (2003): 338–64.

27. There is an analogy here to Husserl's concept of *eidetic* description, where the phenomenon that is experienced is varied in imagination. For more on this topic in broad terms, see Edward S. Casey, "Literary Description and Phenomenological Method," *Yale French Studies*, no. 61 (1981): 176–201.

is itself compatible with, and indeed might in fact require, a variety of content or orientations (or at least, that is what is suggested by the idea that such a position is both "attentive to reality" and "impatient to change it," a simultaneous "engagement and disengagement," the "most separate" and "most committed," and so forth).[28] One way to take this point is to note that such a view of Judaism would by no means argue against the two orientations around which Scholem lodges his rejection of an essentialistic approach to Judaism: fundamentalism and spiritualization (the former is shorthand for locating Judaism's essence in a strictly fundamentalist understanding of the law, while the latter locates Judaism's essence in some "essential spiritual statement").[29] A conception of Judaism as anachronism need not be committed to any particular spiritual precept nor to any rejection or prioritization of the law. What is the significance or even point of such a view? Furthermore, does it even make sense to call it Jewish in any meaningful sense?

If everyone is a little bit Jewish—if Judaism is a modality of being human—then why delineate "being Jewish" specifically? Why play this game, seemingly relegated to a question of rhetoric, and dangerously close to—if not outright flirting with—chauvinism?[30] As a preliminary answer, let me note

---

28. This is one way to situate the idea—explored by Guy Stroumsa—that, during the rise of monotheism in late antiquity, there actually was never a pure monotheism, whether Jewish, Christian, or Muslim (Guy G. Stroumsa, *The Making of the Abrahamic Religions in Late Antiquity* [Oxford: Oxford University Press, 2015], 16).

29. Scholem, "What Is Judaism?," 115.

30. This seems to be Jacques Derrida's tempered critique of Levinas on this front. I say "tempered" because Derrida also takes it that Levinas gestures toward a possibility beyond it ("dreams" of such a possibility, in Derrida's words). For more on this, see Sarah Hammerschlag, "Another, Other Abraham: Derrida's Figuring of Levinas's Judaism," *Shofar* 26, no. 4 (2008): 74–96. For an excellent study of the relationship between Derrida and Levinas, see also Sarah Hammerschlag, *Broken Tablets: Levinas, Derrida, and the Literary Afterlife of Religion* (New York: Columbia University Press, 2016).

that Levinas first begins to formulate this conception of Judaism in response to Hitler and the Nazi regime. In notebooks that he kept during his time as a prisoner of war held by the Nazis,[31] he writes that "in persecution I find the original meaning of Judaism, its original emotion . . . revelation of an order different from the natural order—real despite all the failures of the natural order."[32] These notebooks already often show Levinas referring to Judaism as a "category (*catégorie*)" of being.[33] There is much more to say about Levinas's intellectual development,[34] but what can be flagged now is the simple meaning behind these words: According to Levinas, the persecution that a Jew experiences reveals a potential order different from the current order. Persecution, and the suffering it engenders, suggests that the world ought not be like this and, furthermore, that it might be different. Or, as Theodor W. Adorno, another Jew and philosopher who experienced the Nazi genocide, will put it, "woe speaks: go."[35]

31. Levinas was captured by German forces at Rennes in 1940. Captured formally as a French officer (he had been serving as an interpreter), he was a prisoner of war until 1945. For more on Levinas's prison notebooks, see Howard Caygill, "Levinas's Prison Notebooks," *Radical Philosophy* 160 (2010): 27–35; Sarah Hammerschlag, "Levinas's Prison Notebooks," in *The Oxford Handbook of Levinas*, ed. Michael Morgan (Oxford: Oxford University Press, 2018), 21–35.

32. Emmanuel Levinas, *Carnets de Captivité: Suivi de Écrits sur la Captivité; et, Notes Philosophiques Diverses* (Paris: Grasset and Fasquelle, 2009), 179–80. My attention, like that of many others, was first drawn to this note by Hammerschlag, "Splinter in the Flesh," 402–3.

33. Levinas, *Carnets de Captivité*, 75. One finds this later, in connection with Levinas's reading of Franz Rosenzweig, in Levinas, "'Between Two Worlds' (the Way of Franz Rosenzweig)," trans. Seán Hand, in *Difficult Freedom: Essays on Judaism* (Baltimore, MD: Johns Hopkins University Press, 1960), 183.

34. See Michael Fagenblat, "'The Passion of Israel': The True Israel according to Levinas, or Judaism 'as a Category of Being,'" *Sophia* 54, no. 3 (2015): 297–320; Hammerschlag, "Splinter in the Flesh"; Samuel Moyn, "Judaism against Paganism: Emmanuel Levinas's Response to Heidegger and Nazism in the 1930s," *History and Memory* 10, no. 1 (1998): 25–58.

35. Theodor W. Adorno, *Negative Dialectics*, trans. E. B. Ashton (New York: Seabury, 1973), 203.

This pushes the various problems here back another step: do not others experience persecution? As Muslims, as Blacks, as Christians, and so forth? Doesn't the problem mentioned here—of a sort of chauvinism—remerge again in a different context, by means of a prioritization of the Nazi genocide over other historical sites of brutality?[36] The impulse here cannot be the prioritization of particular forms or sites of suffering.[37] To elevate Jewish suffering during the Nazi genocide in order to diminish other examples of historical suffering—say the brutality of chattel slavery or colonialism or imperialism (just to name a few)—is problematic, odious. To note this, however, is exactly to stress the phenomenological nature of the account that's pursued here: it applies to all humans. Judaism is conceived as a category of being (human). At the same time, to ignore entirely the way in which such suffering has emerged within and informed any understanding of Judaism and Jewishness in the last century is problematic, albeit in a different way: it refuses to acknowledge the extent to which the development of Western rationality has imagined itself by means of an opposition to Judaism.[38] Let me be clear that I am not aiming to reprioritize Judaism or Jewishness as an exemplar of suffering; I am instead noting the fact that, even as it is right to note

36. See, for example, Aimé Césaire, *Discourse on Colonialism*, trans. Joan Pinkbaum (New York: Monthly Review Press, 2000), 36; Charles W. Mills, *The Racial Contract* (Ithaca, NY: Cornell University Press, 1997), 102–3. Césaire and Mills both highlight the way in which the Nazi genocide is often taken as the premier case of human suffering, or how it confronts whites as shocking, even though horrendous evils had been visited on nonwhite populations before the Nazi genocide. There is also here the temptation of trying to rank suffering (to be clear, not something that either Césaire or Mills pursues). See Lauren Berlant, "The Subject of True Feeling: Pain, Privacy, and Politics," in *Cultural Studies and Political Theory*, ed. Thomas R. Kearns and Austin Sarat (Ann Arbor: University of Michigan Press, 1999).

37. On this point, see Berlant, "Subject of True Feeling."

38. On this point, see the Conclusion and also David Nirenberg, *Anti-Judaism: The Western Tradition* (New York: W. W. Norton, 2013).

that the Nazi genocide can usefully be seen as a return of tortures first applied "only to non-European peoples,"[39] the Nazi genocide cannot be understood solely in that context. The brutality of Western society toward Judaism—albeit not *exclusively* Judaism—both (1) stretches back millennia and (2) takes on a distinct register because of the centrality of Judaism to the Nazi worldview (put another way: what's coming into focus here is not exclusively or primarily suffering, but rather the rationality that leads to or pursues such suffering, a rationality implicated in the long history of Western antisemitism).[40] The experience of the Nazi genocide, but equally also of other genocides, and other terrors, demands—ethically, experientially—that a phenomenology of anachronism be constructed. It is a moral imperative not to feel at home in such a world. Such atrocities ought not be—and so, anachronism. What might it mean to take this as a central feature of Judaism, of being human? In such a case, the philosophical project may then itself even critique (historical) Judaism: that particular institutional forms may fall short of the phenomenological modality of Jewishness.[41]

39. Césaire, *Discourse on Colonialism*, 36.

40. Both these points are explored by Arendt in the first part of Hannah Arendt, *The Origins of Totalitarianism* (London: André Deutsch, 1986).

41. This is one way to understand Derrida's invocation of a "Torah before Sinai" in Jacques Derrida, *Adieu to Emmanuel Levinas* (Palo Alto, CA: Stanford University Press, 1999), 65. On this point, see Hammerschlag, "Another, Other Abraham," 87. I take it that the idea that there may be gap between Jewishness and Judaism is a similar idea—see Fagenblat, "Passion of Israel," 301. One way to register this point is to highlight a particular—perhaps not entirely historical, but not thereby unhistorical—understanding of the prophetic tradition of the Hebrew Bible. Think about the way that tradition is invoked in even more contemporary works like Stefano Harney and Fred Moten, *The Undercommons: Fugitive Planning and Black Study* (London: Minor Compositions, 2013); Cornel West, *Prophetic Fragments: Illuminations of the Crisis in American Religion and Culture* (Grand Rapids, MI: William B. Eerdmans, 1993). For a sketch of such an understanding of the Jewish prophetic tradition, see Abraham J. Heschel, *The Prophets* (New York: Harper Collins, 2001).

This leads Levinas to say provocatively that "Jews are people who doubt themselves, who in a certain sense, belong to a religion of unbelievers."[42] If suffering is where we find "the revelation of an order different from the natural order," then implied with this thought is the idea that such a different order can be suggested across a range of phenomena in the world, both empirically (as in, it can be found in the sufferings of any human), and philosophically (as in, other phenomena apart from suffering may equally well disclose it and that even the methods of disclosure can themselves be variable).

This last point is central to the procedures of *How to Measure a World?* The book presents a conception of Judaism as anachronism that, while ethically sensitive, is not exclusively concerned with suffering. (This is one way to understand why this isn't a book solely about Levinas—my claim is that central elements of such an anachronism have nothing to do with suffering and are found in other thinkers within the Jewish tradition.) Because the focus of the book is this conceptualization of Judaism as anachronism, the various stakes of what it would mean to reconfigure our understanding of Judaism in light of such a perspective—of how it would alter our understanding of Judaism's relationship to the other monotheistic traditions, indeed to religion itself, even more broadly to spirituality or philosophy, and more narrowly to the Jewish legal tradition, and so forth—are generally left aside, pursued here only in the Introduction and in the Conclusion. In part this has to do with the gravity of what it would mean to address such a shift (explored briefly in the Conclusion), but in part it also has to do with the philosophical tensions in such a task: the whole thrust of the argument is that a philosophical anachronism of this sort persistently reorients our view toward ourselves and others and thereby

---

42. Levinas, "Reality Has Weight," 164.

demands constant reappraisal and exploration of the historical record of our world. Such a constant reorientation is just an expression of what it means to be a free human being—to be (a little bit) Jewish—and it requires persistent attention to the relationship, and the potential patterns of dissonance, between self and world and what might be beyond both; in short, then, it is a story that has yet to be written and that will have to be written time and time again.

In addition to Levinas, the chapters that follow consider the twelfth-century philosopher Moses Maimonides; the twentieth-century Frankfurt School critical theorist, Theodor W. Adorno, and his colleague Walter Benjamin; and the recently deceased Anglophone philosopher Stanley Cavell. Such a grouping likely doesn't strike readers as immediately obvious (although, controversially, each of these thinkers can be cast as fitting into a tradition of apophatic or negative theology—the idea that our access to ultimate reality is only ever negative).[43] The aim of *How to Measure a World?* is to present an analytic conception of Judaism as anachronism. The view is presented through this constellation of thinkers who, when put together, produce the full range and scope for such a novel conception. The Jewish philosophical record is incredibly vast, and every (Jewish) tradition declares something in and something else out (rationalism as opposed to mysticism, legalism as opposed to literalism, and so forth). In a text from the 1960s, Adorno writes that a "critical relation to tradition as the medium of its preservation is not only concerned with the past but also with . . . the present."[44] Apart from what it has produced, equally important for any

---

43. For more on such a philosophy, see William Franke, *On What Cannot Be Said: Apophatic Discourses in Philosophy, Religion, Literature, and the Arts* (South Bend, IN: University of Notre Dame Press, 2007); William Franke, *A Philosophy of the Unsayable* (South Bend, IN: University of Notre Dame Press, 2014).

44. Theodor W. Adorno, "On Tradition," *Telos* 1992, no. 94 (1992): 80.

tradition is also what it can and will (continue) to produce. In short, let's be self-conscious about our—any—relation to tradition. To do so is to realize that every new production has the potential to alter our very understanding of the tradition from which it arises. The constellation of thinkers presented here just is such a new tradition; I leave it to others to decide what else it might produce. Proceeding in this way suggests not just alternative possibilities for Judaism but also for philosophy, showing how the possibilities of each are much more heterodox than is often thought (more on this shortly).[45] Let me say now a little about how the argument of the book unfolds.

The linchpin for the book is a novel reading of the towering twelfth-century Jewish thinker Moses Maimonides (for a sense of his stature within Judaism, note that his epitaph reads, "from Moses to Moses, there was none like Moses").[46] I argue that Maimonides employs a phenomenological approach, a claim that is not as ahistorical as it may sound if Maimonides's Muslim milieu and his background

---

45. Although a proper comparison here is beyond my scope, there are interesting points of commonality here with the sort of "Marrano strategy" proposed in Agata Bielik-Robson, *Jewish Cryptotheologies of Late Modernity: Philosophical Marranos* (London: Routledge, 2014), and Agata Bielik-Robson, "Marrano Universalism: Benjamin, Derrida, and Buck-Morss on the Condition of Universal Exile," *Telos* 186 (2019): 25–44. Where the points of tension emerge are in her stress on secrecy and on the understanding of this strategy as a third way. This seems to me to cede too much to a sort of sociological analysis of the possibilities of philosophy and its outside (that—sociologically—it has been seen as "Greek" and Judaism as "Hebrew"). But the question at hand here is not one purely of sociology; there is, for lack of a better word, an important philosophical dimension to what philosophy can be that simply cannot be settled sociologically (the analogy here is to the way in which terms like *analytic* and *continental* get deployed . . . but these terms don't really track anything philosophical; they are in fact primarily, if not only, sociological).

46. For an interesting thought experiment about how different things would be if Moses Maimonides hadn't lived, see Menachem Kellner, "From Moses to Moses," *Rambam Maimonides Medical Journal* 1, no. 2 (2010): 1–5.

in Aristotle's thought is properly understood as the source for his phenomenological approach. Both the Qur'an and the eleventh-century Muslim philosopher al-Ghazālī (who was likely the source for the title of Maimonides's *Guide for the Perplexed*)[47] evince phenomenological motifs, especially in how they understand the notion of certainty. Aristotle (also a well-known source for Maimonides) similarly can be understood to have phenomenological commitments. Maimonides's phenomenological approach depends on revealing how a not wholly cognitive, but rather practical, embodied relationship with the world—what philosophers might call a prepredicative relationship—is expressive equally of a practical orientation to something perpetually and entirely distinct from the world (God) and of a fundamentally positive attitude that invites us perpetually to engage in an exploration of the world. Acknowledging this phenomenological core allows us to see Maimonides's *Guide* in a new light and, as a consequence of Maimonides's standing, to construct a bridge, if we so desire, between the conception of Judaism as anachronism presented here and more traditional conceptions of Judaism. Tradition is thereby affirmed even as it is categorically altered (as Adorno puts it, "only that which inexorably denies tradition may once again retrieve it").[48] At the same time, it is important to note that Maimonides remains a controversial thinker to this day (a fact that, to my mind, serves to confirm his importance for a construction of Judaism as anachronism). On one hand, his profound effect on Judaism is indisputable, felt chiefly through his summation of Jewish law in his *Mishneh Torah* (literally, "reiteration of the Torah" or more plainly, "second to the Torah"). On the other hand, the desire to provide such a summation was immediately

---

47. Al-Ghazālī was a significant influence on Maimonides, accounting likely even for the name of the *Guide*. On this point, see footnotes 16, 17, and 18 in chapter 1.

48. Adorno, "On Tradition," 82.

met by disapproval, with many claiming that it would lead to ignorance of the Talmud (the *Mishneh Torah* generally avoids citing particular sources for its claims).[49] Although Maimonides maintained he never intended to replace the study of the Talmud, it is notable that his introduction to the *Mishneh Torah* states that it is called such so that "when one studies the *Torah* first and thereafter reads this work, he obtains from it a complete knowledge of the oral *Torah, having no need to read any other book in between them*."[50] The statement makes Maimonides's thought subject to suspicion. Every belief that Maimonides marshals as essential to Judaism has been subject to dispute,[51] while a debate about the *Guide* continues to occupy scholars, with the work seen as everything from an apologia for Judaism to the esoteric work of a closet atheist.[52] Adjudicating these issues is far beyond my scope, but noting them strikes me as worthwhile in order to highlight an earlier point: the range of disciplinary or institutional responses to Maimonides highlights the importance of stressing the philosophical—phenomenological and therefore formal—qualities of his thinking.

Maimonides's phenomenological claims are connected with related phenomenological claims in Adorno (chap. 2), and then in Cavell and Levinas (chap. 4). (All these figures,

49. For a discussion of this point, see Isadore Twersky, *Introduction to the Code of Maimonides (Mishneh Torah)* (New Haven, CT: Yale University Press, 1980), 30 37.

50. The relevant Hebrew reads וְאֵינוּ צָרִיךְ לִקְרוֹת סֵפֶר אַחֵר בֵּינֵיהֶם. See the introduction to the *Mishneh Torah*, 1: 42. Emphasis added. For useful discussions of the issues—which are legion, including most notably Maimonides's relationship both with the Jewish legal tradition and with the Muslim one—see Sarah Stroumsa, *Maimonides in His World: Portrait of a Mediterranean Thinker* (Princeton, NJ: Princeton University Press, 2009), 62; Isadore Twersky, "The *Mishneh Torah* of Maimonides," *Proceedings of the Israel Academy of Sciences and Humanities* 5 (1976): 265–95.

51. Marc B. Shapiro, *The Limits of Orthodox Theology: Maimonides' Thirteen Principles Reappraised* (Oxford, UK: Littman Library of Jewish Civilization, 2004).

52. For more on this controversy, see footnote 4 in chapter 1.

it might be noted, in one way or another, have important engagements with phenomenology.)[53] The basic analytical thought around which the book is organized is the idea that a conception of Judaism as anachronism requires, at a very high-altitude view, a conception of the world as the sort of thing to which one practically takes either an orientation of awed wonder or an orientation of moral outrage. Either orientation requires a prior assessment (even if only practical) of the world. An assessment in either direction—with the demand for appreciation or the warrant for ethical critique—requires that the world, as a rich phenomenological source, be more than what it presently is: we desire to understand the wondrous world better, or we wish to judge how the wicked world could be better. In either case, it is the world that is ultimately capable of sustaining such approaches (or not). The sheer density of the world, as a human world, requires a consideration of its (human) history, as a feature central to any such density, and therefore to any such assessment (the subject of chap. 3). Again at a very high altitude, such historical density—history itself—does not come premade, it is fashioned through human interaction. Chapter 4 therefore takes up philosophy of language in this context. With Levinas and Cavell, chapter 4 shows how a proper understanding of language as a natural human ability (albeit one that may be shared with nonhumans) always already points beyond what presently is, revealing, already at the heart of language,

---

53. This is likely most controversial in the case of Adorno, whose dialectical thought is often conceived as fundamentally opposed to phenomenology (a conception Adorno might be unlikely to dispute, as his own criticisms of both Husserl and Heidegger suggests). Phenomenology, however, is a diverse method, and there are striking ways in which Adorno can be linked to figures within phenomenology, most notably Levinas, but also—despite his polemics against him—Heidegger. On the rapprochements between Levinas and Adorno, see footnote 66 in chapter 2. On rapprochements with the latter, see many of the essays collected in Iain Macdonald and Krzysztof Ziarek, *Adorno and Heidegger: Philosophical Questions* (Palo Alto, CA: Stanford University Press, 2008).

a structural analogy to the sense of anachronism developed throughout. In response to this discovery, Levinas and Cavell both strikingly speak of a "trace" of something more, and Cavell plainly terms it "the trace or scar of the departure of God."[54] Hannah Arendt captures what emerges here with the thought that what's at stake is "the specifically human way of being alive; for every single person needs to be reconciled to a world into which he [sic] was born a stranger and in which, to the extent of his distinct uniqueness, he always remains a stranger."[55]

To conclude, let me note that for quite some time now, there has been debate about what Jewish philosophy might amount to,[56] and especially whether there can,[57] or even ought to be,[58]

---

54. Stanley Cavell, *The Claim of Reason: Wittgenstein, Skepticism, Morality, and Tragedy* (Oxford: Oxford University Press, 1979), 470.

55. Hannah Arendt, "Understanding and Politics," in *Essays in Understanding, 1930–1954: Formation, Exile, and Totalitarianism*, ed. Jerome Kohn (New York: Schocken, 2011), 308.

56. See Daniel Frank and Oliver Leaman, "What Is Jewish Philosophy?," in *History of Jewish Philosophy*, ed. Daniel Frank and Oliver Leaman (London: Routledge, 1997).

57. See the classic claim by Isaac Husik that "There are Jews now and there are philosophers, but there are no Jewish philosophers and there is no Jewish philosophy" (Isaac Husik, *A History of Mediaeval Jewish Philosophy* [New York: Harper and Row, 1966], 432).

58. See Yitzhak Y. Melamed, "Salomon Maimon et l'échec de la philosophie juive moderne," *Revue Germanique Internationale*, no. Winter (2009): 175–87. See Melamed's claim that "If we accept the thesis that until the 19th century (and actually until today) most Jewish texts are made up of the Talmud, its commentaries and rabbinic literature, and if indeed, my assertion is true (that the kings of modern Jewish philosophy were as bare as when they were born in terms of knowledge of the Talmud and rabbinical literature), then one can appreciate the dose of charlatanism necessary for the pursuit of such a project" (182). On this point, see Samson Hirsch's 1835 letter to Z. H. May—see Samson Raphael Hirsch, *Horeb: A Philosophy of Jewish Laws and Observances* (London: Soncino, 1962), cxli–cxlv. Melamed eschews any sort of essentialist approach to Judaism (184), and suggests that Salomon Maimon is the "sole modern Jewish philosopher worth the title," because he was the only one who possessed the requisite amount of knowledge (of traditional Jewish texts) so as to offer "a well-argued and informed account of Jewish religious and

something like "modern Jewish philosophy."[59] Recently it has been claimed that the entire idea of a Jewish philosophy is really little more than the process of inventing Judaism by "using the languages and categories of other cultures."[60] The response is then to pursue something that might be called "Jewish metaphilosophy," whose aim is to "permit reflection on the task, means, and ends" of such activity.[61] *How to Measure the World* nowhere explicitly engages with these broader issues in this sociological register (about conceptions of Jewish or Judaism as much as conceptions of philosophy),[62] opting instead to construct a distinct tradition of thinking of Judaism as anachronism. Nonetheless, it is useful to note in

cultural beliefs and practices" (176). In suggesting this latter criterion as central, Melamed is very much following in the footsteps of Julius Guttmann, *Philosophies of Judaism: The History of Jewish Philosophy from Biblical Times to Franz Rosenzweig*, trans. David Silverman (New York: Schoken, 1973). My approach in this book is to try to toe a middle line between (1) Melamed's suggestion that essentializing Judaism is impossible because of the diversity of viewpoints and figures within it—see, for example, Melamed's invocation by R. Levi-Yitzchok of Berdichev's irreverence (184n23)—one could just as easily cite R. Menachem Mendl of Kotzk here, or countless others, and (2) his suggestion that "most Jewish texts" are "made up of the Talmud, etc." First, it seems to me that much more goes into "Jewish religious and cultural beliefs and practices" than such Jewish texts, and, second, and more fundamentally, the range of what is a "Jewish" text is itself what's under question (something Melamed considers on 183n20, but pushes it as a possibility into the far future): my sense is that this latter category is far broader than Melamed suggests. What this means for the broader story about modern Jewish philosophy is then what I suggest above: that its conception as an anachronism is in part essentialist, but not wholly so exactly because such anachronism demands constantly shifting content.

59. For an excellent overview of the various stages of such a discussion, both analytically and disciplinarily, see Martin Kavka, Introduction to *The Cambridge History of Jewish Philosophy: The Modern Era*, ed. Martin Kavka, Zachary Braiterman, and David Novak, 1–35 (Cambridge: Cambridge University Press, 2012).

60. Aaron W. Hughes, *Rethinking Jewish Philosophy: Beyond Particularism and Universalism* (Oxford: Oxford University Press, 2013), 118.

61. Ibid., 126, xi.

62. A point raised already in this context in Kenneth Seeskin, *Jewish Philosophy in a Secular Age* (Albany, NY: SUNY Press, 1990), 7.

conclusion that there is a dialectical position available between these extremes. On one hand, Judaism as anachronism is sort of essentialist position,[63] but it is an essentialism that stresses the form and not the content of Judaism. It is impossible ultimately—ethically, politically, aesthetically, religiously—to feel "at home" in the world. On the other hand, central to any such conception of Judaism is the eschewal of a fixed content to Judaism. The form is unwavering in its ethical orientation, but the content is infinitely variable in response to the form: there just is no way to delimit the possibilities of human relationship and being together;[64] and it is equally impossible to

63. I say "sort of essentialist" here exactly to highlight the extent to which it is not an essentialist account in any plain sense of the word: the whole basis of this anachronism—as will emerge—is noncognitive, indeed preexperiential and, therefore, it is hardly essentialist in the sense that it subscribes to some doctrinal understanding of Judaism. Focused as it is on form, it is a sort of *modality*, as Levinas suggests (for more on this, see the earlier discussions in this introduction and the conclusion of this book). In this way, my approach has some points of commonality with the way in which Seeskin (cited in the note just above) responded to these same worries (marshaling the work of Steven Schwarzschild), but I drop the very idea of trying to do philosophy in a "Jewish way" and agree, instead, with Hughes (cited in note 58), that we are defining Judaism and thereby doing philosophy in a Jewish way all at the same time; I part company with Hughes in believing that "Jewish metaphilosophy" is the price for doing so. Quite the contrary: we could do (Jewish) philosophy more responsibly by admitting what we're doing, but by also claiming that we're doing it because we think it is true (i.e., it is not a merely cynical or cynical but uninformed procedure). For more on philosophy in a "Jewish way," see Steven Schwarzschild, "An Agenda for Jewish Philosophy in the 1980s," in *Studies in Jewish Philosophy*, ed. Norbert Samuelson (Lanham, MD: University Press of America, 1987). Another way to put these points, and to put my cards on the table, is to note that I am quite sympathetic to Nancy Levene's suggestion that our "powers of distinction" ought not to be avoided or downplayed, but that, at the same time, they cannot be sublimed, taken as somehow beyond reproach (Nancy Levene, *Powers of Distinction: On Religion and Modernity* [Chicago: University of Chicago Press, 2017]).

64. Although this is likely really the only point of comparison, compare with a "living" approach that is sought after in Michael Wyschogrod, *The Body of Faith: God and the People of Israel* (New York: Seabury, 1996), 52–53. And in this way, it is also comparable to the way in which Judaism

delimit the possibilities of being Jewish (and even if only a little bit). Required is a persistent "attention to the present" that is matched only by "an eternal distance in relation to the contemporary world."[65] Such an orientation is not "learned like a catechism or summarized like a credo" but is rather "acquired through a way of living," comparable to the "training of a fighter."[66] Any training regimen gauges the possibilities of the human body, and here notably we might also gauge the possibilities of philosophy, understanding "Jewish" philosophy as itself already an enterprise that allows us to "rethink the project of philosophy . . . to reimagine it critically."[67] What counts thereby as a philosophical problem and what counts as a Jewish one in each case expands, shrinking and blurring the distance between the two, suggesting that each is intimately related to the other, just like the resemblances between family, no matter how distant.

---

is pursued as a "way of life" in Hilary Putnam, *Jewish Philosophy as a Guide to Life: Rosenzweig, Buber, Levinas, Wittgenstein* (Bloomington: Indiana University Press, 2008).

65. Levinas, "Judaism and the Present," 213.
66. Ibid.
67. Willi Goetschel, *The Discipline of Philosophy and the Invention of Modern Jewish Thought* (New York: Fordham University Press, 2013), 6.

I

HAVING A WORLD

1

WONDER AND WORLD

MAIMONIDES'S PHENOMENOLOGY

§ 1. Introduction:
Setting Up the Importance of Worldhood

Maimonides's *Guide for the Perplexed* (ca. 1190) is incredibly complex and, after millennia, is still subject to controversy.[1] In what follows, I do not explicitly engage all the well-known (and well-worn) debates about this text. Albeit thereby less ambitious, the aims of this chapter are nonetheless controversial: I argue that Maimonides—at key points—relies on a phenomenological method. Although this premise will require more clarification, at the outset let me note that such a method signals the importance of the ontological category of *world*. "Ontological" ought to be understood as the idea that what is under consideration is not the existence of any particular being, but rather the possibility of there being anything at all: the idea is to think through how

---

1. For an overview, see Aviezer Ravitzky, "Maimonides: Esotericism and Educational Philosophy," in *The Cambridge Companion to Moses Maimonides*, ed. Kenneth Seeskin (Cambridge: Cambridge University Press, 2005).

anything so much as comes to be.² And "world" ought to be understood not as the cataloguing of any number—even a very great number—of objects, but rather the exploration of how any object first appears: how is it that a world of objects emerges in the first place? Think of the guiding question here as a question that Thoreau poses in *Walden:* "Why do precisely these objects which we behold make a world?"³

Putting forward my chief claim at once, I will show that central to Maimonides's procedure in the *Guide*—and therefore central to his deepest aspirations as a philosopher and a theist—is an estimation of these questions, ultimately, an exploration of how a world is both to be judged and accounted for, and of how such a judgment or account is possible in the first place. What emerges is a dialectical relationship between our engagement with these phenomenological questions and our conception of ultimate reality. Any understanding of the latter requires a persistent exploration of the former. The very project of a phenomenological exploration of the world thereby itself becomes a spiritual project; indeed, it is, for Maimonides, the chief spiritual project. That last claim may strike many as misguided if not wrong (at the very least it threatens to reignite or call to mind all of the Straussian debates about Maimonides's deepest commitments as a philosopher).⁴ I have no interest in adjudicating these debates. Instead, my aims in this chapter are to present a novel reading

---

2. For the notion of ontology in mind here, see Martin Heidegger, *Being and Time*, trans. Joan Stambaugh (Albany: State University of New York, 1996), §4.

3. Henry D. Thoreau, *Walden* (Princeton, NJ: Princeton University Press, 1971), 225.

4. The literature here is almost too vast to cite, but the central texts by Strauss have recently been collected in Leo Strauss, *Leo Strauss on Maimonides: The Complete Writings* (Chicago: University of Chicago Press, 2013). For discussions, see Kenneth Hart Green, *Jew and Philosopher: The Return to Maimonides in the Jewish Thought of Leo Strauss* (Buffalo, NY: SUNY Press, 2012); Kenneth Hart Green, *Leo Strauss and the Rediscovery of Maimonides* (Chicago: University of Chicago Press,

of the *Guide* in order to argue for understanding Maimonides as a distinct type of phenomenological thinker. In doing so, I do believe that from such an interpretation there are interesting conclusions to be drawn for the study of Maimonides (and of Arabic philosophy more broadly), but I leave that for another day (and perhaps for others to do). My aim is instead to make the case for my reading of Maimonides in order to insert him into the constellation of thinkers required to make the broader claims of *How to Measure a World?*

One final note before beginning. It is worthwhile to get clear on my invocation of phenomenology in this context. There are at least two ways in which Maimonides has occasionally been understood to have a "phenomenology" or a "religious phenomenology." One initial way might be to highlight Maimonides's invocation of the history of religions as a means of understanding the evolution of religion as a human category; this might be called a sort of phenomenological (or philosophical) anthropology of religion.[5] Another way to acknowledge a phenomenology in Maimonides's thought is to examine how he thinks belief in God arises, or ought to arise; this might be termed a sort of moral phenomenology of religion (or moral psychology of religion). My approach differs from both of these. Note above all that the concept of "world" being invoked here is a concept that is most prominently expressed in the philosophical movement now termed as phenomenology (represented in what follows chiefly

---

2013); Joseph A. Buijs, "The Philosophical Character of Maimonides' 'Guide'—a Critique of Strauss' Interpretation," *Judaism* 27, no. 4 (1978): 448–57; Marvin Fox, *Interpreting Maimonides: Studies in Methodology, Metaphysics, and Moral Philosophy* (Chicago: University of Chicago Press, 1995), 56; Joel Kraemer, "The Medieval Arabic Enlightenment," in *The Cambridge Companion to Maimonides*, ed. Steven B. Smith, 137–71 (Cambridge: Cambridge University Press, 2009).

5. See, for example, the fourth chapter of Sarah Stroumsa, *Maimonides in His World: Portrait of a Mediterranean Thinker* (Princeton, NJ: Princeton University Press, 2009).

through reference to the work of Martin Heidegger, but, as a method, encompassing quite a range of approaches and methods, ranging across the humanities and even to neuroscience).[6] My methodology might strike readers as entirely foreign to Maimonides's philosophical background. To mitigate such concerns, let me stress that on a particular reading of the philosophical tradition, the origins of phenomenology—or at least the version on offer by Martin Heidegger,[7] whom I chiefly invoke here as an interlocutor—can be traced to an interpretation of and engagement with Aristotle, who, of course, is a central figure for the Islamic philosophical context that influences Maimonides (and this context is represented in what follows chiefly through the work of one of Maimonides's leading Islamic influences, al-Ghazālī).[8]

My own approach, while differing from the two more standard "phenomenological" approaches to Maimonides's work, can nonetheless be presented by turning briefly to the second strand that I have labeled moral psychology. The point of commonality between this approach and my own is a consideration of the weight that Maimonides gives to exploring the parameters for believing in God. Maimonides's negative theology—surely one of his best-known ideas—urges that

---

6. On this point, see the Introduction and also the range of projects countenanced as "phenomenological" and note the diversity of quite a few recent texts that employ a phenomenological method: Shaun Gallagher, *How the Body Shapes the Mind* (Oxford: Oxford University Press, 2006); Lisa Guenther, *Solitary Confinement: Social Death and Its Afterlives* (Minneapolis: University of Minnesota Press, 2013); Serena Parekh, *Hannah Arendt and the Challenge of Modernity: A Phenomenology of Human Rights* (London: Routledge, 2008); Jill Stauffer, *Ethical Loneliness: The Injustice of Not Being Heard* (New York: Columbia University Press, 2015).

7. Walter Brogan, *Heidegger and Aristotle: The Twofoldness of Being* (Buffalo, NY: SUNY Press, 2012); Ted Sadler, *Heidegger and Aristotle: The Question of Being* (London: Athlone, 2000); Thomas Sheehan, "Heidegger, Aristotle and Phenomenology," *Philosophy Today* 19, no. 2 (1975).

8. On this point, see footnotes 17, 18, and 19.

one's speech, especially when it comes to God, ought to be entirely negative, revolve around "the unsayable and indefinable."[9] And it is exactly around this issue that one of the most well-known puzzles about the *Guide* emerges. The puzzle is that Maimonides appears to be committed both to his negative theology *and* to stating that one can prove the existence of God (which certainly seems like a strong—perhaps the strongest possible—positive statement about God). Here's what he writes:

> For according to me the correct way, which is the method of demonstration about which there can be no doubt, is to establish the existence and the oneness of the deity and the negation of corporeality through the methods of the philosophers, which methods are founded upon the doctrine of the eternity of the world. This is not because I believe in the eternity of the world or because I concede this point to the philosophers; *but because it is through this method that the demonstration becomes valid and perfect certainty is obtained. . . . I mean the existence of the deity.* (*Guide*, 1.71, 180–81, emphasis added)

This passage, refers, above all, to Maimonides's proof of the existence of God at *Guide* 2.1-2.[10] Note that this passage quite obviously stands in stark contrast to Maimonides's claim in *Guide* 2.24 that it is ultimately impossible to have knowledge of God (the latter claim exemplifying a negative theological strategy): "For it is impossible for us to accede

---

9. William Franke, *A Philosophy of the Unsayable* (South Bend, IN: University of Notre Dame Press, 2014), 15. Franke has written one of the most impressive and comprehensive analyses of apophasis, religious and otherwise.

10. There are many reconstructions of this proof available now; two recent lucid ones are Tamar M. Rudavsky, *Maimonides* (Oxford, UK: Blackwell, 2009), 48–58, and Josef Stern, *The Matter and Form of Maimonides' Guide* (Cambridge, MA: Harvard University Press, 2013), 148–59.

to the points starting from which conclusions may be drawn about the heavens; for the latter are too far away from us and too high in place and in rank. And even the general conclusion that may be drawn from them, namely, that they prove the existence of their Mover, is a matter the knowledge of which cannot be reached by human intellects" (*Guide*, 2.24, 327). Making sense of this apparent contradiction has been a sort of holy grail for Maimonides scholarship.[11] Dealing with this contradiction, however, I believe also offers an entry point into the distinct sense of phenomenology—and, more important, a notion of world—that Maimonides invokes. Let me start with the philological issues in the first passage (1.71). Note especially Maimonides's use of the word *certainty* (יקינא [*yakina*] in Judeo-Arabic and يقين [*yaqeen*] in Arabic). Earlier in the *Guide*, Maimonides had given this definition of certainty in the context of belief: "If, together with ... belief, one realizes that a belief different from it is in no way possible and that no starting point can be found in the mind for a rejection of this belief or for the supposition that a different belief is possible, there is certainty" (*Guide*, 1.50, 111). In making sense of what Maimonides is after with this claim, scholars have generally taken issues of epistemology to be central,[12] with a sort of consensus emerging that

11. For a discussion, see Warren Zev Harvey, "Maimonides' First Commandment, Physics, and Doubt," in *Hazon Nahum: Studies in Jewish Law, Thought, and History Presented to Dr. Norman Lamm on the Occasion of His Seventieth Birthday*, ed. Jeffrey S. Gurock and Yaakov Elman (New York: Yeshiva University Press, 1998). For an even deeper discussion, one that precedes an entire journal issue dedicated to the topic (found in the same issue as the citation that follows), see Gad Freudenthal, "Maimonides on the Knowability of the Heavens and of Their Mover (Guide 2:24)," *Aleph* 8, no. 1 (2008): 151–57.

12. Shalom Rosenberg, "The Concept of Belief in the Thought of Maimonides and His Successors (Hebrew)," *Bar-Ilan Yearbook*, no. 22–23 (1987–1988): 351–89; Rosenberg, "The Concept of '*Emunah* in Post-Maimonidean Philosophy," in *Studies in Medieval Jewish Thought and History*, ed. Isadore Twersky, 2: 273–308 (Cambridge, MA: Harvard University Press, 1987). See also Charles H. Manekin, "Belief, Certainty,

what's necessary for resolving this apparent contradiction is the Aristotelian distinction between "*propter quid*" and "*quia*" demonstrations (*Pos. Analytics*, I.13, 78a25).[13] On such a view, the "gap between certainty and knowledge" is exploited in order to suggest that Maimonides argues that God exists (*quia*), but without implying that Maimonides believes that you can argue why or how (*propter quid*) God exists; there is certainty that God exists without *knowledge* of the same. (It is "an inference to the best explanation.")[14]

I do not oppose such a reading of Maimonides; in fact, I take it to be a virtue of my account that, in broad strokes, it is compatible with such a reading. Nonetheless, I do think that the reading that I develop fits better with and expresses more prominently Maimonides's chief aims and aspirations, which intimately involve presenting (his) philosophy as a way of life, as a sort of spiritual exercise.[15] The book is, after all, a guide, and is written, at least putatively, as a guide to his student, Joseph ben Judah of Ceuta. To be clear on this point, my suggestion is not that an epistemological stress is here incorrect, but rather that it is too narrow, missing the pathos of Maimonides's thinking, which, as I will show, has its beginnings in a particular phenomenological stance toward the world, and which equally aims at a particular phenomenological stance in or attunement to the world as its preeminent goal (where one "becomes calm" and where one's thoughts "are not troubled"—see *Guide*, 3.13, 456). It

and Divine Attributes in the *Guide of the Perplexed*," *Maimonidean Studies* 1 (1990): 117–41.

13. The version of Aristotle cited in the body of the text throughout is Aristotle, *Complete Works of Aristotle*. 2 vols. (Princeton, NJ: Princeton University Press, 2014). For a compelling account of how Maimonides's thought allegedly trades on this distinction, see Stern, *Matter and Form*, 141.

14. Ibid., 162.

15. For this latter conception, see Pierre Hadot, ed., *Philosophy as a Way of Life: Spiritual Exercises from Socrates to Foucault* (Oxford, UK: Wiley-Blackwell, 1995). For a reading of Maimonides that presents this view, see Stern, *Matter and Form*, 148, and 181.

is this prior point about the phenomenological beginnings of Maimonides's project that has received insufficient—indeed, no—attention.

Before elaborating this point, note also that explaining Maimonides's use of the notion of certainty chiefly through reference to Aristotelian distinctions like "*propter quid*" and "*quia*" is imprecise in another way: it overlooks Maimonides's more immediate philosophical context. I say this not because Aristotle is unimportant for Maimonides (quite the contrary, of course, as I have myself already noted), but rather because the term *certainty*—notably the Arabic: يقين [*yaqeen*]—plays an important role in Muslim theology and philosophy from the *Quran* onward, especially in al-Ghazālī,[16] who was a significant influence on Maimonides (to the point of likely even being the source for the title of the *Guide*).[17] To prioritize the

---

16. For an excellent introduction, see Eric Ormsby, *Ghazali* (Oxford, UK: Oneworld, 2007).

17. On the former point, see the sort of hedging that Stern must perform ("Maimonides himself nowhere explicitly mentions the [Aristotelian] terminology . . . but the distinction was so ingrained in Aristotelian logic and epistemology that he must have known of it and recognized its importance"—see Stern, *Matter and Form*, 163). To be clear, though, I think Stern has presented a remarkable reading of Maimonides on this point and I view my own as largely reinforcing his, even as I also think my own actually complements the rest of Stern's story better than his own. On the latter point, there is now an extensive literature on this; see especially Steven Harvey, "Alghazali and Maimonides and Their Books of Knowledge," in *Be'erot Yitzhak: Studies in Memory of Isadore Twersky*, ed. Jay M. Harris, 99–117 (Cambridge, MA: Harvard University Press, 2005); Hava Lazarus-Yaffeh, "Was Maimonides Influenced by al-Ghazālī?," in *Tehillah Le-Moshe: Biblical and Judaic Studies in Honor of Moshe Greenberg*, ed. Mordechai Cogan, Barry L. Eichler, and Jeffrey H. Tigay, 163–93 (Winona Lake, IN: Eisenbrauns, 1997); Amira Eran, "Al-Ghazālī and Maimonides on the World to Come and Spiritual Pleasures," *Jewish Studies Quarterly* 8, no. 2 (2001): 137–66; Alfred L. Ivry, "The *Guide* and Maimonides's Philosophical Sources," in *The Cambridge Companion to Moses Maimonides*, ed. Kenneth Seeskin, 58–82 (Cambridge: Cambridge University Press, 2005). On the point about the title, see Avner Gil'adi, "A Short Note on the Possible Origin of the Title *Moreh ha-Nevuchim* (Hebrew)," *Tarbiz* 48 (1979): 346–47.

Islamic context over the Aristotelian one is not to deny the latter, but instead to stress that Islamic thought and culture would have likely been more immediate to Maimonides's thinking,[18] and that his very knowledge of Aristotle would have itself been filtered largely through Muslim intellectual history. And because of his forced conversion,[19] we can confidently claim that Maimonides had an intimate familiarity with a large variety of Islamic thought.

§ 2. The Islamic Phenomenological Background: Certainty in the Qu'ran and al-Ghazālī

To sketch the contours of the phenomenological view I have in mind, take the Qur'an and its invocation of certainty. There, the term *certainty* (يقين [*yaqeen*]) occurs twenty-eight times, where its uses revolve exactly around what might be termed, in the phenomenological language I want to use (and which I will shortly elaborate), the mood or attunement of certainty. In the usage of the Qur'an, *certainty* describes not merely some epistemological position as when I am certain that I locked the door or that I know the answer to this mathematical problem, but rather the use of *certainty* refers to something more properly termed existential, as bearing on the ultimate meaning of human existence. So, for example, often a concern with ultimate punishment and hellfire is invoked as a certainty for a particular type of individual (see notably, for example, Sura 56:95 and Sura 102:5, 7, but also

---

18. On this point, see especially Gil Anidjar, *"Our Place in al-Andalus": Kabbalah, Philosophy, Literature in Arab Jewish Letters* (Palo Alto, CA: Stanford University Press, 2002); S. Stroumsa, *Maimonides in His World*.

19. On the forced conversion, see S. Stroumsa, *Maimonides in His World*, 59–61. Note especially footnote 31, where Stroumsa provides an argument that Maimonides likely had memorized the Qur'an. For hesitations about Maimonides's conversion (which Stroumsa addresses), see Herbert A. Davidson, *Moses Maimonides: The Man and His Works* (Oxford: Oxford University Press, 2010), 9–28.

others). Similarly, Sura 15:99 invokes *certainty* in the context of "*the* certainty" (ٱلْيَقِينُ [*al-yaqeen*]), that is, as a stand-in for death. The resonances here are very much with the way in which Martin Heidegger has understood the phenomenological certainty of death as concretizing individual human possibility and existence.[20] In *Being and Time*, written in 1927, Heidegger stresses that, with death, an individual "stands before itself in its ownmost potentiality-of-being."[21] Heidegger notes how death is a "nonrelational possibility" that cannot "be bypassed" (§50), and that death must, above all, be understood "as the possibility of the impossibility of existence in general" (§53, 242). Note that the way in which death is being invoked here is not merely as a claim about a psychological state one experiences (say, the "fear of death"),[22] but rather as announcing an existential-phenomenological point about what it means to be mortal, to know that one's possibilities, at some point—*inevitably*, often without one's control or despite one's best predictions—will come to an end, and do so *certainly*, without even the slightest possibility of doubt.[23] As Heidegger analyzes, and as the Qur'an states, that is *the* true certainty; it cannot be disputed, no matter how clever or wise one might be. Compare, in this context, the

20. Kindred views about death can also be found in the modern Jewish thinker Franz Rosenzweig. See Franz Rosenzweig, *The Star of Redemption* (Madison: University of Wisconsin Press, 2005). On this point, see especially Peter E. Gordon, *Rosenzweig and Heidegger: Between Judaism and German Philosophy* (Berkeley: University of California Press, 2003), 33: 168.

21. The version cited is Martin Heidegger, *Being and Time* (New York: Harper and Row, 1962), §50, 232. Occasionally it is cited directly in the body of the text.

22. Cf. *Being and Time* §50, 232–33.

23. And all this with the equal possibility that there may be life after death. On this point, see Martin Heidegger, *History of the Concept of Time: Prolegomena* (Bloomington: Indiana University Press, 1992), 314. Heidegger's point is a phenomenological one: that one's death is the negation of a *world*, i.e., the negation of meaning and possibility; an afterlife would only be *another* world, it, too, with its (new) distinct possibilities.

alleged statement by Ali ibn Abi Talib (considered by Shia Muslims to be the first imam and by Sunni Muslims to be the final holy caliph) that "there is nothing greater in certainty than death," with Heidegger's own statement in *History of the Concept of Time* (1925) that "this certainty, that 'I myself am in that I will die,' is *the basic certainty* . . . it is a genuine statement . . . while *cogito sum* [I think, therefore I am] is only the semblance of such a statement."[24] In considering these passages seriously, it strikes me as simply *inappropriate* to gloss the certainty invoked as oriented solely or primarily around epistemological concerns. Such a gloss is not incorrect, but it ignores the pathos of these claims, which are fundamentally existential (the point is not to stress the *certainty* of death, but to stress the certainty of *death*). Something unique—and uniquely radical—happens to someone upon the realization that he or she is mortal. It matters in a concrete way, not merely as a species or bit of knowledge. And it is exactly this phenomenological context—which, as I'll shortly show, need not be restricted to the certainty of death—that ought to be seen as informing Maimonides's own use of *certainty*.[25]

24. Ibid., 316–17. This is a lecture course Heidegger delivered in 1925 and is what *Being and Time* is based on.

25. Furthermore, even though I have used Heidegger to make a case for the Islamic context of the word's use, it is also undeniable that the basic existential point was available to anyone versed in the Jewish textual tradition, above all in the book of Ecclesiastes. On this point, see Martin Shuster, "Being as Breath, Vapor as Joy: Using Martin Heidegger to Re-read the Book of Ecclesiastes," *Journal for the Study of the Old Testament* 33, no. 2 (2008): 219–44. And Maimonides, we know, was familiar enough with Ecclesiastes to affirm its status in the canon. On this point, see Michael J. Broyde, "Defilement of the Hands, Canonization of the Bible, and the Special Status of *Esther*, *Ecclesiastes*, and *Song of Songs*," *Judaism* 44, no. 1 (1995): 65. Finally, it is likely no accident that Maimonides's translator, Samuel ibn Tibbon, made it almost a life's work to focus on Ecclesiastes as *the* philosophical text of Judaism. See James T. Robinson, *Samuel ibn Tibbon's Commentary on Ecclesiastes: The Book of the Soul of Man* (Tübingen, Ger.: Mohr Siebeck, 2007).

To bring into clearer focus Maimonides's use of *certainty*, I want to turn to an intermediary between the Qur'an and Maimonides, namely the aforementioned context of Islamic philosophy, specifically the work of al-Ghazālī. Here are a few striking ways in which al-Ghazālī invokes the term *certainty* in his writings:

> Those who are gifted with spiritual insight have really grasped this truth as a fact of experience, and not a merely traditional maxim. Their clear perception of it leads them to the conviction that he by whom it was spoken was a prophet indeed, just as a man who has studied medicine knows when he is listening to a physician. This is a kind of certainty which requires no support from miracles such as the conversion of a rod into a snake, the credit of which may be shaken by apparently equally extraordinary miracles performed by magicians.[26]

> Rather, what is secure from error should be so closely associated with certainty, that if someone tried to show that it was false by turning stone into gold or a stick into a snake, for example, that would not make it doubtful or refute it. Thus, if I came to know that ten is greater than three, and someone said to me: "No, three is greater than ten, in proof of which I will turn this stick into a serpent," then went on to do so in plain view, I would not as a result of that come to doubt what I was cognizant of. The only outcome would be wonderment at how he is able to perform such a feat.[27]

> This is the way to seek certainty in prophecy, not in the turning of a stick into a serpent or the cleaving of the moon.

---

26. Al-Ghazālī, *Alchemy of Happiness*, 132. *The Alchemy of Happiness* was written sometime in 1105. Field's translation comes from the Hindustani (Urdu), but the word for *certainty* is the same in Urdu and Arabic.

27. This is from al-Ghazālī's autobiography, *Deliverance from Error*, written sometime around 1100 a.d. The translation I have used is Muhammad Ali Khalidi, *Medieval Islamic Philosophical Writings* (Cambridge: Cambridge University Press, 2005), 61. For a standalone and complete version of the book, see Richard J. McCarthy, *Freedom and Fulfillment: An Annotated Translation of al-Ghazālī's al-Munqidh Min al-Ḍalāl and Other Relevant Works of al-Ghazālī* (New York: Macmillan, 1980).

For if you rely only on such things, and do not assemble innumerable pieces of evidence, you may one day come to assume that they are magic or fantasy, or even that they might be confusion sent by God Almighty, who "confuses whom he wishes and guides whom he wishes." Thus, the whole issue of miracles will be thrown back at you. If your faith in prophecy is based solely upon statements supported by the evidence of a miracle, then that faith will be broken by statements designed to render that miracle dubious and suspect. Let such exceptional occurrences be just one of the proofs and indications that figure in the *totality* of your theoretical speculation, so that you will come to have necessary knowledge whose grounds cannot be narrowly specified. You will be like someone who has heard a report recurrently corroborated by a whole group of people. *The certainty associated with the report cannot be said to derive from a single specific statement, but rather in an indefinite way. Although it does not derive from anyone outside the group, it cannot be traced back to any single individual.*[28]

A few points ought to be noted. It is both impossible and unnecessary at this juncture and in this context either (1) to pursue a comprehensive inquiry into the way in which al-Ghazālī invokes "certainty" (يقين [*yaqeen*]) in his writings or (2) to outline conclusively how this term functions for al-Ghazālī in relation to other concepts (the most notable of which would be the Sufi notion of "taste" ذوق [*dawq*], which al-Ghazālī invokes frequently for the sort of immediate or direct experience that interests him).[29] This is because what

28. Ali Khalidi, *Medieval Islamic Philosophical Writings*, 86. Emphasis added.
29. For the use of this term in al-Ghazālī and Sufi mysticism, see Caner K. Dagli, *Ibn al-'Arabī and Islamic Intellectual Culture: From Mysticism to Philosophy* (London: Routledge, 2016); Fadlou Albert Shehadi, *Ghazali's Unique Unknowable God* (Leiden: Brill, 1964), 44. For its inheritance in Jewish philosophy, especially the work of Judah Halevi, see Diana Lobel, *Between Mysticism and Philosophy: Sufi Language of Religious*

I want to highlight is a relatively modest point: that certainty within al-Ghazālī's corpus, as in the Qur'an (and as in Heidegger) is not solely an intellectual matter. When al-Ghazālī discusses certainty in the first quote above, he draws an analogy to how one can recognize a (fellow) physician when one has studied medicine.

It is crucial—for the present argument and for the broader argument of this chapter—to understand that any such recognition is not a matter of *knowing* some particular fact or even set of facts (although this, too, is obviously involved), but more properly a factor of being *attuned* in a particular way.[30] The idea is that I recognize a fellow doctor not because I wait for them to display their knowledge in a "doctorly" situation or even myself quiz them about their knowledge of medicine, but rather that they comport themselves in the way in which doctors comport themselves (in earlier centuries this may have had to do with evincing care for someone suffering or some other illustration of a commitment to the principles of the Hippocratic oath, engaging in the sort of curiosity associated with being committed to medicine, while in the present US moment it may be more closely tied to the sort of values and comportments that insurance companies and our distinct medical systems may reinforce—a commitment, say, to "not having my time wasted" and to feeling as if one's deepest career aims are perpetually besieged by one's working conditions, combined with the aforementioned doctorly traits, and many others besides).[31]

Experience in Judah ha-Levi's "Kuzari" (Buffalo, NY: SUNY Press, 2000), 89ff. For Maimonides's familiarity with Halevi, see Howard Kreisel, "Judah Halevi's Influence on Maimonides: A Preliminary Appraisal," *Maimonidean Studies* 2 (1991).

30. For the sense of attunement I have in mind here, see Stanley Cavell, *The Claim of Reason: Wittgenstein, Skepticism, Morality, and Tragedy* (Oxford: Oxford University Press, 1979), 115 and throughout.

31. My few lines obviously cannot capture what a rich phenomenological account would need to capture about such comportment, but I hope that they give the reader a sense of how one might proceed. Some memoirs and likeminded accounts might be useful here. For example, see Eliza

With such an example, it is never the case that there is any particular fact that a physician reveals that leads someone else (who is also a physician) to conclude that the person speaking is a physician. Instead, such a conclusion may be drawn from a wide array of things: the way in which they comport themselves, the way in which they tie various strands of knowledge together, the way in which the view the world and themselves in it, the way in which they prioritize certain things over others, the things that are salient to them and those that are not, the fact that they aim to help others, and so forth. In short, to once again draw an analogy to Heidegger, it is their entire practical engagement with and in the world that is important (as opposed to, say, their theoretical approximation of the world).[32] In the case of the doctor, what's important is a specific sort of practical existence within the world; there are other sorts of practical existence that are available to individuals, each of them depending on what other professions or modes of worldly engagement one is talking about (understand that no matter their individual personalities, the things that are salient to a doctor merely are different from those that are salient to a physics professor or a lawyer or a construction worker).

This broader point about certainty can also be exemplified by broaching another philosophical analogy, this time to something Ludwig Wittgenstein states in *On Certainty* (ca. 1950): "If you tried to doubt everything you would not get as far as doubting anything. The game of doubting itself presupposes certainty (*Gewißheit*)."[33] Heidegger's and Wittgenstein's suggestion is

---

Lo Chin, *This Side of Doctoring: Reflections from Women in Medicine* (Oxford: Oxford University Press, 2002); Michael J. Collins, *Blue Collar, Blue Scrubs: The Making of a Surgeon* (New York: St. Martin's Griffin, 2009); Tracy Kidder, *Mountains beyond Mountains* (New York: Random House, 2009); Sherwin B. Nuland, *The Soul of Medicine: Tales from the Bedside* (New York: Kaplan, 2009).

32. See *Being and Time*, §14–18.

33. Ludwig Wittgenstein, *On Certainty* (New York: Harper and Row, 1969), 115, 18.

that even the most technical epistemological investigations presuppose,[34] indeed are parasitic on, a lived engagement with the world, a sort of "absorbed coping,"[35] where one moves and acts within the world without the intrusion of doubt (and this without claiming that doubt cannot intrude). Such a practical, engaged certainty is how to make sense of al-Ghazālī's second quote: even the production of apparent miracles is not enough to discredit the sort of certainty that makes possible that one have a world, that is, that makes possible the production of such practical certainty in the first place. To my mind, there is here a strong link between the Arabic (يقين [yaqeen]) that I have been translating as certainty and what often gets translated as "unconcealment" or "factuality" (or truth) in ancient Greek (ἀλήθεια [aletheia]).[36] I mention this link in order to further strengthen the comparison to Heidegger, because, as is well known, Heidegger frequently proposes the notion of *aletheia* (ἀλήθεια [aletheia]) in exactly the sort of phenomenological context that I have been arguing is most appropriate here. For Heidegger, ἀλήθεια [aletheia] denotes a "primordial truth" or a "clearing" that, in turn, "makes truth claims *possible*."[37] Truth claims of whatever sort presuppose the fact of being embedded within a particular form of life that allows certain saliences to register, and that serves as a condition of the possibility for raising those truth claims.[38] One way to think about this in the

34. There is now an incredibly large range of literature comparing and contrasting these two figures. For the most recent and likely most extensive treatment, see Lee Braver, *Groundless Grounds: A Study of Wittgenstein and Heidegger* (Cambridge, MA: MIT Press, 2012).

35. Hubert Dreyfus, *Being-in-the-World: A Commentary on Heidegger's "Being and Time," Division I* (Cambridge, MA: MIT Press, 1991), 58.

36. This point is suggested, albeit in another and very different philosophical context, in Franz Rosenthal, *Knowledge Triumphant: The Concept of Knowledge in Medieval Islam* (Leiden, Neth.: Brill, 1970), 25.

37. Dreyfus, *Being-in-the-World*, 270. Compare Dreyfus's elaboration to Heidegger, *Being and Time*, 44; Martin Heidegger, *On Time and Being*, trans. Joan Stambaugh (Chicago: University of Chicago Press, 2002), 70.

38. There is a lot more to be said about ἀλήθεια (*aletheia*) in Heidegger's corpus, and indeed, the picture I have presented in the last few

context of medicine, pursued thus far, is that even to begin to doubt a particular bit of medical knowledge (say, this or that claim about our health is incorrect) or a particular individual's knowledge of medicine (say, this person isn't a doctor at all!), is first to have a fundamental certainty about what *counts* as certain in this realm, what the methods are for accounting for this, what evidence, what concern, what observation, and so forth; particular knowledge claims are always parasitic on broader embodied practices (for better and for worse). Taking such a position is one way to understand why al-Ghazālī speaks of a totality in the third quote above and stresses how there is no single source for the certainty involved; again, the certainty involved is the certainty that makes possible a world and so could never revolve around or involve simply one or even a collection of distinct facts.

What's striking, then, is that al-Ghazālī exactly suggests the puzzling possibility of having certainty, albeit without having truth. In fact, this is a prospect that he had considered as early as his logic text, *Criterion of Knowledge in the Art of Knowledge* (ca. 1095),[39] where, for example, in considering whether death follows decapitation, he points out that while it is certain that it does, it need not do so necessarily, that is, it may come to be *false* that it does—miracles just are (logically) possible.[40] A similar sentiment underwrites what

---

sentences is overly simplistic from that perspective. But my aims here are not to engage in any meaningful fashion with Heidegger scholarship. In that vein, I point the reader to Hayim and Rivca Gordon, *Heidegger on Truth and Myth: A Rejection of Postmodernism* (Bern: Peter Lang, 2006), 83–99; Robert Bernasconi, *The Question of Language in Heidegger's History of Being* (New York: Springer, 2016), 24ff; Werner Marx, *Heidegger and the Tradition* (Evanston, IL: Northwestern University Press, 1982), 145–52.

39. Al-Ghazālī, *Mi'Yar al-'Ilm* (Cairo: Dar al-ma'arif, 1965).

40. Ibid., 58. For a discussion of this point, and of the broader issues it suggests about causality in al-Ghazālī, see Michael Marmura, "Ghazali and Demonstrative Science," *Journal of the History of Philosophy* 3, no. 2 (1965): 183–204. For the broader issue of causality, see Lenn E.

al-Ghazālī writes in his autobiography (from which I've already quoted), when he claims that "certainty reached by apodeictic proof is *knowledge*. Intimate experience of that very state is *immediate experience*. Favorable acceptance of it based on hearsay and experience of others is *faith*. These, then, are three degrees, or levels, of knowledge—'God raises in degrees those of you who believe and those to whom knowledge is given'" (Qur'an, 58.12).[41] I take the first part of this quote—that there is a certainty reached by apodictic proof that can therefore be called knowledge—to suggest that there could be certainty that is *not* knowledge (i.e., that hasn't been verified or vouchsafed by apodictic proof).[42] This is why elsewhere al-Ghazālī speaks of there being "*verified* certainty,"[43] again implying that there could be certainty that hasn't been verified by means of proof. This is a point

---

Goodman, "Did al-Ghazali Deny Causality?," *Studia Islamica*, no. 47 (1978): 83–120. For the point about miracles, see Richard Swinburne, *The Concept of Miracle* (Dordrecht, Neth.: Springer, 1970); Richard Swinburne, *The Existence of God* (Oxford: Oxford University Press, 2004), 273–93.

41. McCarthy, *Freedom and Fulfillment*, 95–96. Translation modified. There is, of course, a lot more to be said about the notion of certainty in Islamic theology in general, especially the idea of the three degrees of certainty that are allegedly found in the Qur'an. Obviously, dealing with this topic is far beyond my scope here, but I do refer the reader to Rashid al-Din Maybudi's commentary on the Qur'an. It was initiated around 1126 a.d. and reflects well what's in the air at the time and what Maimonides likely would have been familiar with. See Rashid al-Din Maybudi, *The Unveiling of the Mysteries and the Provision of the Pious*, trans. William Chittick (Louisville, KY: Fons Vitae, 2015), 90–91, 249–50, 262–63, 309, 552. Thanks to Amer Latif for these references.

42. And this, without denying, that in Islamic philosophy, certainty for the most part was closely associated with knowledge, see Josef Van Ess, *Die Erkenntnislehre des 'Adudaddin al-Ici: Übersetzung und Kommentar des ersten Buches seiner Mawaqif* (Weisbaden, Ger.: Steiner, 1966), 101. The same is true of Jewish philosophy after Maimonides. Indeed, Maimonides's translator, ibn Tibbon, translates the Judeo-Arabic יקינא' in Maimonides as "true belief" (אמתית אמונה).

43. This is also from the *Deliverance from Error*, quoted in Rosenthal, *Knowledge Triumphant*, 62. Emphasis added.

that I take to be important for understanding Maimonides, and I have wanted to stress this background and backdrop to Maimonides's thinking in order to suggest a way (1) to make sense of the alleged tension earlier above between negative theology and proof of God and also (2) to understand Maimonides's general intuitions about what it means to be "certain" of God's existence, all in order (3) to set up Maimonides's distinct use and understanding of phenomenology and world.

§ 3. Aristotle and the Greeks as a Phenomenological Source

I take it that when Maimonides invokes God as a "first existent,"[44] he is invoking this sort of practical sense of certainty, wherein one may be certain without apodictic proof. In the context of Islamic thought of this period, a "first existent," ought to be most closely associated with the ancient Greek notion of an "axiom" (ἀξίωμα [*axíoma*]).[45] On this point, a thought of Heidegger's is again instructive. In his lectures on Leibniz's principle of sufficient reason, Heidegger notes that while we tend to use terms like *axiom* and *principle* interchangeably (as in "fundamental principle"—i.e., "first existent"), the two are conceptually distinguishable (although there is enough overlap for them to be plausible as translations). Heidegger stresses that "the Greek ἀξίωμα comes from ἀξίω [*axió*], 'I find something worthy.'"[46] In the ancient Greek context, however, "finding worth" is not something that is

---

44. מעקול אול—see, for example, *Guide* 2.2 and 3.51, among others.

45. See Herbert A. Davidson, *Alfarabi, Avicenna, and Averroes on Intellect: Their Cosmologies, Theories of the Active Intellect, and Theories of Human Intellect* (Oxford: Oxford University Press, 1992), 51. See also Joel L. Kraemer, *Maimonides: The Life and World of One of Civilization's Greatest Minds* (New York: Doubleday, 2010), 71.

46. Martin Heidegger, *The Principle of Reason*, trans. Reginald Lilly (Bloomington: Indiana University Press, 1996), 15.

best explained or understood through the human conferment of value (indeed, Heidegger radically claims that the Greeks did not engage in such an undertaking until fairly late in their history). Heidegger alleges that for the ancient Greeks, it was the object itself that presented its value: an object stands forth—shines—and thereby allows other objects to emerge from its light. In such a view, "an axiom is that which is in the highest regard (*höchsten Ansehen*), and *not as a consequence of an estimation by humans and granted by them*. That which is in the highest regard brings its standing from out of itself. This regard rests on its individual aspect (*Aussehen*)."[47] My aims here are not to assess the merits of this position as a view about objects or about axiology—neither as an interpretation of the ancient Greeks nor as a claim about the production of value—but rather only to present this view as a plausible way of understanding Maimonides's own stance toward God.[48] To put the whole of my proposal forward at once: Maimonides takes it that in examining one's world—*the* world—one is inevitably led to the certainty of God's existence, where certainty carries the valence sketched above, as not merely or exclusively a category of knowledge, but rather something like a practical certainty. We might say that through an *acknowledgment* of the complex and amazing ways in which the elements of this world hang together, we are (practically) led to an acknowledgment—made *certain*—of the "light" that makes all this appear, shine forth.[49]

---

47. Ibid., 16. Translation modified and emphasis added.

48. For an exploration of Heidegger on this point, see John Caputo, *The Mystical Element in Heidegger's Thought* (New York: Fordham University Press, 1986). For hesitations about Heidegger's views of the ancient Greeks, see Glenn Most, "Heidegger's Greeks," *Arion* 10, no. 1 (2002): 83–98. For extensive discussion of Heidegger's relationship with the ancient Greeks, see Drew Hyland and John Manoussakis, *Heidegger and the Greeks: Interpretive Essays* (Bloomington: Indiana University Press, 2006).

49. There is a complex issue here about the relationship between knowledge and acknowledgment. Useful here is the work of Stanley Cavell,

The context of these claims by Heidegger about the ancient Greeks should not be overlooked: they are proposed as an elaboration of Leibniz's thought.[50] Since the 1861 publication of Leibniz's study notes on Maimonides by Foucher de Careil, it has been known that Leibniz studied Maimonides quite closely, in fact seeing himself as developing elements of his thought.[51] Such a connection between these thinkers makes plausible that the view that Heidegger describes here is one that might be found in Maimonides. To be clear: my claim is not that Leibniz was after all simply reworking or paraphrasing Maimonides, or that, in turn, Heidegger was

who proposes two important points. First, Cavell notes that knowledge and acknowledgment cannot be separated: the latter involves the former, which does not thereby imply that acknowledgment is simply a matter of agreement or contract. As Cavell notes, "I do not propose the idea of acknowledgement as an alternative to knowing but rather as an interpretation of it, as I take the word 'acknowledge,' containing 'knowledge,' itself to suggest (or perhaps it suggests that knowing is an interpretation of acknowledging)." See Stanley Cavell, *In Quest of the Ordinary: Lines of Skepticism and Romanticism* [Chicago: University of Chicago Press, 1994], 8. Important in this context is also Cavell's entire locus of investigation on the varieties of skepticism, notably the idea that "skepticism suggests . . . that since we cannot know the world exists, its presentness to us cannot be a function of knowing. The world is to be accepted; as the presentness of other minds is not to be known, but acknowledged." Later in the same text, Cavell stresses that the "methodological expression" of missing this point about how we "have" a world is the idea that we must pursue "an investigation of our knowledge of the external world by an investigation of a claim that a particular object exists" See Stanley Cavell, "The Avoidance of Love," in *Disowning Knowledge in Seven Plays of Shakespeare* [Cambridge: Cambridge University Press, 2003], 95, 96.

50. For an analysis of the relationship between Heidegger and Leibniz, see Renato Cristin, *Heidegger and Leibniz: Reason and Faith* (Dordrecht, Neth.: Kluwer Academic, 1998).

51. Louis-Alexandre Foucher de Careil died in 1891. A fervent Catholic, he also published, in addition to his publication of Leibniz's notes on Maimonides, a book on Leibniz's relationship with Kabbalah. See Louis-Alexandre Foucher de Careil, *Leibniz, la Philosophie Juive et la Cabale: Trois Lectures à l'Académie des Sciences Morales et Politiques avec les Manuscrits Inédits de Leibniz* (Paris: Durand, 1861). For a translation and analysis of Leibniz's notes, see Lenn E. Goodman, "Maimonides and Leibniz," *Journal of Jewish Studies* 31, no. 2 (1980): 214–36.

doing the same with either Leibniz or Maimonides. Instead, I have wanted to raise this possible connection in order to make even more plausible a particular reading of a philosophical influence and ancestor that all these figures share: Aristotle.[52] My argument will not be that Maimonides or Islamic philosophers or Heidegger all explicitly argued for a particular understanding of Aristotle. The sources are too varied, the contexts and concerns of the philosophers too different, and the projects too distinct to make such a claim convincingly. Nonetheless, I do think that presenting a *particular reading* of Aristotle makes it even more plausible that these figures share a fundamental approach that has its origin in Aristotle, an approach that I will argue prioritizes the phenomenological notion of world that I have been developing. The locus for these issues is Aristotle's notion of οὐσία [*ousia*], which has variously been translated as "substance" or "essence." It may be, however, that these translations are already warping a possible, more original, understanding of the term.

Here's how Heidegger develops his understanding of οὐσία [*ousia*] in Aristotle and the ancient Greeks. In a 1928 lecture course, *The Metaphysical Foundations of Logic*, he alleges that, "οὐσία itself has a twofold meaning."[53] Drawing a distinction between οὐσία [*ousia*] in the sense of a "modus existendi" (a mode of existence) and a "modus essendi" (the essence of something), Heidegger stresses that the former denotes *that* something is, while the latter denotes *what* something is; the former implies questions of ontology, of how something *is*, while the latter implies questions of an

---

52. The importance of Aristotle to Heidegger, Maimonides, and the Muslim philosophical context is well known; Leibniz, it should be noted, also had a complex and long-standing relationship with Aristotle. On this point, see Christia Mercer, *Leibniz's Metaphysics: Its Origins and Development* (Cambridge: Cambridge University Press, 2001), 63.

53. Martin Heidegger, *The Metaphysical Foundations of Logic*, trans. Michael Heim (Bloomington: Indiana University Press, 1984), 145.

empirical bent: what it is, how it originates, and so forth. According to Heidegger, such a dual understanding is innate to the Greek word οὐσία [*ousia*], which equally connotes "useful items, the homestead, property assets, possessions, that which is at hand anytime for everyday use, that which is *immediately and for the most part always present* [*Anwesende*])" and as something "πρότερον (earlier) than beings."[54] Although this latter claim might initially appear mysterious, Heidegger's point is that *any* understanding of οὐσία [*ousia*] highlights how it presents or brings forth particular beings. Heidegger notes in a later course, *An Introduction to Metaphysics*, that both senses of οὐσία [*ousia*] emphasize how "something is present to us. It stands steadily by itself and thus manifests itself. It is. For the Greeks 'Being' basically meant this standing presence."[55] This invocation of presence should be explicitly connected to the earlier discussion of an axiom, and its function in "presencing," and therefore to ἀλήθεια [*aletheia*] as unconcealment *of* such presence (similarly the original association between οὐσία [*ousia*] and valuables or property should exactly make plausible the earlier connection between an axiom and "finding something valuable or worthy"). Heidegger emphasizes that a "presence that is not yet mastered in thought, wherein that which is present manifests itself as an essent. *But this power first issues from concealment*, that is, in Greek *aletheia* (unconcealment) *when the power accomplishes itself as a world*."[56] The idea here is that it is the presence of worldhood—that there is a world—that makes such unconcealment possible, in fact, that makes beings—anything—possible. Or, as he puts

---

54. Ibid., 145, 146. I left in the German *"Anwesen"* in exactly for the same reason as Heidegger: that its meaning is akin to the Greek one as denoting both these valences.

55. Martin Heidegger, *An Introduction to Metaphysics*, trans. Ralph Manheim (New Haven, CT: Yale University Press, 1959), 61.

56. Ibid., 61. First and second emphasis mine.

it, "it is *through world* that essent first becomes essent."⁵⁷ In the words of one commentator, "*Ousia* is understood as that which constitutes the being-there of beings. Beings are present. Their thereness is signaled out from the wider original meaning of *ousia* as that which one owns. *Ousia* is what makes possible that humans can claim properties and possession as their own. It gives rise to the availability of beings."⁵⁸

As should be apparent from earlier remarks, it is not my aim here to adjudicate questions of Aristotle scholarship or to argue for Aristotle as the originator or precursor of Heidegger's own account of ontological difference.⁵⁹ Instead, I want to draw attention to book 2 of the *Physics*, where Aristotle himself claims that "nature (Φύσις) then is what has been stated. Things have a nature which have a principle of this kind. Each of them is a substance; for it is a subject, and nature is always in a subject" (*Physics*, 192b34–35). Note that the translator of the edition of Aristotle that I am citing has made a lot of important decisions about key terms. To see this, let me note how Heidegger translates this same passage: "Φύσις, therefore, is what has been said. Everything that includes this kind of origin and unity 'has' Φύσις. And each of these things *are* (have being) of the manner called beingness (οὐσία). In such a case, Φύσις presents of and by itself, and is always present in such a way (as a lying-forth from out of itself)."⁶⁰ Here is the Greek: φύσις μὲν οὖν ἐστὶ τὸ ῥηθέν· φύσιν δὲ ἔχει ὅσα τοιαύτην ἔχει ἀρχήν. καὶ ἔστιν πάντα ταῦτα οὐσία· ὑποκείμενον γάρ τι, καὶ ἐν ὑποκειμένῳ ἐστὶν ἡ φύσις ἀεί. All I want to suggest is that Heidegger's translation is not

57. Ibid. Emphasis mine.
58. Brogan, *Heidegger and Aristotle*, 51.
59. On this point, see Heidegger, *Metaphysical Foundations*, 10.
60. Martin Heidegger, *Wegmarken* (Frankfurt: Klostermann, 1976), 9: 259. Cf. Brogan, *Heidegger and Aristotle*, 47. The edition of Aristotle I quoted is *Complete Works of Aristotle*, 2 vols. (Princeton, NJ: Princeton University Press, 2014).

implausible. The key line is καὶ ἔστιν πάντα ταῦτα οὐσία (*kai éstin pánta tâuta ousia*). It strikes me as plausible to translate this as "each of these beings is in the manner of beingness (οὐσία)." Such a translation would make available exactly the original sense(s) of οὐσία [*ousia*] that Heidegger claims to reveal: that οὐσία [*ousia*] is that which allows beings to come forth, it is that "which is always already there."[61] Even if one disagrees, my discussion should highlight that Aristotle is sufficiently complex and that contemporary translations are influenced by centuries—millennia—of reading Aristotle's text in a particular way, and especially in light of particular Latin translations (and thereby philosophical moves and interpretations). Furthermore, and more crucial for present purposes, is the simple fact that the Muslim philosophers important to Maimonides's own development would have occupied a philosophical (not to mention religious, social, economic, and political) position quite different from these later Latin interpreters and interpretations.

This does not, of course, imply that these Muslim philosophers shared Heidegger's interpretation of Aristotle. Indeed, to develop such a point in detail would be its own book-length project.[62] My aims instead, especially in tandem with and in

---

61. See *Metaphysics*, 1007a22: ὅλως δ' ἀναιροῦσιν οἱ τοῦτο λέγοντες οὐσίαν καὶ τὸ τί ἦν εἶναι. The edition I've been citing translates this as "And in general those who use this argument do away with substance and essence," but with an alternative understanding, it seems just as likely to translate it (as Walter Brogan does) as "In general, those who talk like this, do away with οὐσία as that which is always already there" (Brogan, *Heidegger and Aristotle*, 51).

62. For an entry into such a project, see Nader el-Bizri, *The Phenomenological Quest between Avicenna and Heidegger* (Buffalo, NY: SUNY Press, 2000); Nader el-Bizri, "Being and Necessity: A Phenomenological Investigation of Avicenna's Metaphysics and Cosmology," in *Islamic Philosophy and Occidental Phenomenology on the Perennial Issue of Microcosm and Macrocosm*, ed. Anna-Teresa Tymieniecka (Dordrecht, Neth.: Springer, 2006), 243–61. El-Bizri's work is powerful and makes these analogies both plausible and fruitful, but to present what I am hinting at here comprehensively would require tracing the various permutations of

light of the account of certainty in al-Ghazālī just sketched, is just to make plausible a particular orientation to Aristotle, one that would thereby further make conceivable that the notion of world that I have been developing is important to an understanding of Maimonides ("world" understood as the idea that it is having a world, in this phenomenological sense, that reveals particular beings to us; that such a phenomenological understanding of world clarifies how there is anything for us at all).

Because of the importance of another Muslim philosopher, ibn Sīnā (Avicenna), to Maimonides's thought,[63] and also to the story I am telling, let me also therefore sketch how ibn Sīnā fits into this story about Aristotle and worldhood. Ibn Sīnā is crucial to Maimonides and this period of the history of philosophy for introducing a particular "synthesis between . . . two opposed accounts—the metaphysics of being *as an eternal given*, bearing within itself its logic and its law, and the creationist metaphysics of radically contingent being."[64] Inherent in this synthesis is the basic distinction between essence and existence that is also implicit in Heidegger's reading of Aristotle and important for Heidegger's entire project.[65] So, for example, ibn Sīnā will note that "the nature of existence *qua* the nature of existence is

---

how, for example, οὐσία gets ported into Arabic under the Persian loan-word جوهر (گوهر) in Persian; גוהר in Judeo-Arabic—a word, incidentally, that exactly shares the original, twofold sense of Greek as referring to both possession and essence).

63. See David B. Burrell, *Knowing the Unknowable God: Ibn-Sina, Maimonides, Aquinas* (South Bend, IN: University of Notre Dame Press, 1992); Davidson, *Moses Maimonides*, 102; Dov Schwartz, "Avicenna and Maimonides on Imortality," in *Medieval and Modern Perceptions on Jewish-Muslim Relations*, ed. Ronald Nettler (Luxembourg: Psychology Press, 1995).

64. Lenn E. Goodman, *Avicenna* (Ithaca, NY: Cornell University Press, 2006), 61.

65. To be clear: this does *not* imply that Heidegger subscribes to the idea that "existence precedes essence" as many existentialists do. Indeed, Heidegger ultimately attempts to sketch a position that tries to question the introduction of this distinction altogether, but this is all exactly *to* stress

a single account in definition and description, and that ... essences are different from the nature of existence itself because they are things."⁶⁶ And this is a distinction that Maimonides affirms and takes up.⁶⁷ In this view, God is that which allows beings to shine forth, to present themselves; God is that which is "always already there." My suggestion is that in making use of this distinction in order to advance such a view of God (a position, again, that's already been well developed in the literature on Maimonides and his Muslim influences), Maimonides also takes up a stance that stresses world and worldhood, much as Heidegger does. Worldhood is what allows beings to come forth to us, allows them to be unconcealed to us.⁶⁸ Here's Heidegger on the point: "And the world? Is it the sum of what is within the world? By no means.... World is not something subsequent that we calculate as a result from the sum of all beings. The world comes not afterward but *beforehand*, in the strict sense of the word. Beforehand: that which is unveiled and understood already in advance ... before any apprehending of this or that being, *beforehand as that which forth as always already unveiled to us*."⁶⁹ For Maimonides as much as for Heidegger,

---

the importance of Aristotle and the ancient Greeks and to conceive of the history of philosophy as a history of various proposals for how to navigate this distinction. On this point, see especially Martin Heidegger, "Letter on Humanism," in *Basic Writings*, ed. David Farrell Krell (New York: Harper Collins, 1993), 231 and throughout.

66. Ibn-Sina, *The Physics of the Healing: Books I and II*, trans. Jon McGinnis (Provo, UT: Brigham Young University Press, 2009), 34.

67. On this point, see Burrell, *Knowing the Unknowable God*.

68. Notably, apart from one exception, which I will discuss shortly, Maimonides essentially *does* conceive of God as *another* being, albeit categorically different; in this way, the case might be made that he falls prey to Heidegger's critique of ontotheology. I'll say more about this shortly, but I do want to note already that nothing about my reading hinges on defending Maimonides on this point.

69. Martin Heidegger, *The Basic Problems of Phenomenology*, trans. Albert Hofstadter (Bloomington: Indiana University Press, 1988), 165. Emphasis added.

it is a particular acknowledgment of the practical role that the world plays for any human being that allows other philosophical insights to emerge (for the former, about God, for the latter, about Being).

§ 4. On the Importance of Worldhood to Maimonides

Keeping in mind this broad sketch of the importance world or worldhood, turn to Maimonides's famous parable of the ruler (*Guide*, 46). In response to a question about how one might be able to prove whether there is a ruler in a particular area, Maimonides answers, proposing an imagined exchange between a diminutive money changer and a poor giant:

> You shall tell him, this proof is to be found in the fact that while this money-changer is, as you see, a weak and small man and this great amount of dinars is placed before him, this other big, strong, and poor individual is standing in front of him and asking him to give him as alms a carob-grain and that the money-changer does not do this, but reprimands him and drives him off by means of words. For, but for his fear of the ruler, the poor man would have been quick to kill him or to drive him away and to take the wealth that is in his possession. Accordingly, this is a proof of the fact that this city has a king. Thus you would have proved the existence of the king through the orderliness of the circumstances of the city, the cause of which is the fear of the ruler and the anticipation of the punishment he metes out. (*Guide*, 1.46, 97–98; translation modified)

Generally, Maimonides's proof is taken as an example of an inference to the best explanation.[70] As with the earlier case of "*propter quid*" and "*quia*" arguments, such a reading is not incorrect, but it once again strikes me as insufficiently

---

70. See Stern, *Matter and Form*, 172.

nuanced. Note two things. First, that while it *appears* as if the idea that a larger, stronger man in the context of anarchy would kill those weaker and take their possessions, it is by no means obviously true (or "natural" as some might like to think).[71] Indeed, it is itself a normative claim that presupposes an entire context—or more accurately, world—of significance (of what's important, what's not, what counts, what doesn't, what's strength and what isn't, what appears, what doesn't, which principles orient one's view, which don't, moral, psychological, social, political, and so forth). In short, what's being presupposed between the giant and the money changer is not a mere *fact* (that a ruler exists), but rather an entire *world* (that rulers and authority function in this way, and not others; that these things thereby become and were salient; that there are these conceptual connections and not others; that there is this relationship between violence and authority and not another; that *this* counts as evidence; that strength is *this* and not that; and so forth).[72] This is why it is important *not* to introduce the less literal language that Shlomo Pines introduces by glossing elements of the Arabic

---

71. As at least a plausible rejoinder to this "natural" thought, refer to Rousseau's famous argument against Hobbes's state of nature as a "war of all against all" in the second discourse. Hobbes famously postulates that perhaps there is nothing "natural" about war (since natural resources would have been bountiful and pride nonexistent), and that Hobbes is instead projecting the war of all against all of his contemporary society back into the state of nature. See Jean-Jacques Rousseau, "Discourse on the Origin of Inequality," in *Basic Political Writings*, ed. and trans. Donald A. Cress (Indianapolis: Hackett, 1987). For a recent philosophical development of Rousseau's philosophical thought along these lines, and especially his prioritization of the social aspects of self-love (*amour propre*), see Frederick Neuhouser, *Rousseau's Theodicy of Self-Love: Evil, Rationality, and the Drive for Recognition* (Oxford: Oxford University Press, 2008).

72. I am here making recourse to the way in which Heidegger has presented the phenomenological notion of world and worldliness as involving individuals in a practical engagement with the world (as discussed in section 3). For an elaboration of this point in Heidegger, see Dreyfus, *Being-in-the-World*, 88–107, especially 98–99.

with the phrase that "you would have proved the existence of the king through the *fact* that matters in the city proceed in an orderly fashion" (*Guide*, 1.46, 97, emphasis mine). As Pines himself notes, it literally reads: "you would have proved the existence of the king through the orderliness [באנתטאם / *b'anit'tam*] of the circumstances of the city" (*Guide*, 1.46, 98). The idea that the Arabic word النظام (*aniẓam*) is meant to denote is the idea of a systemic orderliness, as the root, نظام (niẓām), with its meaning of "system" suggests; it is therefore no mere or sole or single fact that betrays the existence of the ruler but rather an entire world. Second, if you take the phenomenological approach I have been invoking above, then the certainty involved here is neither, say, "subjective" nor "objective,"[73] where we focus on subjective properties within a world or objective ones, but rather the sort phenomenological, embodied *practical* certainty involved with having a world (i.e., the conditions that make possible the distinction between subject and object in the first place); it is a *gestalt*, a certainty originating from how the subjective and objective elements of experience *hang together*. And it is this certainty that allows anything to appear—to be—in the first place: a money changer, strength, weakness, relations of power, exchange, and so forth. Furthermore, and with analogy to the position of al-Ghazālī sketched earlier, such certainty could turn out to be false: there is nothing that would prevent the world of the money changer and the brute being such that absent a ruler, the brute would still not kill the money changer.[74] With analogy to the way in which the

---

73. This is contrary to Manekin's assertion take on certainty in Maimonides (apart from this philosophical point, it is also linguistically the case that the uses by Maimonides he cites in his footnote are not as obvious as he suggests; Manekin, "Belief, Certainty, and Divine Attributes," 127, footnote 29).

74. If you'd like, think of this simply in possible-world semantics: there just *is* a world in which such is the case. On the philosophical picture I'm

above interpretation of οὐσία [*ousia*] worked: Maimonides's parable is meant to acknowledge that it is a particular understanding of world that points to the existence of a ruler; in other words, it is not a particular understanding about this or that object or person or even relationship between several particular objects, but instead—again—the existence of a whole *world* that suggests the presence of a ruler. In the same way, it is a whole world that suggests the existence of God.

And exactly this point about worldhood can make sense of Maimonides's gloss on Exodus 33:13. In this passage, Moses famously asks God to show him all God's ways.[75] According to Maimonides, when God responds that he will show Moses all his goodness, he means all creation (*Guide*, 1.54, 124).[76] As Maimonides writes, "This dictum—*All my goodness*—alludes to the display to him of all existing things of which it is said: *And God saw every thing that He had made, and, behold, it was very good*. By their display, I mean that he will apprehend their nature and the way they are mutually connected . . . that is, he [Moses] has grasped the existence of all My world with a true and firmly established understanding (*Guide*, 1.54, 124). Maimonides's suggestion is that the world was revealed to Moses, that is, all of creation, all the ways in which everything hangs together, but not merely as the revelation of a collection of objects or stuff ("what") but rather also all the various lines of salience that tie these things together, that make them what they are ("how" and "why").

---

referencing here, see David Lewis, *On the Plurality of Worlds* (Oxford, UK: Blackwell, 1986).

75. For an excellent recent analysis of this passage, see Sarah Pessin, "On Glimpsing the Face of God in Maimonides: Wonder, 'Hylomorphic Apophasis' and the Divine Prayer Shawl," *Tópicos (México)*, no. 42 (2012):75–105.

76. Maimonides is explicitly connecting Exodus 33:19 and Genesis 1:31.

Strikingly, one finds an analogous view of things in the *Mishneh Torah*, where Maimonides also comments on Exodus 33. Maimonides writes that "Moses, our teacher, asked that the existence of the Holy One, blessed be He, be distinct in his mind from the existence of everything else that exists, so that he would know the truth of His existence as it is."[77] In other words, it is the world that is to be made distinct from God (and vice versa) *in order to* give Moses a certain sort of knowledge. Maimonides continues by noting that, in response, God is unable to directly offer such knowledge and instead offers Moses a different sort of "knowledge" in the form of a revelation that shows God as "distinct in Moses's mind from everything else that exists, as one man will be distinct from other men when he sees his own back and knows of his own body and his clothing as his own in distinction to other bodies."[78] What Moses is given is not exactly knowledge but rather a certainty of the sort I have described, a certainty that is fundamentally practical in nature (and the Hebrew root of דעת is one that can easily carry this valence given its own practical connotations and its stress on acquaintance and acknowledgment). This is the tenor in which one should read 1:1 of Maimonides's *Yesodei ha-Torah*, where he writes, "The foundation of all foundations and the pillar of wisdom is to know that there is that which first brings out into being all of existence. All the beings of the heavens, the earth, and what is between them, could not be save for the truth of what brings them forth."[79]

---

77. See *Mishneh Torah, Sefer ha-Madda, Yesodei ha-Torah*, chapter 1:10.

78. Ibid. The Hebrew reads כמו שיפרד אחד מן האנשים שראה אחוריו והשיג כל גופו ומלבושו בדעתו משאר גופי האנשים.

79. In this way, the claim that these opening remarks in the *Mishneh Torah* are "heavily indebted to Aristotle and the Islamic *falāsifah*" must be qualified. The former may indeed be distinct from the latter to the extent that the latter relies heavily on the aforementioned existential themes and qualities within the Qur'an. For this quote, see Yehuda Halper, "Does

The Hebrew reads

יסוד היסודות ועמוד החכמות לידע שיש שם מצוי ראשון והוא
ממציא כל נמצא וכל הנמצאים משמים וארץ ומה שביניהם לא
נמצאו אלא מאמתת המצאו.

The use of *know* (ידע) and *truth* (אמת) should not imply any sort of narrow epistemological stance, for both these terms have quite concrete and embodied connotations in biblical Hebrew (the former being tied also to the word for intimate sexual encounter, and the latter carrying the valence of "firmness" and "support"). Similarly, the various uses of "bring out" (יצא), which are generally translated as some permutation of "cause" should be understood less abstractly and rationalistically. The original sense of the Hebrew root here means "to come out" or "go out of," with uses in early Phoenician suggesting going out from a source of water (i.e., a source of life). It is that valence that ought to be stressed here. The idea is that one practically grasps something—becomes certain of something—by means of something else: thus, only through an acknowledgement of and a meditation on the world does one grasp ontological difference (Heidegger); in the same way, one grasps God only through an acknowledgment of and meditation on the world (Maimonides). And in neither case is it a matter of grasping a cause, as if God or Being is merely the first being in a string of beings.[80]

I want to pause here to reflect on what is actually being said; there are three important points to stress. First, there is something discomforting, perhaps maddening, about this

Maimonides's *Mishneh Torah* Forbid Reading the *Guide of the Perplexed*? On Platonic Punishments for Freethinkers," *AJS Review* 42, no. 2 (2018): 351–79.

80. Although (as far as I know), I am the first to draw this analogy between Maimonides and Heidegger and the former's fundamentally phenomenological orientation, I am not the first to employ a conception of ontological difference to think about God in the Jewish context. On this point, see Arthur Green, *Radical Judaism: Rethinking God and Tradition* (New Haven, CT: Yale University Press, 2010). Obviously, also relevant is Jean-Luc Marion, *God without Being: Hors-Texte* (Chicago: University of Chicago Press, 1995).

picture, in that it presupposes a perspective that is fundamentally inhuman. *Our* perspective always depends on having a world, that is, *one* single set of saliencies (our world), but what appears to be revealed to Moses are *all* the possible saliencies available at a particular moment. Second, it might be tempting to understand my gloss on these passages from Exodus as suggesting a distinction between, say, "a human view on the world" and view of the world "as it really is," suggesting that the latter as what is revealed to Moses. This temptation needs to be resisted. The distinction is not between a particular take on the world and the world "as it is" (so that, say, what is revealed to Moses is what best or wholly corresponds to "the world");[81] rather, what is revealed to Moses is the range of then-current primordial possibilities about how a world—any world—can exist in the first place (another way to put this point is to stress that "as it really is" need not be understood narrowly simply as congruent with the idea of "the world as it corresponds to natural science" or "the natural (physical) world," since both of these are particular views within a world).[82] Third, my use of

81. For the sort of point I have in mind here, see Richard Rorty, "The World Well Lost," in *Consequences of Pragmatism: Essays, 1972–1980* (Minneapolis: University of Minnesota Press, 1982).

82. Here's Heidegger on this point from his 1927 lectures *The Basic Problems of Phenomenology* (in a passage already quoted earlier): "Nature—even if we take it in the sense of the whole cosmos as that which we also call, in ordinary discourse, the universe, the whole world—all these entities taken together, animals, plants, and humans, too, are not the world, viewed philosophically . . . rather, the universe of being is—or, to speak more carefully, can be—the *intraworldly*, what is *within the world*. And the world? Is it the sum of what is within the world? By no means. Our calling nature, as well as the things that surround us most closely, the intraworldly and our understanding them in that way already presuppose that we understand world. World is not something subsequent that we calculate as a result from the sum of all beings. The world comes not afterward but beforehand, in the strict sense of the word. Beforehand: that which is unveiled and understood already in advance . . . before any apprehending of this or that being, beforehand as that which stands forth as always already unveiled to us," Heidegger, *Basic Problems*, 165.

the word *primordial* might suggest that these possibilities are somehow fixed, but that is not the case. Instead, the possibilities themselves are temporally indexed, potentially evolving over time. One could use the word *normative* here, but with the caveat that what's really under discussion is what makes normativity itself possible, and that, at the very least, it is not merely a range of propositional stances, but also bodily comportments.[83] As a further point of clarification, I can note that the temporally indexed nature of this revelation allows for a quite seamless connection to well-known passages in the Talmud (surely also an important reference point for Maimonides). In this context, take, for example, Menachot 29b or Baba Mezi'a 59a, with the former presenting a picture of Akiba as introducing worldly possibilities that derive from the Mosaic revelation, but which were not available to Moses himself, and the latter presenting an account of how this process works altogether, historically and legally.[84]

To develop this point, note also the important point that Maimonides alleges that God's revelation of the world to Moses was unique in the history of prophecy and revelation, and its uniqueness consisted of the fact that God's revelation on this point did not require the mediation of the imaginative faculty (*Guide*, 2.46, 403). There is a lot to be said about the imagination in Maimonides's corpus,[85] but what I

---

83. For more on this point and the distinction I'm drawing on, see Carl Sachs, *Intentionality and the Myths of the Given: Between Pragmatism and Phenomenology* (London: Routledge, 2016).

84. Such a train of thought is given a robust philosophical elaboration in Joseph B. Soloveitchik, *Halakhic Man*, trans. Lawrence Kaplan (Philadelphia: Jewish Publication Society, 1983). This sort of standpoint isn't exclusive to "rationalistic" versions of Judaism; one finds a similar idea in mystical sources. See, for example, the way in which reincarnation is discussed in Haim Vital, *Sha'ar Hagilgulim* (Jerusalem: Yeshivat Kol, 1981).

85. For more on the imagination in Maimonides, see Oliver Leaman, "Maimonides, Imagination and the Objectivity of Prophecy," *Religion* 18, no. 1 (1988): 69–80. For an excellent consideration of some of the broader issues in "imaging," see Zachary Braiterman, "Maimonides and the Visual

want to stress in this context is the extent to which the imagination is involved in understanding any world. To be clear: without the sort of revelation offered to Moses, it is up to every individual to attempt to see, to draw, and to elaborate the connections, actual and possible, between worldly phenomena. Each person must attempt to figure out how they hang together. Notably, the sort of examples that we might refer to here are not exclusively scientific, but also include the various "attributes"[86] that one might discover within the world (see, for example, Maimonides's example of kindness and the embryo in *Guide*, 1.54, 125). They reveal a potential network of connections, in a variety of domains. This is why Maimonides stresses Isaiah 6:3, which states that "the *whole earth* is full of God's glory" (*Guide*, 1.64, 157, emphasis added) and highlights that "the true way of honoring Him consists in apprehending His greatness" (*Guide*, 1.64, 157). Furthermore, and most important, "*all that is other than God* . . . honors Him" (*Guide*, 1.64, 157, emphasis added). In this way, *all* of existence offers the opportunity for the human imagination to draw connections between its contents.[87]

I want to pause here for a moment to note how this connects to my broader ambitions in *How to Measure a World?* Note that Maimonides's views, as I have been developing them, reveal a perpetual anachronism with the world; because the world's saliences and wonders are essentially

Image after Kant and Cohen," *Journal of Jewish Thought and Philosophy* 20, no. 2 (2012): 217–30.

86. For more on attributes in Maimonides, see Kenneth Seeskin, "Metaphysics and Its Transcendence," in *The Cambridge Companion to Moses Maimonides*, ed. Kenneth Seeskin (Cambridge: Cambridge University Press, 2005), 84.

87. In this sense, I agree with an element of Pessin's point about this being analogous to the sort of wonder expressed in ancient Greek thought, but I don't follow her in her assessment that this offers any sort of positive understanding of God (more on this shortly) or restrict this merely to an "intellectual" movement as she claims (Pessin, "On Glimpsing the Face of God," 91).

innumerable—the sum of potential knowledge by means of such aforementioned connections is infinite—no investigation can ever be final. Instead, every investigation raises the necessity for others, multiplying always into the future (anachronism). In the ntroduction—at least provisionally—I noted that Levinas suggests that suffering offers a site for anachronism, for a rejection of the world as it presently stands. Maimonides's philosophy offers the same—anachronism—but instead through a reliance on wonder: it is our wonder and awe before the world, in all its glory, that demands that we understand that whatever present account we have is fundamentally incomplete. Exploration sparks more exploration; wonder sparks more wonder.

Every individual is importantly already in a world and in this way already occupies—practically and theoretically, bodily and conceptually—the sort of (worldly) space that allows, indeed likely (at least at certain moments) requires, her to undertake what Maimonides suggests.[88] Because our knowledge is not complete, indeed can never be complete (assuming the saturated nature of any world and the persistent temporal variability of the same), any such inquiry inevitably allows for a persistent increase in the connections one might draw. Regardless of the scope of one's inquiry, the very fact that one is in a world combined with the potentially infinite scope of what that amounts to (am I merely a professor? A husband? A father? A citizen? A human? An earthling? A consciousness?) suggests that all of existence is potentially implicated in and fodder for such an inquiry. Furthermore, and again regardless of the scope actually undertaken, my being in a world immediately suggests a question of how a

---

88. As a reason such curiosity might arise in even the most unphilosophical or uncurious of minds, one might cite Heidegger's insight that when our involvement with the world breaks down or when things go awry, then we are led to reflect on the various structures and references that hold a world together. See *Being and Time*, §16.

world is possible, and not causally (of how a world came to be), but rather ontologically (of how a world can be at all). And the ultimate answer to that can never be anything in the world (it is, to speak somewhat loosely, a question akin to a kind of transcendental inquiry, if that term be understood as an inquiry concerned after the conditions of possibility). In this way, Maimonides's invocation of a first existent is meant exactly to capture *this* question and mystery. God—as something utterly distinct from the world—is the only thing that can account for a world; God cannot in any way be worldly; indeed, God is perpetually and categorically different from the world. God therefore must both "be present" and yet can have no presence. Such a position is exactly comparable, as I've suggested, to al-Ghazālī's claim that "first principles are not sought but are present."[89] It is ultimately an acknowledgment of this point that leads Maimonides to stress that even the predicate of existence cannot apply to God (without thereby implying that nonexistence does apply—God is simply such that there are no predicates that might apply; and again, this is why the aforementioned quote by al-Ghazālī continues with the claim that "if what is present is sought it will be lost and will disappear").[90]

Before turning to the implications of this view, let me try to present another analogy that may help give substance to the view emerging. The task that Maimonides sets for any individual encountering a world has an analogy to the position

---

89. Ali Khalidi, *Medieval Islamic Philosophical Writings*, 64.

90. Ibid. Putting things in this way suggests a position quite similar to the sort sketched in Marion, *God without Being*. See especially, for example, 41, and the discussion that follows. In light of this analogy, even Alvin Reines's suggestion about God's "absolute transcendence" is likely improper (Alvin J. Reines, "Maimonides's True Belief concerning God: A Systematization," in *Maimonides and Philosophy: Papers Presented at the Sixth Jerusalem Philosophical Encounter*, ed. Shlomo Pines and Yirmiyahu Yovel [Dordrecht, Neth.: Martinus Nijhoff, 1986], 24–36). Truly, silence becomes the only proper linguistic act—see *Guide*, 1.59.

that Kant outlines in the *Critique of Judgment* (1790) about reflective judgment.[91] For Kant, natural beauty reveals "a technique of nature, which makes it possible to represent nature as a system in accordance with laws *the principle of which we do not encounter anywhere in our entire faculty of understanding.*"[92] It is important that Kant highlights how it is natural beauty itself, not some merely accidental feature of our psychology or subjectivity, that suggests such a system to our faculties. In being struck by natural beauty and the seeming interconnectedness of all phenomena, we do not know—indeed, with our discursive understanding, cannot know—the law of the whole of nature, but nonetheless are driven to suggest, indeed try to discover, that law. In the case of beauty, however, there can be no such discovery, for what defines beauty (and therefore natural beauty) is the fact that our understanding (which normally supplies a concept for any particular manifold) enters into a "free play" with our imagination (which is what, according to Kant, supplies a unified manifold to our understanding). With beauty, there just is no concept that exhausts the manifold in question, and so there is a vivification of our faculties where no particular concept exhausts the manifold in question.[93] For Maimonides, the world is such that we are invariably led to think that

91. Maimonides scholarship, following Shlomo Pines's original suggestions, has located the analogy to Kant almost exclusively on Kant's First Critique. Obviously, I think this is a mistake. For arguments for a Kantian connection, see Warren Zev Harvey, "Maimonides' Critical Epistemology and Guide 2: 24," *Aleph* 8, no. 1 (2008): 213–35. See that same issue of *Aleph* for additional essays both pursuing the analogy (Carlos Fraenkel and Josef Stern) and disputing it (Herbert Davidson, Joel Kramer, and Y. Tzvi Langermann). For the original suggestion, see Shlomo Pines, "The Limitations of Human Knowledge according to al-Farabi, ibn Bajja, and Maimonides," in *Studies in Medieval Jewish History and Literature*, ed. Isadore Twersky (Cambridge, MA: Harvard University Press, 1979), 1–82.
92. Immanuel Kant, *Critique of the Power of Judgment*, trans. Paul Guyer and Eric Matthews (Cambridge: Cambridge University Press, 2000), 5:246. Emphasis added. Throughout I cite the German pagination.
93. On this point, see especially ibid., 5:316.

there is—must be—an *explanans* for the world, but we can literally have no knowledge of that *explanans*; our description of it can only be silence, indeed even saying such an *explanans* exists is already saying too much (*Guide*, 1.59). The procedures that are involved in such an assessment of the world or stance within the world can profitably be understood as of a kind with the sort of mechanics Kant locates with a reflective judgment about natural beauty.[94]

Maimonides's negation of any and every godly attribute is therefore uncompromisingly categorical; his position toward God is entirely negative, utterly apophatic. In light of our acknowledgment of the world and its *worldliness*, there is suggested to us an understanding that such a world, our worldliness, is possible only through something that is not this world, not of this world, not in any way like the world—indeed, something that "is" wholly and utterly and completely distinct from it (and even saying "is" is already to say too much). To maintain any sort of fidelity to the aforementioned insight about the world and worldliness, one must categorically deny any predicate—*every* predicate—to the "what" that emerges from that insight, that emerges as the *explanans* for the world, an *explanans* that is not merely causal, but indeed existential, in the robust sense discussed above (we might say, again with the proper caveats, "transcendental"). Of course, to deploy even these terms (*explanans*, "what," and so forth) is already to say too much. This is how to understand Maimonides's claim that even when applying negations to God, they are applied "from the

---

94. There is a lot more to be said here about the comparison, and especially about the function of imagination in Kant and Maimonides, and the issues between them more broadly. The thinker that likely thought most about the comparison is Salomon Maimon, but pursuing it is beyond my scope here. See David Rapport Lachterman, "Mathematical Construction, Symbolic Cognition and the Infinite Intellect: Reflections on Maimon and Maimonides," *Journal of the History of Philosophy* 30, no. 4 (1992): 497–522.

following point of view[:] ... one sometimes denies with reference to a thing something *that cannot fittingly exist in it*. Thus we say of a wall that it is not endowed with sight" (*Guide*, 1.58, 136, emphasis mine). This is the sense in which Maimonides doesn't merely attribute negations to God, but in fact attributes the negation even of negations. Much in the same way that the wall is not "not-seeing" (i.e., blind), just so God is not "not-*x*." In a deep sense, there is literally nothing more to be said on this point.

Note, though, the importance of *world* to this entire procedure.

§ 5. Conclusion: Spiritual Exercises

Let me return to an earlier point. According to Maimonides, only Moses was granted a vision of the world in its interconnectedness. It should be obvious now that, even in being granted such a vision, Moses was not thereby granted access to what might be termed God. This is what Maimonides means by the fact that Moses's second demand (to see God's essence) was not granted (Maimonides here quotes Exodus 33:20, where God says, "you cannot see my face, for no one may see me and live"—see *Guide*, 1.52, 124; and the case is analogous in the passage I quoted above from the *Mishneh Torah*).

Because only Moses was granted this vision, everyone else operates with an epistemic deficiency that guarantees the necessity of perpetually having to multiply potential worldly connections. Contemporaneously, the passage of time itself further guarantees such a multiplication: the world changes; and our worldhood itself changes, as does our access to that worldhood (this would be one way to understand Heidegger's late work). I mention this in order to acknowledge that Moses's vision was indexed to a particular time. Such revelation carries a temporal dimension to it, and this is one way to understand why, after a discussion of the aforementioned encounter between Moses and God, Maimonides moves to a discussion of the divine name, the Tetragrammaton (*Guide*, 1.63–64). In refusing to attempt to multiply the potential connections that the world offers, the option remains open that one might simply give fealty to this original encounter through tradition, through a remembrance.[95] So, Maimonides claims that "knowledge of God . . . [is] . . . given to the multitude in all the books of the prophets and also in the *Torah*" (*Guide*, 1.46, 98). (This is one way to understand the story of Moses in Menachot 29b, where things are presented as "identical" to the Mosaic revelation but nonetheless appear initially entirely foreign to Moses.)

Within Jewish tradition, the following of Jewish law might thereby be seen as the practical analogue to the sort of philosophical stance that Maimonides proposes. In carrying out Jewish legal tasks within and for this world, one inevitably acknowledges more than the world, one occupies oneself with something else "than with matters pertaining to this

---

95. Emmanuel Levinas presents such a reading of Maimonides in a Talmudic commentary. He writes, "The first book of the famous Tractate in which Maimonides, in the twelfth century, summarizes and systematizes the Talmud, begins in fact as follows: 'The foundation of the foundation and the pillar of wisdom consists in knowing that the Name exists and that it is the first being.'" See Emmanuel Levinas, *Beyond the Verse: Talmudic Readings and Lectures*, trans. Gary D. Mole (London: Continuum, 1994), 118. Levinas is vocalizing the opening of Maimonides's *Mishneh Torah*'s use of שם as שֵׁם (name) rather than שָׁם (there) in Maimonides's text (replacing "there" with "name" in reading "there exists a being and it is the first being"). For a powerful analysis of this point in Levinas and Maimonides, and of Maimonides in general, especially of the idea of "glory" in Maimonides, see Michael Fagenblat, "Levinas and Maimonides: From Metaphysics to Ethical Negative Theology," *Journal of Jewish Thought and Philosophy* 16, no. 1 (2008): 95–147. See also especially the fourth chapter in his recent book Michael Fagenblat, *A Covenant of Creatures: Levinas's Philosophy of Judaism* (Stanford, CA: Stanford University Press, 2010). My understanding of the function of glory in Maimonides's corpus has been greatly influenced by Fagenblat and by Levinas on these points.

world" (*Guide*, 3.51, 622).⁹⁶ In this way, Jewish law and the philosophical stance that Maimonides proposes are alleged to be two sides of the same coin: where one's task is to multiply the connections of this world in order to point to more than the world, all while acknowledging that the content of this "more" cannot be anything in the world, indeed, from the perspective of the world—of objects and things—cannot even be described as emptiness.⁹⁷ As Maimonides puts it, "it is from this point of view that one ought to come nearer to an apprehension of God by means of investigation and research: namely, in order that one should know the impossibility of *everything* that is impossible with reference to God" (*Guide*, 1.59, 139, emphasis added). In this way, when "you make an affirmation ascribing . . . [any] . . . thing to God, you become more remote from God in two respects: one of them is that everything you affirm is a perfection only with reference to us, and the other is that God does not a possess a thing" (*Guide*, 1.59, 139).

One therefore realizes that existence simply is, and that even as it points beyond itself, such a gesture implies no teleology, indeed, paradoxically implies both nothing *and* everything more than what presently is. This is what I take Maimonides to suggest when he writes that "this is what one ought to believe. For when man knows his own soul, makes no mistakes with regard to it, and understands every being according to what it is, he becomes calm and his thoughts

---

96. This point is developed in Yirmiyahu Yovel, "God's Transcendence and Its Schematization," in *Maimonides and Philosophy: Papers Presented at the Sixth Jerusalem Philosophical Encounter*, ed. Shlomo Pines and Yirmiyahu Yovel (Dordrecht, Neth.: Martinus Nijhoff, 1986), 269–83. It also connects well to the position that is outlined in Soloveitchik, *Halakhic Man*.

97. On this point, see Franke, *Philosophy of the Unsayable*, 63. Franke writes, "If denial becomes determinate, it then disbelieves some*thing* and has become just another form of belief in a finite, articulated discourse: it believes in what it says rather than in what it cannot say, and that changes everything."

are not troubled by seeking a final end for what has not that final end; or by seeking any final end for what has no final end except its own existence" (*Guide*, 3.14, 456). Because of the complexity of the world, and the connections that might be drawn within it, it would not be improper, in this context, to call such an investigation a "spiritual exercise,"[98] where what that means, above all, is a practice that intends "to bring about a transformation of the individual, a transformation of the self."[99] Such a practice, however, is by no means exclusively Jewish. Furthermore, it suggests a view of "religious understanding" as denoting a sort of achievement, to be obtained through a repertoire of approaches and means that would multiply our appreciation of how elements of our world(s) hang together, a way ultimately "of making sense of things relative to our own experience,"[100] where the latter should be understood in exactly the phenomenological terms I have sketched herein, as centering above all on notions of world, notions themselves grounded on a fundamentally positive attunement to and assessment of the world. The world just is the sort of thing that can sustain and invite such practices. And such practices never fully exhaust the world, nor finally satisfy the individuals carrying them out; thus anachronism and the question of how to measure a world remains as long the world remains and humans in it.

98. Josef Stern has powerfully drawn this analogy to Pierre Hadot in Stern, *Matter and Form*, 312.

99. Pierre Hadot, *The Present Alone Is Our Happiness: Conversations with Jeannie Carlier and Arnold I. Davidson*, trans. Marc Djaballah and Michael Chase (Palo Alto, CA: Stanford University Press, 2009), 87.

100. Stephen Grimm, "The Value of Understanding," *Philosophy Compass* 7, no. 2 (2012): 113. Grimm provides an excellent overview of the literature on understanding, and I endorse his concluding sentiments, except only with the caveat that "subjective" here must be understood in the robust way that I've suggested in footnote 73 and the surrounding discussion in the body.

2

SUFFERING AND WORLD

ADORNO'S NEGATIVITY

§ 1. Introduction: Relations to the World

Maimonides suggests a spiritual undertaking wherein we approach the world with a sense of awe or wonder, multiplying our inquiries into, connections among, and saliences within the world. The world is fundamentally understood in such a way as to invite us to proceed in this way and ultimately to see it as capable of sustaining such interest; there is a sort of fit between our capacities and the world (and this is one way to understand the analogy to Kant's understanding of natural beauty that I drew in chap. 1). Only through such inquiry—negatively—do we have access to ultimate reality (God), which is *not* anything that would fall under our investigation (or its negation); ultimate reality is not any *thing* at all. An acknowledgment and assessment of the world in these terms—which are not purely cognitive, but rather terms that suggest that our very "bones necessitate this belief"—lead to the sort of "rest" and "calm" that Maimonides highlights, all even despite the perpetual desire to multiply what's said and concomitantly what also cannot be said.¹ There is a fruitful analogy here to be had with certain ways to think about a text and what might be said of that text:

> There is no such thing as beginning, only having begun . . . because the end cannot be said, saying can have no end. Where the text ends it is unfinished, because although its end has come it is still unsaid, and when the text says it, it has not yet come to an end, since it is still in the middle of saying that it has. Writing, which must always already have begun in order to be able to say that it has, must always continue in order to be able to say that it is ending. It always ends too early or too late, and therefore does not end at all.²

The world itself is an ultimate text, bearing within itself all others, actual and possible, now and into the future. Every novelty, whether textual or otherwise, expands the possibilities and actualities of that world, altering what might be said about and seen within the world. Such a procedure reveals the ultimate reality of what lies beyond the world; a silence more robust than any imaginable silence is the only means to capture the discovery.

There are, however, other conceptions of the world, especially in the modern period, with its distinct calamities and brutalities (as *the* modern evil, one might invoke everything from Lisbon to Auschwitz).³ Maimonides, of course, was no stranger to evil and suffering (one might cite here the drowning of his brother David on a trading voyage just as easily as his forced conversion), but it is worth asking after an

---

1. Moses Maimonides, *The Guide of the Perplexed*, trans. Shlomo Pines (Chicago: University of Chicago Press, 1963), 1.64, 157; 3.14, 456.

2. Hans-Jost Frey, *Interruptions*, trans. Georgia Albert (Buffalo, NY: SUNY Press, 1996), 23.

3. See, for example, Michael L. Morgan, *Beyond Auschwitz: Post-Holocaust Jewish Thought in America* (Oxford: Oxford University Press, 2001); Susan Neiman, *Evil in Modern Thought: An Alternative History of Philosophy* (Princeton, NJ: Princeton University Press, 2002).

entirely different approach to our fundamental understanding of the world. My aim in this chapter is to introduce such a fundamental understanding of the world by reference to the thought of Theodor W. Adorno, a German-Jewish thinker who wrote explicitly in the wake of the Nazi genocide, orienting his thought around the ills of that catastrophe and the world that made it—and continues to make it—a possibility. In such a view, the world cannot sustain awe or wonder, but instead proposes moral indignation or resistance. The omnipresence of suffering and the difficulty of (finding) meaning forecloses exactly the sort of procedures Maimonides suggests. The world is cruel and inhospitable, and to proceed in the way Maimonides suggests is an ethical betrayal that inflicts additional suffering on the vanquished and oppressed.

Before turning to an elaboration of such a view, it is worthwhile to return to a central term from chapter 1: the notion of mood (*Stimmung*) or attunement (*Bestimmung*). In the *Fundamental Concepts of Metaphysics* (1929–30), Heidegger notes that moods are not "side-effects," but rather "something which in advance determines our being with one another," indeed, that with moods "an attunement is in each case already there, so to speak, like an atmosphere in which we first immerse ourselves in each case and which then attunes us through and through."[4] A mood is not a mere psychological state of affairs, it rather sets the entire horizon for an agent: of what appears and can appear, what's significant and what's not, what's possible and what's not—in short, it is what allows psychological states of affairs to arise in the first place. The aim of this chapter is to sketch a mood that runs almost exactly opposite in its pathos to the mood sketched in chapter 1. Despite this

---

4. Martin Heidegger, *The Fundamental Concepts of Metaphysics: World, Finitude, Solitude*, trans. William McNeill and Nicholas Walker (Bloomington: Indiana University Press, 2001), 67. Think also of the way in which Heidegger invokes the idea of "*Befindlichkeit*" in *Being and Time*—finding oneself in the world in a particular way. See Martin Heidegger, *Being and Time*, trans. Joan Stambaugh (Albany, NY: SUNY Press, 1996), §29.

fundamental distinction, what's striking, as will emerge clearly in what follows, is the extent to which *both* Maimonides and Adorno locate their views in conversation with Aristotle, highlighting, to my mind, their common phenomenological source and the basic ontological plausibility of each view.

Finally, what's also remarkable is that despite their diametrically opposed orientations, Maimonides and Adorno employ related if not analogous notions of negativity and negation. To begin to see how they relate, note that, at the most fundamental level, Adorno begins with a basic observation about the world: there is useless or needless suffering, and registering this suffering demands a rational—ethical—response from me. This is true to the extent that Adorno proposes an entirely new categorical imperative: that we arrange our thoughts and actions in such a way that Auschwitz will not repeat itself;[5] furthermore, Adorno explicitly ties the possibility of philosophy—what he also sometimes calls simply dialectical thinking—to the acknowledgment of suffering. In the opening lines of *Negative Dialectics* (originally published in 1966) we read "Philosophy, which once appeared obsolete, sustains itself because the moment for its actualization has been lost."[6] Philosophy once appeared obsolete because it seemed like needless human suffering was on the verge of disappearing. The promises of the revolutionary ideals of modernity, however, turned concretely into their opposite, and thus philosophy is now needed more than ever.

---

5. On this point, see J. M. Bernstein, *Adorno: Disenchantment and Ethics* (Cambridge: Cambridge University Press, 2001), 384–96; Martin Shuster, *Autonomy after Auschwitz: Adorno, German Idealism, and Modernity* (Chicago: University of Chicago Press, 2014), 71–99; Oshrat Silberbusch, *Adorno's Philosophy of the Nonidentical* (Dordrecht, Neth.: Springer, 2018), 57–122.

6. Theodor W. Adorno, *Negative Dialectics*, trans. E. B. Ashton (New York: Seabury, 1973), 16.

§ 2. *Adorno and the Negative: Orienting Ourselves*

Picking up on this revolutionary thread, note how in the eleventh thesis on Feuerbach, Marx remarks that "philosophers have only *interpreted* the world, in various ways; the point, however, is to *change* it."[7] Adorno takes up this thought, noting that because the revolution never came, the need for philosophy still exists,[8] and therefore philosophy continues. In a state of utopia or redemption, philosophy would be unnecessary.[9] Adorno's story about the continuation of philosophy, however, also importantly revolves around the conceptual act or process of determination within and about the world. Most fundamentally, after all, on what grounds can it be determined that anything—let alone the world—*ought* to be different? We must determine that the present world contains suffering in order to claim that it *ought not* be so. Understanding Adorno's reflections on the entire process of determination (and conceptualization) is thereby central to understanding his broader views about the world and suffering.

In a particularly dense passage in *Negative Dialectics*, Adorno appears to address explicitly the aims of philosophy when he considers the "staging ground" of dialectics or of philosophy: "The unity of what is subsumed under general concepts is entirely different from the conceptually determined particular. With the latter, the concept is always also its negative; what the particular is in itself and what yet

---

7. Karl Marx, *The Marx-Engels Reader*, ed. Robert C. Tucker (New York: Norton, 1978), 145.

8. I explore other dimensions of what's implied for philosophy in such view in Martin Shuster, "Education for the World: Adorno and Cavell," in *Dissonant Methods: Undoing Discipline in the Humanities Classroom*, ed. Ada Jaarsma and Kit Dobson (Alberta: University of Alberta Press, 2019).

9. A theme that's found in a variety of philosophers, including, for example, Rorty. See Martin Shuster, "Rorty and (the Politics of) Love," *Graduate Faculty Philosophy Journal* 40, no. 1 (2019): 65–78.

cannot be named immediately, the concept cuts down [*coupiert*], replacing it with identity. This negative, [the] false, is also however necessary and is the staging-ground [*Schauplatz*] of dialectics."[10] Note the way in which Adorno is casting the entire philosophical procedure in an ethical register:[11] negativity or what he here terms simply "the false" somehow drives philosophy, and thereby the entire philosophical procedure might be seen, again, as a sort of spiritual exercise oriented around an assessment of the world,[12] but this time by means of a particular ethical sensitivity toward that world, a particular sensitivity toward suffering and toward the *lack* of happiness or beauty or wonder or whatever else in the world. Crucial to Adorno's procedure is to distinguish between what is subsumed under a general concept, on one hand, and a "conceptually determined particular (*begrifflich bestimmten Besonderen*)" on the other. Equally clear from Adorno's remarks, however, is that *how* things are determined in these two classes of items is not different. In both cases, the concept "cuts down" or limits what is subsumed, instantiating an identification of the subsumed, in other words, determination.

With all these remarks, Adorno is implicitly invoking the early modern philosopher Spinoza (who, as is now well known, engaged significantly with Maimonides, making the conversation staged between Adorno and Maimonides in the present work even more plausible).[13] When Adorno

10. Adorno, *Negative Dialectics*, 173.

11. For more on the ways in which Adorno connects epistemology and ethics, see Martin Shuster, "Nothing to Know: The Epistemology of Moral Perfectionism in Adorno and Cavell," *Idealistic Studies* 44, no. 1 (2015): 1–29.

12. I pursued this analogy earlier in Shuster, *Autonomy after Auschwitz*, 168–75.

13. See the several essays on this topic collected in Steven Nadler, *Spinoza and Medieval Jewish Philosophy* (Cambridge: Cambridge University Press, 2014); Heidi M. Ravven and Lenn E. Goodman, *Jewish Themes in Spinoza's Philosophy* (Buffalo, NY: SUNY Press, 2012).

describes the negativity cited above as false, he is invoking not only all his various explorations of "the false" in late capitalism (think here most prominently of *Minima Moralia*'s claim that "there is no right living in the false [*Es gibt kein richtiges Leben im Falschen*]"),[14] but also his own earlier engagement with Spinoza. In response to the student movements of the late 1960s, Adorno concludes his 1969 essay "Critique"[15] with an opposition between hasty (and he thinks, dangerous) calls for immediate "political" action and what he calls "a variation of a famous proposition by Spinoza, that the false, once determinately known and precisely expressed, is already an index of what is right and better."[16]

Determining "the false," Adorno thinks, is crucial. It may in fact be the only route available in situations where any action would further contribute to catastrophe.[17] What proposition of Spinoza's, however, does Adorno have in mind?[18] How exactly is Spinoza's—labyrinthine—thought relevant? The answer to this question emerges from a consideration of a discussion Adorno has with his colleague, Ernst Bloch,

14. Theodor W. Adorno, *Minima Moralia: Reflections on a Damaged Life*, trans. Edmund F. N. Jephcott (London: Verso, 2005), 39.

15. See Theodor W. Adorno, "Critique," trans. Henry W. Pickford, in *Critical Models: Interventions and Catchwords* (New York: Columbia University Press, 1998).

16. Ibid., 288. For the background to Adorno's rejection of such immediate action, see Fabian Freyenhagen, "Adorno's Politics Theory and Praxis in Germany's 1960s," *Philosophy and Social Criticism* 40, no. 9 (2014): 867–93.

17. This point has been recently developed most forcefully in Fabian Freyenhagen, *Adorno's Practical Philosophy: Living Less Wrongly* (Cambridge: Cambridge University Press, 2013).

18. Henry Pickford, the translator of the essay, suggests that this is "presumably" a reference to Spinoza's proposition that "all determination is negation" (*omnis determinatio est negatio*). See Theodor W. Adorno, *Critical Models: Interventions and Catchwords*, trans. Henry W. Pickford (New York: Columbia University Press, 1998), 393n19. As I will demonstrate later in this chapter, however, I do not think this is the proposition that Adorno has in mind, which is significant for the discussion that follows.

about utopia. In a conversation in 1964 that spanned several days, Adorno and Bloch discuss various notions of utopia. Adorno recalls how at one point Bloch had quoted Spinoza in this context, stating, "Yesterday you quoted Spinoza in our discussion with the passage, '*Verum index sui et falsi*' (truth is the index of itself and of the false)."[19] Adorno then continues, modifying Spinoza's principle: "I have varied this a little in the sense of the dialectical principle of the determined negation and have said, Falsum—the false thing—index sui et veri. That means that the true thing determines itself via the false thing, or via that which makes itself falsely known. And insofar as we are not allowed to cast the picture of utopia, insofar as we do not know what the correct thing would be, we know exactly, to be sure, what the false thing is."[20] There are several interesting things going on here, and it is the task of this chapter to unpack them. First, note that Adorno is already explicitly invoking the tradition that I introduced in chapter 1 with Maimonides. There is, in the way that Adorno thinks of utopia, a sort of negative theology here: we are "not allowed to cast the picture of utopia." Second, note that the reference to Spinoza's "principle" by Bloch and Adorno is in fact a humorous quip Spinoza makes in a letter to Alfred Burgh, in which Spinoza aims to defend his philosophy from detractors, pointing out that "if you ask me how I know this [that my—Spinoza's—thought] is true, I reply that I know it in the same way that you know that three angles of a triangle are equal to two right angles. . . . For truth reveals both itself and the false."[21]

---

19. Ernst Bloch, *The Utopian Function of Art and Literature: Selected Essays*, trans. Jack Zipes and Frank Mecklenburg (Cambridge, MA: MIT Press, 1988), 12.
20. Ibid.
21. See Spinoza to Alfred Burgh, December 1675; letter 76 in Baruch Spinoza, *The Letters*, trans. Samuel Shirley (Indianapolis: Hackett, 1995), 949. Translation modified. This letter has an important afterlife in the German philosophical traditions that Adorno was steeped in. For example, the

Adorno's modification is significant. First, it allows us to see clearly, to the extent that the false indexes itself *and* what is true, that Adorno, with Spinoza and an entire tradition of philosophy that follows in his wake,[22] thinks that determination is negation. Any time we determine something, we negate (something else). Relatedly, negation, in the form of the false, determines, albeit not wholly, what is true. Second, the fact that this claim is embedded in a discussion of utopia shows exactly the extent to which Adorno's concerns are not simply logical, merely conceptual, or entirely philosophical, but rather already ethical, political, and—it would not be too much to say—spiritual in nature (they are, we might alternatively say, "basic" or "foundational" in exactly the phenomenological sense developed thus far).

Returning to the earlier quote from *Negative Dialectics*, note how that quote can be harnessed to introduce some larger themes. In what follows, I focus on getting particularly clear on the difference between the sorts of "conceptually determined particulars" that Adorno has in mind and "what we tend to subsume under general concepts" (i.e., on these two, distinct ways of determining). In addition to this focus, however, it is crucial to elaborate the exact nature of the negative, and especially how it is equated with the false and why it "cannot be named immediately (*unmittelbar nicht sich nennen läßt*)." Finally, it is important still to keep in mind the idea—to which we must still return in order to consider it in more depth—that in some sense the negative and the false are

---

letter is quoted by Jacobi in Friedrich Heinrich Jacobi, *Main Philosophical Writings and the Novel Allwill*, trans. George di Giovanni, vol. 18 (Montreal: McGill-Queen's University Press, 1995), 193. It is also quoted by Hegel in Georg Wilhelm Friedrich Hegel, *The Encyclopedia Logic*, trans. Théodore F. Geraets, Wallis Arthur Suchting, and Henry Silton Harris (Indianapolis: Hackett, 1991), 17. I suspect one of these two sources, rather than Spinoza himself, was likely the source for Bloch, Adorno, or both.

22. Eckart Förster and Yitzhak Y. Melamed, *Spinoza and German Idealism* (Cambridge: Cambridge University Press, 2012).

"necessary" and the "staging ground" for dialectics.[23] Getting clear on these distinctions is the means by which a picture of Adorno's own distinct theology comes into focus (Adorno calls it an "inverse theology").[24] Bringing this theology into focus will also introduce another element into the broader story I am sketching around anachronism and Judaism.

§ 3. Materialism as Motor in Adorno

In a subsection titled "Objectivity and Reification" in the "Concept and Categories" section of *Negative Dialectics*, Adorno spends considerable time minimizing the importance of the problem of reification (understood in the traditional Marxist sense of *Verdinglichung*—the idea that human relations in capitalism come to be transformed, ossified, and identified with thing-like relations, and ultimately seen as natural; that is, ultimately use—indeed, really, all—value comes to be determined solely by means of exchange value). Understanding why Adorno aims to minimize this strand of Marxist thought is an effective way to start to address the issues we have presented, and it especially offers a way into his broader views about how to assess the world. Much of Adorno's attack here centers on his rejection of György Lukács's approach in *History and Class Consciousness*,[25] where Lukács extends Marx's ideas far beyond the economic sphere, essentially to all spheres of life. Without wading into

23. See Adorno, *Negative Dialectics*, 173.
24. For more on this, see James Gordon Finlayson, "On Not Being Silent in the Darkness: Adorno's Singular Apophaticism," *Harvard Theological Review* 105, no. 1 (2011): 1–32; Elizabeth A. Pritchard, "Bilderverbot Meets Body in Theodor W. Adorno's Inverse Theology," *Harvard Theological Review* 95, no. 3 (2002): 291–318; Deborah Cook, "Through a Glass Darkly: Adorno's Inverse Theology," *Adorno Studies* 1, no. 1 (2017): 66–78; Christopher Craig Brittain, *Adorno and Theology* (London: Bloomsbury, 2010).
25. See György Lukács, *History and Class Consciousness: Studies in Marxist Dialectics* (Cambridge, MA: MIT Press, 1972).

the complexities that animate the exchange between Adorno and Lukács,[26] I rather want to present a sense of what Adorno takes to be the chief issue between them, namely the issue of how suffering in the world fails to register for an agent. What animates Adorno's concerns is how we ultimately (might) come to ignore suffering.

Adorno writes, "*that* from which human beings suffer, the lament of reification would in the meantime rather glide over than denounce."[27] Adorno's point is that human beings suffer from concrete instances of injustice, not from abstract principles of exchange value. Let me be clear: Adorno is by no means denying that exchange value can run amuck or, indeed, pushed to extremes, become catastrophic. Adorno's point is instead that the problem(s) of late capitalism are not fundamentally with exchange value as a concept, that is, with reification as a category. The problem is not merely with the concept itself. As he puts it earlier in *Negative Dialectics*, it is exactly "*criticism* of the exchange principle as the one identified with thought [that] desires that the ideal of *free and fair exchange* would be realized, but which to this day is still a mere pretext."[28] To focus on reification as the problem is to miss the complexity of late capitalism and to miss the basic point that reification and exchange value themselves carry the promise of happiness: free and fair exchange. As Adorno puts it, "if comparability as a category of measure were simply annulled, [then] the *rationality inherent in the exchange principle*—as ideology, of course, but also as promise (*Verspreche*)—would give way to immediate appropriation,

---

26. For a recent discussion of this debate, see Timothy Hall, "Reification, Materialism, and Praxis: Adorno's Critique of Lukács," *Telos* 155 (2011): 61–82. See also the earlier discussion in Gillian Rose, *The Melancholy Science: An Introduction to the Thought of Theodor W. Adorno* (New York: Columbia University Press, 1978), 35–66.

27. Adorno, *Negative Dialectics*, 190, translation modified.

28. Adorno, *Negative Dialectics*, 147; emphasis added and translation modified.

to force, and nowadays to the crude privilege of monopolies and cliques."[29]

So, what is "that from which human beings suffer" then? Adorno is here referring to his entire assessment of contemporary society, an assessment that depends on understanding that society as a whole is fundamentally wrong, in not only the ways in which its parts hang together but also the ways in which those parts operate individually, as well as the ways in which they socialize and orient the agents within society. It is a broad and sweeping thesis. One recent commentator captures it exceptionally well when he writes that

> The events for which the name "Auschwitz" stands were not something which went against the trend of civilization. Rather, these events were intimately connected to some of the main tendencies of the path which civilization has taken and to the structure of modern society and thinking in particular. The lesson of Auschwitz—at least according to Adorno—is not that culture was replaced by a momentary fallback into a barbaric state; the lesson is that culture itself failed. If Auschwitz was possible in a country with an advanced economy and high culture ("a land of poets and thinkers," as Germany is known); if it happened despite the fact that moral theories reached into the minds of perpetrators (in the way Eichmann claimed that he had lived his whole life according to Kant's categorical imperative of which he seemed to have a decent grasp); if it was carried out not so much by monsters, but ordinary men (and women); if they thought of themselves

---

29. Ibid., 146–47; emphasis added and translation modified. In this way, I disagree with Hall (see the footnote 26). There are three distinct arguments against Lukács in *Negative Dialectics*. I see Adorno's approach as much more unified. Adorno's basic opposition is—as I will shortly elaborate in detail—ethical in nature. In his lectures, Adorno puts it simply as the idea that "there could be no *possibility* even of something different and better, that is, of a rationally organized society, without a means-ends rationality with its domination of nature" (Theodor W. Adorno, *History and Freedom*, ed. Rolf Tiedemann, trans. Rodney Livingstone [Cambridge, UK: Polity, 2006], 55).

not as acting against morality and civilization, but as men of integrity who have taken on a heavy burden to protect them, remaining in their own eyes, with few exceptions, decent and respectful of human life (as Himmler described the work of the SS in his October 1943 speeches at Posen); and if it was not the act of a small group of people, but if a whole society contributed, in one way or another, to it; then it seems not altogether far-fetched to come to Adorno's pessimistic conclusion that Auschwitz was not an accident, but an indication of a deep-seated problem of modern society, civilization, and culture.[30]

A full justification and elaboration of this view is beyond my scope here;[31] instead, the aim of this chapter, and, indeed, of *How to Measure a World?*, is to explore the significance of such a view of things. At this point in my argument, my approach assumes that one either shares this estimation or one does not (and so, the argument *for* such an estimation must be found elsewhere, much in the same way that the *practical* orientation toward God and the world that Maimonides advances is not *argued* for but rather arrived at by means of a practical comportment).

What I want to register at this point is that the radical scope of Adorno's assessment makes it only natural that Adorno would

---

30. Freyenhagen, *Adorno's Practical Philosophy*, 28–29. Adorno himself means for the assessment of society to extend far beyond Auschwitz. As he puts it in his lectures on metaphysics, "Through Auschwitz—and by that I mean not only Auschwitz but the world of torture which has continued to exist after Auschwitz" (Theodor W. Adorno, *Metaphysics: Concept and Problems*, ed. Rolf Tiedemann, trans. Edmund F. N. Jephcott [Stanford, CA: Stanford University Press, 2000], 101). There is now also emerging here the question of social pathology, which Freyenhagen has since explored in this context in Fabian Freyenhagen, "Critical Theory and Social Pathology," in *The Routledge Companion to the Frankfurt School*, ed. Axel Honneth, Espen Hammer, and Peter Gordon (London: Routledge, 2018), 410–24.

31. One of the strongest recent elaborations and justifications of this view is Freyenhagen, *Adorno's Practical Philosophy*, 26–75.

thereby also exhibit deep worries about the very functioning of the critical capacities of human beings as they live under the conditions of such a wrong society. It ought to be no surprise that the functioning of such critical capacities—warped as they are by late capitalism—would be a point of concern for anyone interested in offering alternatives to or possibilities for the current state of affairs.[32] All this leads Adorno to claim in his lectures that the value of the "concept of the negative" is above all that it allows us to "resist . . . habits of thought" that produce deeply unreflective individuals (and so therefore individuals incapable of critical reflection and action).[33]

Many of Adorno's philosophical resources are marshaled toward understanding how, in the conditions of late capitalism—conditions that, as the just-cited lengthy quote suggests, it is not too much to call radically evil—we might come to think more than what presently is, that is, imagine alternative (more just) possibilities and states of affairs. In his *Lectures on Negative Dialectics* (1965–66), Adorno simply states that the "speculative surplus that goes beyond whatever is the case, beyond mere existence, is the element of freedom in thought, and because it is, because it alone does stand for freedom, because it represents the tiny quantum of freedom we possess, it also represents the *happiness* of thought."[34] Exactly this train of thought also underpins Adorno's claim that "metaphysics arises at the point where the empirical world is taken seriously."[35] Adorno's point is that only in taking the empirical world seriously—in other words, critically assessing it, responding to the way in which

32. I discuss elements of this point in more detail in Shuster, *Autonomy after Auschwitz*, 7–42, 102–28.
33. Theodor W. Adorno, *Lectures on Negative Dialectics*, ed. Rolf Tiedemann, trans. Rodney Livingstone (Cambridge, UK: Polity, 2008), 24–25. For these larger claims, see also Freyenhagen, *Adorno's Practical Philosophy*, 162–87, 255–71; Shuster, *Autonomy after Auschwitz*, 71–134.
34. Adorno, *Lectures on Negative Dialectics*, 108.
35. Adorno, *Metaphysics*, 18.

it creates and maintains sites of suffering—can we attempt to move, at least initially within thought, to more progressive configurations. In doing so, we are forced to move beyond that world: to imagine it as different—better—and thereby devoid of these deformities. This is how to understand Adorno's suggestion that "metaphysics attempts to rescue through concepts what it simultaneously calls into question through its critique."[36] As with our earlier example of reification, Adorno is critiquing a problematic instantiation of the concept, that is, the way it occurs in late capitalism, broadly conceived, without arguing that the concept ought to be discarded altogether (*some* notion of reification is actually essential to making sure that it is not merely power that rules the day). In this way, Adorno is using "metaphysics" in a peculiar way, to denote simply something like "more than what is." By virtue of this use, he is indexing the term *metaphysics* to theology. As Adorno puts it explicitly, "metaphysics in the precise sense I have set out here is both a critique and reprise, a resumption, of theology."[37] Note that Adorno is also thereby explicitly orienting his entire approach to an assessment of the world (albeit in negative terms), and thereby to cultivating flashes of how such a world might appear different (in order to be made different).

§ 4. Materialism and Metaphysics

It is worth asking at this point what exactly Adorno means by such an approach. Do we find ourselves in a highbrow version of the metaphysics and theology found in the New Age sections of (some) contemporary bookstores, where metaphysics is cast as astrology or occultism? In fact, Adorno wants to reject exactly this option. Instead, Adorno claims

36. Adorno, *Lectures on Negative Dialectics*, 108.
37. Adorno, *Metaphysics*, 88.

that the defining characteristic of almost everything we call "metaphysics" is the "attempt to save—and to save by means of concepts—what appeared to be threatened precisely by concepts, and was in the process of being disintegrated, or corroded."[38] And in this way, metaphysics, in positing more than what is, is structurally connected to theology. He sketches this story with a gloss on Plato, suggesting that we might read Plato's doctrine of the forms as "a secularization of theology."[39] The idea seems to be something like the following: In Plato's milieu, conceptual activity begins to undermine traditional Greek religious concepts (here primarily the gods of Olympus). That same conceptual activity, however, also leads to the doctrine of the forms, which might be understood as "the gods turned into concepts."[40] Such a process, however, raises questions about the forms, namely the question of their "*relationship* to appearances," and introduces the various "epistemological and logical difficulties with which Plato has to contend."[41] Now, this reading of ancient philosophy, by itself, is quite rushed and not particularly novel or sophisticated. At the same time, it is not entirely implausible. Furthermore, what makes it worth thinking about is how Adorno embeds it in a broader view of metaphysics, one that frames Aristotle's project, as much as Plato's, as oriented around a similar motif.[42] Like Maimonides, then, Adorno's thought orients itself around a particular reading of Aristotle.

38. Adorno, *Metaphysics*, 19.
39. Adorno, *Metaphysics*, 18. Compare *Negative Dialectics*, 297.
40. Adorno, *Metaphysics*, 18.
41. Adorno, *Metaphysics*, 18–19.
42. It is not entirely implausible to read Plato and Aristotle as much closer than often thought. Indeed, Aristotle and Plato were not always viewed as antithetically as they are oftentimes viewed now—for an argument that the two are not antithetical, see Lloyd Gerson, *Aristotle and Other Platonists: Ancient Commentators on Aristotle* (Ithaca, NY: Cornell University Press, 2005).

Adorno's chief claim is that Aristotle, in criticizing Plato, suggests that Plato merely hypostatizes "universal concepts as a duplication of the world."[43] Nonetheless, "at the same time," Aristotle—like Plato—"seeks in his turn to extract an essential being from the sensible, empirical world, and thereby to save it; and it is precisely this twofold aim of criticism and rescue which constitutes the nature of metaphysics."[44] Adorno continues, radicalizing the thesis from one about ancient philosophy to one about history of Western philosophy more broadly, now highlighting how "the polarity between critical rationality, on the one hand, and the pathos of rescue, on the other, points to the essence of traditional metaphysics, or at least has done so throughout its history."[45] He concludes that "metaphysics can thus be defined as the exertion of thought to save what at the same time it destroys."[46] In this view, Aristotle, like Plato, is concerned with taking seriously conceptual activity, which, to Aristotle, seems above all to register the fact of *constant change*, and thereby to undermine the plausibility of the Platonic account.[47] In doing so, however, Aristotle discovers "an extraordinarily important and profound insight, *that all change presupposes something unchangeable, and all becoming something that has not become*."[48] We are here—as with Maimonides—once again thrust into the heart of ancient Greek thought about possibility and actuality, and thereby the world.

43. Adorno, *Metaphysics*, 20.
44. Ibid.
45. Ibid.
46. Ibid.
47. Ibid., 56.
48. Adorno, *Metaphysics*, 57; emphasis added. Adorno also claims that this is "one of Aristotle's most magnificent discoveries, to which we are hardly able to give its due weight because it has become so self-evident to us that we no longer know what an enormous exertion of genius its attainment must have cost" (Adorno, *Metaphysics*, 57).

To elaborate this point, observe—as Aristotle does—the ways in which various artifacts become what they are. An artifact comes about through the actions of an artificer, that is, someone who makes the artifact in question. And the artificer does so because the cause—in Aristotelian parlance, the "for the sake of which" of the artifact—resides in her and is actualized in her making the artifact. So, the artificer initially possesses the form of the artifact in a less actualized state, which she then fully actualizes in the creation of the artifact; the artificer making this artifact is the form of the artifact in the process of becoming what it actually is.[49] Change here occurs by means of a form in action. And the same is true in nature, where a form in action drives a being's becoming what it actually is, whether it is a plant or a cow or whatever else. As Aristotle puts it, "since nature is twofold, the matter and the form, of which the latter is the end, and since all the rest is for the sake of the end, the form must be the cause in the sense of that for the sake of which."[50]

Adorno rightly notes that for Aristotle "form is the true reality . . . reality is actually energy; it is reality only in so far as it is formed reality—and it [true reality] is not the material of that reality." "Matter," on the other hand, "is defined as mere possibility or potentiality, because it must always have within it the possibility of attaining such reality, of attaining its form."[51] As Aristotle puts it, "in all cases . . . it is plain that there must be something underlying, namely, *that which becomes*."[52] If matter is that which becomes—in other words,

49. See Aristotle, *Physics*, 2. 2–3, 194b–95b, in Aristotle, *Complete Works of Aristotle*, 2 vols. (Princeton, NJ: Princeton University Press, 2014).

50. Aristotle, *Physics*, II:8, 199a30.

51. Adorno, *Metaphysics*, 63.

52. Aristotle, *Physics*, I:7, 190a33–4; emphasis added. This need not imply any position on the nature or existence of prime matter, which has been a topic of some dispute within Aristotle scholarship. See S. Marc Cohen, "Alternation and Persistence: Form and Matter in *The Physics* and

potentiality—then form is that which makes matter what it actually is. So much so that, ultimately, because form is that which is actual, first philosophy turns out, at bottom, to be fundamentally the study of actuality and its innermost core is the study of pure actuality, or the prime actuality, that is, the unmoved mover, an eternal and changeless substance that is the final cause of everything else.[53] Adorno stresses this point:

> The unmoved mover is, fundamentally, nothing other than pure form existing in itself, which, as it were, draws everything up towards it. Although itself immobile, it is like a magnet of pure actuality, or pure energy, pulling up everything which is merely potential towards it, and in this way, realizing itself to an ever-increasing degree. That, really, is the core of Aristotle's *Metaphysics*, if the core is defined as the point at which his metaphysics passes over into theology. The central point of any metaphysics is probably to be found where the transition between metaphysics and theology takes place.[54]

In turn, Adorno finds this point deeply objectionable, calling it a "short-circuit or false conclusion."[55] So much so that Adorno presents Aristotle's alleged mistake as in fact informing (or perhaps "infecting") the entire subsequent history and tradition of Western metaphysics. Although there are many examples[56] in Adorno's lectures, some notable ones are the following:

> If I might give you a cross-reference to the later history of philosophy, this doctrine of Aristotle's is a speculation which reappeared at the height of German idealism, in Schelling, where matter is likewise conceived, in an objective

---

De Generatione et Corruptione," in *The Oxford Handbook of Aristotle*, ed. Christopher Shields (Oxford: Oxford University Press, 2012), 221–22.
 53. See especially Aristotle, *Metaphysics*, 1026a23–32 and 1072a20–26.
 54. Adorno, *Metaphysics*, 59.
 55. Ibid., 57.
 56. See esp. ibid., 28–32.

dialectic, as a principle which has the inherent tendency to move towards a higher form.[57]

> The problem with which this work [Kant's *Critique of Practical Reason*] grapples above all ... is how the moral law, which is something purely spiritual, arising from the intelligible world and independent of any empirical determination, manages to act upon the empirical world. ... This problem ... is already fully contained in Aristotle's *Metaphysics*.[58]

> In our own time this doctrine of the eternal character of the relationship of matter and form, and thus the doctrine of the eternity of movement, has cropped up again in Heidegger's theory which seeks to grasp historicity or temporality as an invariant, an *Existenzial*, that is, a basic condition of existence.[59]

> What is astonishing is that the whole *instrumentarium*, if you like, of later idealism is to be found in Aristotle.[60]

Adorno is not deaf to the history of Western philosophy, and he recognizes important differences and distinctions between Aristotle and the philosophy that comes after him.[61] What is crucial for Adorno, however, is that much of the history of metaphysics (and thereby philosophy) recreates the basic structure of Aristotle's (and Plato's) argumentation,[62] which asserts above all that

57. Ibid., 63.
58. Ibid., 27–28.
59. Ibid., 87.
60. Ibid., 90.
61. Most notable in this regard is his point that allegedly "the *infinite* was foreign to antiquity" (Adorno, *Metaphysics*, 57). I take Adorno to mean not that ancient philosophy lacked the notion of infinity (an absurd conclusion, which he himself rejects in *Metaphysics*, 57), but rather that the ancient notion of causation was distinct from modern theories of causation. Such a notion did not rely on causes being held together by events and effects and instead operated on a model of efficient causation where one speaks of things as potentiality on the way to actuality. For more on this point, see Jonathan Lear, *Aristotle: The Desire to Understand* (Cambridge: Cambridge University Press, 1988), 34–36.
62. In one regard, then, Adorno certainly agrees with Whitehead's idea that "the safest general characterization of the European philosophical

(1) *actuality*, that is, form, the *abstract* and *general*, is somehow the most real, and thereby more real than matter;
(2) matter, in being relegated in this way to something less real than form nonetheless regains those qualities that it was meant to lack, since anything indeterminate, by virtue of being undetermined, is paradoxically also *somehow* determined; thus, something entirely formless is thereby given at least *some* form.[63]

For Adorno, such dualisms are both unstable and objectionable because they miscast human experience.

Adorno suggests these points are most obvious in Aristotle's understanding of motion. In book 3 of the *Physics*, Aristotle states that "the fulfillment of what is potentially, as such, is motion (ἐντελέχεια [*entelékheia*])."[64] Adorno glosses this notion as "that which is by virtue of its possibility *becomes* by virtue of its entelechy [motion]; movement is the becoming real of the possible.... The impulse towards movement can only come from something which already

---

tradition is that it consists of a series of footnotes to Plato" (Alfred North Whitehead, "Process and Reality: An Essay in Cosmology" [New York: Free Press, 1978], 39).

63. Adorno, *Metaphysics*, 75–76. Let me mention two points. First, what Adorno says here is equally applicable to Maimonides, who consistently impugns matter as a barrier to comprehension of ultimate reality (for more on this point, see footnote 121 in chap. 3). Second, likely, Adorno overstates his case by suggesting that Aristotle imbues matter with *tyche* (τύχη) and *automaton* (αὐτόματον)—chance and necessity, respectively. Aristotle seems careful to attribute these designations to agents (whether natural or intelligent) as the sources of change (see *Physics*, II.6, 198a1–3). Not much hinges on this point, however, since Adorno's general point still stands. Furthermore, in support of Adorno's claims here, one can look to the extent to which the existence of "prime matter" has generated an immense literature in Aristotle scholarship, ending in a stalemate between arguments for its necessity within Aristotle's system as well as its impossibility for the same. On this point, see, for example, S. M. Cohen, "Alternation and Persistence," 222. Similarly, in *Metaphysics*, Aristotle is clear that matter cannot even exist without form. Whether this confirms or denies Adorno's point depends on how Aristotle's statement is taken.

64. Aristotle, *Physics*, III.1, 201a10.

is."⁶⁵ In defense of Adorno's claim, Aristotle himself stresses that "actuality in the strict sense is identified with movement" (*Metaphysics*, Θ.3, 1047a30–2). Movement, in turn, must be eternal, lest we have a moment without actuality, which, on its face, is impossible, for *being* a moment implies existence. Therefore, Adorno stresses that for Aristotle "under all conceivable circumstances, therefore, movement must be eternal. . . . In this way *the dynamic itself is made an invariant, is made static.*"⁶⁶ In turn, this necessitates the existence of a prime mover and thus, as Adorno elaborates, that "we have made a transition from Aristotelian metaphysics to what might perhaps be called Aristotelian theology."

In relating this story to the history of Western philosophy, Adorno stresses that because form is that which is truly actual, matter—regardless of how much human suffering it necessitates—is always "on its way" toward a trajectory that is, at bottom, justified or justifiable. Such "thinking already has the tendency to justify the world itself in its current state of being so and not otherwise."⁶⁷ Furthermore, because of this implicit justification, something like perfection is always already waiting in the wings. On this point, Adorno suggests a structural analogy between Aristotle's prime mover and ontological arguments for God's existence, where the only distinction between the two is that unlike the latter, which "draw conclusions about existence from the concept of perfection," Aristotle's argument for the prime mover "concludes from the structure of existence that the being of God must arise virtually out of pure thought."⁶⁸

65. Adorno, *Metaphysics*, 82.
66. Ibid., 87; emphasis added. Aristotle's arguments for the eternity of motion are to be found in book 8 of the *Physics*. He offers several arguments, and none is exactly of this form. I am not, however, concerned here with "getting Aristotle right," because I think the standard is only whether Adorno's reading is plausible enough, and it seems to be so.
67. Ibid., 89.
68. Ibid.

Adorno's reading of the history of Western philosophy diagnoses within that tradition a common formal quality, namely, a persistent minimization of the empirical world of concrete (we might even say everyday) life in favor of a somehow more actual world, one that is conceived as already existent, unchanging, and as the telos of the present world, waiting for it at the end of a sequence.[69] This, Adorno thinks, is true as much of Aristotle and Plato as it is of Descartes (with his proof of God and mind-body dualism, as well as with the thought that God and the mind are the "most real"), of Kant (with his stress on rational theology as necessary for self-consciousness, and the telos inherent in the final end of creation),[70] and even of Heidegger (with his stress on temporality as an "invariant" means for grasping Being).[71]

Assessing these claims about the history of philosophy in proper depth is beyond my scope here, but what this story makes clear is Adorno's broader point about theology. As he puts it, "metaphysics is a translation of theological conceptions into categories of reason, that it is a conceptualization of those conceptions."[72] What Adorno means here—at the most basic level—is that metaphysics and theology share a common impulse: the impulse to see in reality more than what

---

69. Adorno also stresses another objectionable element, that the conjunction of these two also implies a solitary unity, and that "truth," "highest purpose," "highest good," and so on, are all used interchangeably (see Adorno, *Metaphysics*, 96–97). I do not pursue this point because I do not view it as necessary to the rest of my argument.

70. For a detailed reconstruction of Kant's rational theology in this regard and Adorno's take on it, see Shuster, *Autonomy after Auschwitz*, 42–70.

71. Although this charge might strike Heideggerians as unfair, it is not entirely implausible. For example, Levinas launches a similar attack on Heidegger and his recourse to the *Neuter* in Emmanuel Levinas, "Philosophy and the Idea of Infinity," trans. Alphonso Lingis, in *Collected Philosophical Papers* (Dordrecht, Neth.: Martinus Nijhoff, 1987), 52. For detailed discussions of the relationship between Heidegger and Adorno, see Macdonald and Ziarek, *Adorno and Heidegger*.

72. Adorno, *Metaphysics*, 98.

presently is there. Theology instantiates such an impulse through fundamentally religious categories and concepts that are understood as themselves originating through a variety of natural, psychological, or nonrational means,[73] while metaphysics arrives at *formally* and *functionally similar* categories and concepts but does so *through the operations of reason*. Both therefore depend on an impulse, not solely cognitive, but equally parts *practical* that conceives—and perceives—the world in a particular way: that sees it ultimately as substance for criticism and for possible improvement.

I have wanted to stress Adorno's reading of Aristotle because it allows us to understand why Adorno thinks that the natural link between metaphysics and theology can go awry, how it ought to be transformed, and when it ultimately must be opposed. Above all, Adorno opposes this Aristotelian story (taken in the expansive sense suggested above, as a story from Aristotle down to the present times) on *ethical* grounds. Here is what Adorno suggests in his lectures in 1965, and I quote him at length:

> You will have noticed from my analyses and expositions of Aristotle's *Metaphysics* . . . how fundamental the affirmative moment is to this whole conception of metaphysics. You will there have seen how far the theory, that *even without divine influence*, being is teleologically orientated towards the divine by its own nature. . . . I mention this to make fully clear the metaphysical problem which concerns me here—that matter, ὕλη [*húlē*], as that which is represented by possibility, must be endowed with some kind of purposiveness; and he argues

---

73. One might cite here the complex story that Max Horkheimer and Adorno sketch in *Dialectic of Enlightenment, Philosophical Fragments*, ed. Mieke Bal and Hent de Vries, trans. Edmund F. N. Jephcott, Cultural Memory in the Present Series (Stanford, CA: Stanford University Press, 2002). See especially their stress on the suffering that nature engenders in early human lives, and how myth arises as a means of coping with such suffering. On this point, see also Owen Hulatt, *Adorno's Theory of Philosophical and Aesthetic Truth* (New York: Columbia University Press, 2016).

this even despite the fact that it is in some contradiction to his own doctrine of possibility as wholly abstract and indeterminate. In face of the experiences we have had, not only through Auschwitz but through the introduction of torture as a permanent institution and through the atomic bomb—all these things form a kind of coherence, a hellish unity—in face of these experiences the assertion that what is has meaning, *and the affirmative character which has been attributed to metaphysics almost without exception*, become a mockery; and in face of victims it becomes downright immoral. For anyone who allows himself to be fobbed off with such meaning moderates in some way the unspeakable and irreparable things which have happened by conceding that somehow, in a secret order of being, all this will have had some kind of purpose.[74]

Adorno's ethical stance here can be compared exactly to the stance outlined a year later in *Negative Dialectics*. There, Adorno writes that our sensitivity "bristles against any claim for the positivity of existence as preachy yammering, an injustice towards the victims."[75] His point is that our concrete experience within our present world—"present" taken here broadly, as can be seen—bars attributing any sort of positivity or justification to existence: there is no secret telos toward which the world moves, no actuality that stands behind the possibility of matter.[76] If anything, quite the contrary. As Adorno notes, "as long as the world is as it is, all pictures of reconciliation, peace, and quiet resemble the picture of death."[77] This ethical stance is underwritten by the idea that rational categories cannot in the first place be divorced from experience (and all this, contrary to both

74. Adorno, *Metaphysics*, 103–4; emphasis added; compare 101–2.
75. Adorno, *Negative Dialectics*, 361, translation modified.
76. As will shortly emerge, an assessment of these metaphysical or ontological states will also necessitate an assessment and engagement with and a conception of history. More on this in chapter 3.
77. Adorno, *Negative Dialectics*, 381.

traditional metaphysics and to critics who, perversely even in light of the experience of Auschwitz, might shy away from invoking a notion of experience).[78] For Adorno, we are always, through and through, embodied creatures, whose mental life depends irreducibly on our physical life, and vice versa. As he puts it, the "supposition of a radical separation, χωρισμός [*khōrísmos*], between the intra-mundane realm and the transcendental, which is one of the keystones of the metaphysical tradition, is highly problematic, *since it is constantly confronted with evidence showing that it has picked out its eternal values, its immutabilities, from the mutable and from experience, and has then abstracted them.*"[79] This stress on experience ought not to be taken as implying something like what is regularly dismissed as "merely" subjective experience, but rather as revealing a commitment to the idea, common to German philosophy from Kant onward,[80] that experience is never merely causal, but perpetually carries a normative component within it.[81]

Materialism—for Adorno—suggests a commitment to this ethical stance, more so than some specific doctrine within a stream of Marxism (although, of course, the two are not

---

78. On the point of experience, Adorno would be in agreement with Marianne Janack's conclusion that (a) a reliance on experience need not lead us toward reductionism and, in fact, (b) such a reliance is essential to understanding ourselves as *human* agents. See Marianne Janack, *What We Mean by Experience* (Palo Alto, CA: Stanford University Press, 2012). For an extensive discussion of Adorno on experience, see Roger Foster, *Adorno: The Recovery of Experience* (Albany, NY: SUNY Press, 2007).

79. Adorno, *Metaphysics*, 100; emphasis added.

80. There are many ways to make a case for this story. For two notable ways, see especially Robert B. Brandom, *Tales of the Mighty Dead: Historical Essays in the Metaphysics of Intentionality* (Cambridge: Cambridge University Press, 2002); John McDowell, *Mind and World* (Cambridge, MA: Harvard University Press, 1994). The most elaborate and sophisticated discussion of Adorno in this context is Bernstein, *Adorno*.

81. Again, this suggests that much more needs to be said about this, especially both at the level of history *and* at the level of individual human agency, points that I pursue in chapters 3 and 4.

mutually exclusive). Rather than "a set of fixed metaphysical or methodological commitments," materialism is "something which could more accurately be named an impulse: the utopian wish for undeluded happiness . . . the wish for an end to suffering."[82] Anchored to a concern about human suffering,[83] Adorno's understanding of materialism is not exclusively a set of ontological theses,[84] even as it relies on a distinct understanding of the tradition of ontology and metaphysics. The way in which Adorno understands materialism is intimately tied to his new categorical imperative and the acknowledgment of human suffering.[85] This is why Adorno stresses that "the bodily [*leibhafte*] moment [of acknowledging suffering] makes explicit [*anmelden*] to cognition [*Erkenntnis*] that suffering ought not to be, that things should be different. 'Woe speaks: "Go."'" Thereby the specifically materialistic converges with what is critical, with socially transformative praxis."[86] Our conceptual capacities are—in the form of an ethical sensitivity—always already bound up with our bodily comportments. What drives such ethical assessments of the world is not a commitment to some sort of moral principles (although, of course, such a commitment

---

82. Simon Jarvis, "Adorno, Marx, Materialism," in *The Cambridge Companion to Adorno* (Cambridge: Cambridge University Press, 2004), 80.

83. Adorno is likely influenced by Max Horkheimer, "Materialism and Morality," trans. G. Frederick Hunter, Matthew S. Kramer, and John Torpey, in *Between Philosophy and Social Science* (Cambridge, MA: MIT Press, 1993). For more on this point, see Shuster, "Nothing to Know."

84. I am not suggesting that such ontological theses that arise from other concerns cannot be implied. For more on Adorno and his relationship to nature, see Deborah Cook, *Adorno on Nature* (London: Routledge, 2014).

85. For some recent discussions of the new categorical imperative: Bernstein, *Adorno*, 384–95; Freyenhagen, *Adorno's Practical Philosophy*, 133–61; Pritchard, "Bilderverbot Meets Body," 314–18; Shuster, *Autonomy after Auschwitz*, 71–133; Silberbusch, *Adorno's Philosophy*, 57–123.

86. Adorno, *Negative Dialectics*, 203, translation modified.

is not barred or excluded), but rather a distinct ethical sensitivity to concrete cases and forms of suffering.[87]

§ 5. Adorno and/on Negativity

Taking this point seriously, note that by "negativity" Adorno invokes something explicitly opposed to the "positivity" that he diagnoses in Aristotle and the subsequent Western philosophical tradition. Whereas the former posits *some* sort of telos, Adorno rejects that notion because of present historical experience (and again, "some" is accurate here to the extent that it need not be an outright theodicy but can be something as seemingly innocuous as the prioritization of actuality over potentiality, of form over matter, and so forth). Registering the full tenor of the ethical quality of this point is crucial. And this comes out most clearly when a comparison is drawn—as Adorno himself inadvertently suggests—with Heidegger. Heidegger articulates a position quite similar, in which he rejects imbuing reality with any sort of positivity. In his 1931 lectures on the first three chapters of book Θ of Aristotle's *Metaphysics*, Heidegger also uses Aristotle to stage this argument and to argue that Aristotle fundamentally misunderstands the nature of negativity. Heidegger claims that "every production of something, in general every δύναμις μετά λόγου (*dunamis meta logou*), prepares for itself, and this necessarily through its proper way of proceeding, the continually concomitant opportunity for mistaking, neglecting, overlooking, and failing; thus every force carries *in itself* and *for itself* the possibility of sinking into *un-force*. *This negativum does not simply stand beside the positive force as its opposite but haunts this force in the force itself, and this because every force of this type according to its essence is*

---

87. This, of course, raises the question of how such assessments might be justified or understood. On this point, see footnote 85.

invested with divisiveness and so with a 'not. '"[88] Heidegger's chief example here is human action, and his claim is that the persistent possibility of failure just is a part of such action. Failure is not merely an accidental feature of such action or a possible lack that may or may not occur in its unfolding; rather, the possibility for failure is an inherent feature of understanding the deepest meaning of human action, thereby making it what it is. And so negativity is always embedded in all human action.[89] In *Being and Time*, Heidegger puts it simply as the idea that "existing as thrown ... means *never* to gain power over one's ownmost being from the ground up. This *not* belongs to the existential meaning of thrownness."[90] According to Heidegger, at the very foundation of what it means to be Dasein—human—is the following twofold idea: that, first, I am thrown into a particular history, not entirely of my own making, and, second, that this history, and therefore the history of my life, gains its "meaning" only from its end, that is, from my death, which, at its core, is ultimately nothing because it can never be incorporated into any system of meaning for me—it represents the impossibility of my

88. Martin Heidegger, *Aristotle's Metaphysics Θ 1–3: On the Essence and Actuality of Force*, trans. Walter Brogan and Peter Warnek (Bloomington: Indiana University Press, 1995), 131–32; second emphasis added.

89. There are many issues here, including likely most critically Aristotle's own notion of στέρησις (*lack*). Heidegger gives a reading of the term in *Aristotle's Metaphysics*, 92–93. For a reading of Heidegger on this point, see Karin de Boer, *Thinking in the Light of Time: Heidegger's Encounter with Hegel*, trans. Karin de Boer and Janet Taylor (Buffalo, NY: SUNY Press, 2000), 208. I do not think it is necessary to speak here of striving and counterstriving—as de Boer does—in order to understand what Heidegger is after. Heidegger seems to me to be making the point—which he does more elaborately with his account of guilt in *Being and Time*—that human action must be understood always on the horizon of the possible failure of care and the possibility of an ultimate failure of meaning to one's being. One of the best discussions of this point is Robert B. Pippin, "Necessary Conditions for the Possibility of What Isn't: Heidegger on Failed Meaning," in *The Persistence of Subjectivity* (Cambridge: Cambridge University Press, 2005), 57–79.

90. Heidegger, *Being and Time*, §58.

existence. As Heidegger puts it, somewhat clumsily, but certainly aptly, "*Dasein* finds itself *faced* with the nothingness of the possible impossibility of its existence."[91]

The reason I claim that Adorno inadvertently suggests a comparison to Heidegger here is that Adorno describes a structurally similar occurrence.[92] In response to the calamitous brutality of the modern world, Adorno points out that "those who continue to engage in old-style metaphysics, without concerning themselves with what has happened [i.e., with Auschwitz], keeping it at arm's length and regarding it as beneath metaphysics, like everything merely earthly and human, thereby prove themselves inhuman. . . . It is therefore *impossible, I would say, to insist after Auschwitz on the presence of a positive meaning or purpose in being*. Here, too, though from a totally different context, I would like to say quite candidly that I am entirely of one mind with Sartre."[93] There are important differences between Heidegger and Sartre.[94] But what Adorno is stressing here—and it is a point on which Heidegger and Sartre agree—is that at the core of existence is nothing; there is no ultimate meaning.[95] What is important, however, is the difference in their modes of evaluation. What Sartre and Heidegger diagnose is a structural

---

91. Heidegger, *Being and Time*, §53. This is the phenomenon Heidegger dubs "anxiety" (*Angst*).

92. There is a lot more to be said here about Heidegger and Adorno, especially with respect to Adorno's own invocation of guilt. The best discussion of these issues is Iain Macdonald, "Ethics and Authenticity: Conscience and Non-Identity in Heidegger and Adorno, with a Glance at Hegel," in *Adorno and Heidegger: Philosophical Questions*, ed. Iain Macdonald and Krzysztof Ziarek, 6–21 (Palo Alto, CA: Stanford University Press, 2008).

93. Adorno, *Metaphysics*, 101; emphasis added; compare 105.

94. These are outlined by Heidegger in Heidegger, "Letter on Humanism." For analysis of this text, see Stefanos Geroulanos, *An Atheism That Is Not Humanist Emerges in French Thought* (Palo Alto, CA: Stanford University Press, 2010), 222–50.

95. Jean-Paul Sartre, *Being and Nothingness*, trans. Hazel E. Barnes (New York: Philosophical Library, 1956), 3–47.

feature of human agency. As one commentator on Heidegger puts it, the "nothing" that they diagnose at the core of being "is neither bridgeable nor fillable, and the difference it makes essential to existence always remains so, no matter how Dasein pursues its projects."[96] Adorno's diagnosis, however, operates in an entirely different register, one that is ethical in orientation. As he puts it, "unless one makes oneself wholly insensitive one can hardly escape the feeling—and by feeling I mean experience which is not confined to the emotional sphere—that just by continuing to live one is taking away that possibility from someone else, to whom life has been denied; that one is stealing that person's life."[97]

To understand what Adorno is after, we might consider the way in which things are arranged in the contemporary world. A recent commentator on the current state of affairs is worth citing here at length:

> Turn off the lights. Use compact fluorescent bulbs (even if they produce an ugly glare). Drive a small, fuel-efficient car. Drive less. Take public transportation. Don't fly unless you really need to (no more trips to international conferences, no more exotic vacations). Turn down the thermostat in winter. Turn off the air-conditioning in summer. Make sure your appliances are energy efficient. Take cooler showers. Eat local (except sometimes; find out when). Don't eat factory-farmed meat; leaving aside harm to animals, producing it is not energy efficient. Don't buy Chilean sea bass, or salmon, or . . . (fill in the blank, depending on which sea food is overfished at any given time). Don't drink bottled water—the energy costs of producing and transporting it are wasteful (leaving aside that only 14 percent of bottles are recycled). Don't use plastic bags (not paper bags either!). Recycle. Compost. Don't use chemical fertilizers on your lawn; better still, get rid of your lawn. In this new world in which we find ourselves, "each

96. Macdonald, "Ethics and Authenticity," 15.
97. Adorno, *Metaphysics*, 112–13.

bite we eat, each item we discard, each e-mail message we send, and each purchase we make entails a conversion of fossil-fuel carbon to carbon dioxide," with possible deleterious consequences for others and for the globe. Apart from the environmental consequences of our actions, which disproportionately affect poor people, other kinds of harms also loom. Don't buy clothing made in sweatshops. (Find out which those are.) Was your oriental rug knotted by eight-year-olds? (Find out.) Do you own stock in a company that exploits its workers? (Find out.) Is the coltan in your cell phone fueling wars in the Congo?[98]

Adorno's point, like the one of the commentator, is that late capitalism is both globally ubiquitous and also wholly pervasive of our lives, as private or public as they might be.

Furthermore, our present form of capitalism, by virtue of being what it is, breeds suffering, and it does so both mercilessly and inescapably: there simply is no refuge, no island to which one can retreat and not be somehow implicated. As Adorno famously puts it, "there is no right living in the false [*Es gibt kein richtiges Leben im Falschen*]."[99] Such suffering, which is omnipresent, prohibits the construction of any overarching—moral—meaning to or justification for the

---

98. Judith Lichtenberg, "Negative Duties, Positive Duties, and the 'New Harms,'" *Ethics* 120, no. 3 (2010): 559.

99. Adorno, *Minima Moralia*, 39; translation modified. This is one way in which Adorno's thought both connects to and radically departs from similar lines of thought in contemporary Anglo-American philosophy. Ever since Peter Singer's essay (Peter Singer, "Famine, Affluence, and Morality," *Philosophy and Public Affairs* [1972]: 229–43), contemporary Anglo-American thought has recognized something like the problem that Adorno recognizes here (witness Judith Lichtenberg's wonderful description just quoted). In response, the debate has centered on the *scope* of Singer's strong (and weak) principle. Adorno, however—and I would suspect *shockingly* in the eyes of Anglo-American scholars—would take even Singer's strong principle to be insufficiently radical since it doesn't affect the basic *way* in which the world is organized, instead affecting the ways in which money circulates within it.

social or historical whole.[100] The prohibition against such a construction, is not, however, chiefly an epistemological or logical one (where what is being diagnosed is a structural feature of our human finitude), but rather an ethical one, where what bars such a construction is the experience of bodily suffering. What is most real is matter, which, above all, has the capacity to reveal human suffering. It is only in the acknowledgment of such suffering that Adorno thinks morality, "the demand for right living," lives on; that is, it may live on in only such "openly materialist motifs."[101] Adorno's invocation of materialism here, however, ought not be understood as endorsing any sort of bald realism. As Adorno puts it, the idea is not to put such material back on the "orphaned royal throne" formerly occupied by the subject.[102] Adorno is clear that "what would be beyond [our conceptual apparatus], appears only in the materials and categories inside."[103] The acknowledgment of suffering is a somatic process, but it is not one that is divorced from our conceptual capacities. Instead, it is one that is intimately involved with such capacities, delineating routes of moral salience and vectors of ethical engagement. It is therefore a sort of judgment, but one initially "bodily" in nature (and therefore potentially initially "unconscious"),[104] that is, a judgment that is for that reason

100. This does not mean that a *negative* meaning to history cannot be construed. See Adorno, *Metaphysics*, 320. For a discussion, see also Shuster, *Autonomy after Auschwitz*, 153–55.

101. Adorno, *Metaphysics*, 117.

102. Adorno, *Negative Dialectics*, 181.

103. Ibid., 140.

104. "Unconscious" is understood here in the way in which Kant's "I think" is unconscious—not perpetually barred from conscious engagement, but rather meant to designate the possibility of *becoming* conscious. On this point, see Immanuel Kant, *Critique of Pure Reason*, trans. Paul Guyer and Allen W. Wood (Cambridge: Cambridge University Press, 1998), B131–32. Highly relevant here is Yannik Thiem's elaboration of an "emotionality that is the medium of thinking" (Annika Thiem, "Adorno's Tears: Textures of Philosophical Emotionality," *MLN* 124, no. 3 [2009]: 593).

"indispensably sustained by ... perceptions and feelings and thoughts that are open to criticism" and that is therefore "based on norms that are open to criticism."[105] In short, there is here, as in Maimonides, a sort of prioritization of a type of practical orientation toward or mood—*Stimmung*—within the world. Where Maimonides sees plenitude and the world as perpetually ripe for our exploration, Adorno sees lack, registering the suffering that he claims fundamentally defines that world.

To return to the passage from *Negative Dialectics* that opened my entire inquiry into negativity in Adorno, note that ultimately a "conceptually determined particular" is one in which "the concept is always also its negative."[106] "Negativity" in this case means that our somatic experience of suffering always suggests a state of affairs where such suffering does not exist. In this way, as Adorno argues, the false indexes the true (*falsum index sui et veri*).[107] Negativity is the rejection of the present world as justified or justifiable, and all by virtue of the experience of suffering. Such negativity, however, cannot be "named immediately" because it exactly requires the experience of and the encounter with human suffering. Because of a fundamental avoidance of materiality and suffering, "it is almost as if philosophy—and most of all the great, deep, constructive philosophy—obeyed a single impulse: to get away from the place of carrion, stench and putrefaction."[108] The common modern philosophical refrain from Kant onward—that "determination is negation"—cannot, for Adorno, mean that one delineates elements of

---

105. David Wiggins, "A Sensible Subjectivism?," in *Foundations of Ethics: An Anthology*, ed. Russ Shafer-Landau and Terence Cuneo (Oxford, UK: Wiley-Blackwell, 2007), 208.

106. Adorno, *Negative Dialectics*, 173, translation modified.

107. On this point, compare with Bloch, *The Utopian Function of Art and Literature*, 12.

108. Adorno, *Metaphysics*, 117.

reality without reference to human suffering.[109] Metaphysics follows ethics. This is how to understand Adorno's suggestion that "metaphysics . . . has slipped into material existence.[110] Or, as Adorno puts it in *Negative Dialectics*, "the need to give voice to suffering is a condition for *all* truth."[111] The fundamental structure of such negativity ("the false") and therefore the glimpses of positivity ("the true") that it yields are tied to particular experiences and are therefore incapable of homogenization into an overarching whole, into a picture of the world in the (entirely) right state of things.[112] Such negativity, nonetheless, is entirely necessary because it offers the only clues, as small as they are, for "right living" and opens our eyes to glimpses of utopia. This is what Adorno means when he calls this negativity the "staging ground" (*Schauplatz*) of dialectics. As he points out in *Negative Dialectics*, "the right state of things would be free of dialectics."[113] In other words, in the "right" state of things, there would be no falsity, that is,

109. This raises the question of what determination would look like in utopia—a question that Adorno does not (as far as I know) address anywhere. I take it that any answer must acknowledge the point that above all (1) we don't know, and (2) that determination in utopia may not involve negation.

110. Adorno, *Metaphysics*, 117. One can tease out strong connections to the thought of Emmanuel Levinas. On this point, see Hent de Vries, *Minimal Theologies: Critiques of Secular Reason in Adorno and Levinas*, trans. Geoffrey Hale (Baltimore, MD: Johns Hopkins University Press, 2005); Asher Horowitz, "'By a Hair's Breadth' Critique, Transcendence and the Ethical in Adorno and Levinas," *Philosophy and Social Criticism* 28, no. 2 (2002): 213–48; Nick Smith, "Adorno vs. Levinas: Evaluating Points of Contention," *Continental Philosophy Review* 40, no. 3 (2007): 275–306; Carl Sachs, "The Acknowledgement of Transcendence: Anti-theodicy in Adorno and Levinas," *Philosophy and Social Criticism* 37, no. 3 (2011): 273–94; Eric Nelson, *Levinas, Adorno, and the Ethics of the Material Other* (Buffalo, NY: SUNY Press, 2019).

111. Adorno, *Negative Dialectics*, 17–18 6:29; translation modified and emphasis added. Compare Adorno's claim that "the historical trace on things, words, colors and sounds is always of past suffering," in Theodor W. Adorno, Adorno, "On Tradition," *Telos* 94 (1992): 78.

112. Jay Bernstein aptly calls this "fugitive experience" in his work; see the discussion in (Bernstein, *Adorno*, 437–51).

113. Adorno, *Negative Dialectics*, 11.

no negativity, and therefore no alternative picture where such suffering is no longer present. Despair, therefore, is unavoidable, but it is also never total or final. Adorno puts this beautifully with the idea that "consciousness could not even despair over the gray, if it did not shelter the concept of a different color, whose dispersed traces are not absent from the negative whole."[114]

§ 6. On the Emergence of Theology

These traces should exactly be seen as analogous to the procedures of metaphysics and theology. As Adorno notes, both suggest "more than what is." This is why Adorno can say that metaphysics slips "into material existence"[115] and even more forcefully with respect to theology, that "where materialism is at its most materialistic [*materialistischesten*], it comes to agree [*kommt er dort überein*] with theology."[116] The acknowledgment of bodily suffering always suggests more than what presently is, and in this way, formally, it is of one kind with theology (the two are thereby intimately linked, each suggesting more than what presently is).

It is crucial to understand, though, that such traces are spurred entirely by contingent historical events, not by metaphysical (and therefore unchanging) principles. As Adorno emphasizes explicitly in introducing the new categorical imperative, Hitler has forced (*aufzwingen*) such an imperative on humankind. And in this way "the content of the moral principle, the categorical imperative, constantly changes as history changes."[117] This is why, as I have mentioned,

---

114. Ibid., 377, translation modified.
115. Adorno, *Metaphysics*, 117.
116. Adorno, *Negative Dialectics*, 207, translation modified.
117. Adorno, *History and Freedom*, 205. Fabian Freyenhagen's discussion of this point drew my attention to this passage; see Freyenhagen, *Adorno's Practical Philosophy*, 136–38.

Adorno had early on in his writing career called his theology an "inverse theology."[118] The inversion consists of two things. First, as we have seen, with its invocation of the body and of history, it reverses the origin point for entering into any conceptualization of more than what presently is, and therefore of utopia and anything even remotely tied to the possibility of what's beyond this world. This is one way to understand Adorno's suggestion that what is required presently is "an extreme loyalty to the prohibition of images, far beyond what this once originally meant."[119] The prohibition now applies to even the remotest picture of that which is more than what presently is because the further we move into such pictures, the more we move away from present historical details, and above all, the proper registering of suffering requires a deep attachment to the minutest of historical details. Everything matters. This is why Adorno speaks of mysticism and the "infinite relevance of the intra-mundane, and thus the historical, to transcendence, and to any possible conception of transcendence."[120] With an eye toward contemporary discussions, this is one way to understand the myriad ways in which forms of structural suffering are persistently ignored by various systems of thought.

Second, because of this focus on the intramundane, it is an inverse theology because any such picture of utopia or of more than "what presently is" is incomplete and by nature indeterminate. "Determination is negation" . . . but is not once and for all complete. This is another way of saying that all such determinations are never finished, subject to perpetual revision in the face of new historical circumstances. Hannah Arendt captures a similar thought well when she notes that

---

118. He does so in a letter to Walter Benjamin: Theodor W. Adorno and Walter Benjamin, *The Complete Correspondence, 1928–1940* (Cambridge, MA: Harvard University Press, 2001), 67.

119. Adorno, "Reason and Revelation," 142.

120. Adorno, *Metaphysics*, 100.

"the event illuminates its own past; it can never be deduced from it."[121] Such historical revision, perpetually conducted as history itself unfolds, is captured by the process of dialectics, which itself—until the world is redeemed—always responds to an "ontology of the wrong state of things."[122] In any world short of utopia, any ossification of categories in permanence betrays the demand for a continual responsiveness to suffering and therefore is, in Adorno's stark image, akin to "the nature of the musical accompaniment with which the SS liked to drown out the screams of its victims."[123]

This claim highlights a feature of the image that Adorno uses to make this point in the aforementioned letter where he also mentioned inverse theology. There, discussing Kafka, Adorno mentions an earlier piece of his on Kafka (since lost, and not the same as the "Notes on Kafka"). He writes that "I claimed he [Kafka] represents a photograph of our earthly life from the perspective of a redeemed life, one which merely reveals the latter as an edge of black cloth, whereas the terrifyingly distanced optics of the photographic image is none other than that of the obliquely angled camera itself."[124] Generally, commentators read this passage as suggesting something like the idea that "the perspective of negativity is the inverted image projected by the light of

---

121. Hannah Arendt, "Understanding and Politics," in *Essays in Understanding, 1930–1954: Formation, Exile, and Totalitarianism*, ed. Jerome Kohn (New York: Schocken, 2011), 319.

122. Adorno, *Negative Dialectics*, 11.

123. Ibid., 365. There are important caveats to be had here: sometimes in the face of administrated and homogenizing categories—categories that shrink the range of experience—it may be important to retain certain earlier categories, concepts, and forms of thought. See the way in which Max Pensky develops the thought of Adorno's "late style" in Wendy Brown, Peter E. Gordon, and Max Pensky, *Authoritarianism: Three Inquiries in Critical Theory* (Chicago: University of Chicago Press, 2018). This does not mean that their constellation stays static, however. They need to be developed as suffering itself develops.

124. Adorno and Benjamin, *Complete Correspondence, 1928–1940*, 66.

redemption."[125] Yet, if one looks closely at the image Adorno uses, this reading is unwarranted. Instead, I take it that Adorno is referring—as he would likely be in 1934—to an older type of "view camera," where a front and rear standard are separated by a bellows. The front standard holds the lens and shutter and the rear standard has a glass that allows the photographer to focus the image before opening the shutter. Generally, a black cloth was used at the back glass in order to shield it from any extraneous light, thereby making the image clearer.[126] Adorno's point is that, when speaking of theology, the image we are presented with is the edge of the black cloth. The way in which the camera is angled reveals equally well that the camera cannot capture anything more than the image before it, and, at best, perhaps the edge of the black cloth (which suggests more but never reveals it). So, in line with Adorno's own suggestion at the end of *Minima Moralia*, we must "try to view all things as they would be represented from the standpoint of redemption."[127] This attempt can succeed only if we base this standpoint on the acknowledgment of human suffering. In that case, as Adorno importantly notes, "the question of the actuality or unactuality of redemption itself hardly matters."[128]

§ 7. Conclusion: History

As with Maimonides, Adorno's assessment of what lies beyond this world hinges on an assessment—fundamentally practical and not merely theoretical—of the world. Adorno

---

125. Pritchard, "Bilderverbot Meets Body," 306. As I have already mentioned, in all respects except the one I am presently outlining, I find Pritchard's piece exemplary. In this case, it is also exemplary in the way others read this passage—to my mind, incorrectly.

126. On this point, see Leslie Stroebel, *View Camera Technique* (Woburn, MA: Focal, 1999), 3.

127. Adorno, *Minima Moralia*, 247, translation modified.

128. Ibid.

measures the world by means of an ethical sensitivity[129] and ultimately finds it wanting; what lies beyond, however, cannot be merely reduced to this ethical impulse.[130] What might be beyond this world—God—is unknowable exactly because our ethical sensibility is "fugitive,"[131] tied locally to particular ills (even as such ills fill a deformed whole). Central to this ethical sensibility is the idea that any theological perspective that would situate these fugitive acts in some broader redemptive whole is suspect, ultimately a betrayal of that very ethical sensitivity. As Adorno puts it, "noble, elevated words" can, after Auschwitz, "no longer be used."[132] To the extent that such words continue to be used by religious zealots and various fundamentalists who have closed themselves off to the acknowledgment of human suffering or committed themselves to violence, if not both, Adorno cautions even more strongly against using such words.[133] In his lectures on moral philosophy, Adorno suggests that, at best, we might "salvage" religious ideas in order to involve them "as ingredients of moral action,"[134] as items for motivation. It is not therefore that Adorno's views of negativity reveal or found a commitment to theological doctrines,[135] but rather

---

129. There is, as far as I know, only one analogue to such a view in modern philosophy, where ethical claims drive conceptions of ultimate reality: Moses Mendelssohn. In *Morning Hours*, Mendelssohn recreates a possible debate about God and concludes with the idea that it depends on different conceptualizations. He urges that instead of argument or further conceptual analysis, we ought to "renounce words, and friend of wisdom, embrace your brother!" (Moses Mendelssohn, *Morning Hours: Lectures on God's Existence* [Dordrecht, Neth.: Springer, 2011], 90).

130. As in certain understandings of Kant, see Hermann Cohen, *Religion of Reason: Out of the Sources of Judaism*, trans. Simon Kaplan (New York: Frederick Ungar, 1972); Eric Funkhouser, "On Privileging God's Moral Goodness," *Faith and Philosophy* 23, no. 4 (2006): 409–22.

131. Bernstein, *Adorno*, 443.

132. Adorno, *Metaphysics*, 123.

133. Ibid.

134. Theodor W. Adorno, *Problems of Moral Philosophy*, trans. Rodney Livingstone (Stanford, CA: Stanford University Press, 2000), 97–98.

135. As in Pritchard, "Bilderverbot Meets Body," 317.

that such theological motifs best capture for Adorno the sort of ethical agency that human experience in late capitalism requires. This formal analogy to negative theology and the ban on images (*Bilderverbot*) appears only when theology has been inverted: been made to focus on historical expressions of suffering, that is, made ethical.

This ethical sensibility is captured by Adorno with an additional, later reference to Kafka and photography. In his 1954 "Notes on Kafka," Adorno structures a reading of Kafka around a ghastly image: "[Kafka's] writing feigns a standpoint from which the creation appears as lacerated and mutilated as it itself conceives hell to be. In the middle ages, Jews were tortured and executed 'perversely'—i.e., inversely. . . . Offenders were hung head down. Kafka, *the land-surveyor, photographs the earth's surface just as it must have appeared to these victims during the endless hours of their dying*."[136] Kafka's procedure is taken by Adorno to be exactly the same as Adorno's own: one acknowledges the suffering of victims and thereby catches glimpses of "more than what is" (so, the inversion, both of traditional history and of traditional religion, an inversion that nonetheless relies on tradition).[137] Adorno follows up his summation of Kafka's procedure with the claim that "it is for nothing less than such unmitigated torture that the perspective of redemption presents itself to him [Kafka]."[138] Such a perspective, however, is fleeting,

---

136. Theodor W. Adorno, "Notes on Kafka," in *Prisms* (Cambridge, MA: MIT Press, 1981), 269; emphasis added.

137. For more on this point, see Adorno, "On Tradition," and Adorno, "Reason and Revelation," tr. Henry W. Pickford, in *Critical Models: Interventions and Catchwords* (New York: Columbia University Press, 1998), 135–43. This is the only place where I would push back on Deborah Cook's take on Adorno's inverse theology in "Through a Glass Darkly." When Cook stresses that Adorno foreshadows a world where religion is no longer needed, I would only want to say that we have taken an entirely too narrow view of religion, and that its archive—for better *and* for worse—is far deeper than merely a response to suffering in the present.

138. Adorno, "Notes on Kafka," 269.

incapable of being either ossified or presented into a redemptive whole (for the reasons just discussed). Adorno suggests, then, that "to include Kafka among the pessimists, the existentialists of despair, is as misguided as to make him a prophet of salvation."[139] Adorno is not a pessimist. In assessing the world and rejecting it as it stands, he acknowledges the world in its minutest details, thereby revealing a sort of love for the world, a love that demands that the world be more than what it currently is. (I am reminded here of Camus's note in his *Notebooks* about "the misery and the greatness of this world: it offers no truths, but only objects for love.")[140] Where, for Maimonides, the world was such that it could invite and sustain wonder and inquiry, for Adorno, the world is such that it can sustain ethical indignation and commitment. For both Maimonides and Adorno, therefore, judgment about—an assessment of—the world is central.

Returning to the broader theme of *How to Measure a World?*, at an eagle's eye view of things, there are now two fundamental paths by which anachronism—distance from the present world—emerges: the world sparks awe and invites an exploration and elaboration of its wonders (Maimonides), or the world sparks moral outrage and invites an

139. Ibid.
140. Albert Camus, *Notebooks: 1935–1942*, trans. Philip Thody (New York: Modern Library, 1963), 93. A related passage from Cavell also comes to mind: "And if you find that you have fallen in love with the world, then you would be ill-advised to offer an argument of its worth by praising its Design. Because you are bound to fall out of love with your argument, and you may thereupon forget that the world is wonder enough, as it stands. Or not" (*Claim of Reason: Wittgenstein, Skepticism, Morality, and Tragedy* [Oxford: Oxford University Press, 1979], 431). I had in mind this quote and the whole Cavell passage from which it comes as an epigraph for *How to Measure a World?*, but there are peculiar requirements for epigraphs, and I was ultimately unable to use it. Perhaps making that fact explicit could be of use to the reader (even if only as a bit of trivia or entertainment).

examination and documentation of its evils (Adorno). Each exploration leads to more than what presently is (and this "more" is something for which God can serve as shorthand, but only if this idea is understood as connected to but as also fundamentally distinct from religion as it is traditionally conceived). What needs to be stressed in conclusion, however, is that each of these paths is available only to the extent that the world is such that it is capable of sustaining and inviting these respective approaches. Events in the world cannot therefore be understood solely as exemplars of general lawful relations, discovered once and for all (although, of course, such are not prohibited), but rather must be understood as consistently evolving and expanding in their concrete specificity, wherein human action perpetually reveals "newness ... [as] the realm of the historian who—unlike the natural scientist ... is concerned with ever-recurring happenings—deals with events which always occur only once."[141] Arendt captures the entire point well when she notes that

> Each event in human history reveals an unexpected landscape of human deeds, sufferings, and new possibilities which together transcend the sum total of all willed intentions and significance of all origins. It is the task of the historian to detect this unexpected *new* with all its implications in any given period and to bring out the full power of its significance. He must know that, though his story has a beginning and an end, it occurs within a larger frame, history itself. And history is a story which has many beginnings but no end. ... For whatever the historian calls an end, the end of a period or a tradition or a whole civilization, is a new beginning for those that are alive.[142]

141. Arendt, "Understanding and Politics," 318.
142. Ibid., 320.

It is essential to understand how a particular conception of history is required in order to understand the density that the procedures of Maimonides and Adorno appear to exhibit and to require.[143]

---

143. I am implicitly suggesting that something like Hannah Arendt's notion of *amor mundi*, as a sort of love for the world, underwrites the two positions vis-à-vis the world that I have presented. This requires some clarification. I am not suggesting—and neither is Arendt—that "love of the world" be understood simply as blind acceptance or desire for the world as it is. *Amor mundi* is not *amor fati* (love of fate). Instead, as Arendt notes, loving the world amounts to a certain education into and about the world in which "education is the point at which we decide whether we love the world enough to assume responsibility for it and by the same token save it from . . . ruin" (Hannah Arendt, "The Crisis in Education," in *Between Past and Future: Eight Exercises in Political Thought* [New York: Penguin, 2006], 193). In her *Denktagebuch* (Notes), she suggests that "we are not attached to life, which is exhausted by itself, we are attached to the world for which are perpetually willing to give our life" (Hannah Arendt, *Denktagebuch: 1950 bis 1973*, 2 vols., ed. Ursula Ludz and Ingeborg Nordmann [Munich: Piper, 2002], 1: 539). Compare the claim that "what is most difficult is to love the world as it is, with all the evil and suffering in it" (Hannah Arendt, *Thinking without a Banister: Essays in Understanding, 1953–1975* [New York: Schocken, 2018], xvi). For a sustained engagement with elements of Arendt's notion of *amor mundi*, see the essays collected in James William Bernauer, ed. *Amor Mundi: Explorations in the Faith and Thought of Hannah Arendt* (Dordrecht, Neth.: Springer, 2012). Finally, many would likely be quite skeptical of any attempts to bring Adorno and Arendt together. In this context, I only want to note their shared common source in Walter Benjamin, essentially the focus (by means of Adorno) of the next chapter and my elaboration of history. For opposition to linking Arendt and Adorno, see Idit Dobbs-Weinstein, *Spinoza's Critique of Religion and Its Heirs: Marx, Benjamin, Adorno* (Cambridge: Cambridge University Press, 2015), 7–12. For suggestions that they can be brought quite closer together, see the essays collected in Dirk Auer, Lars Rensmann, and Julia Schulze Wessel, eds., *Arendt und Adorno* (Frankfurt: Suhrkamp, 2003); Lars Rensmann and Samir Gandesha, eds., *Arendt and Adorno: Political and Philosophical Investigations* (Palo Alto, CA: Stanford University Press, 2012). Finally, for the connections between Arendt and Benjamin, see Annabel Herzog, "Illuminating Inheritance: Benjamin's Influence on Arendt's Political Storytelling," *Philosophy and Social Criticism* 26, no. 5 (2000): 1–27.

11

PRECONDITIONS OF HAVING A WORLD

3

HISTORY AND WORLD

BENJAMIN AND ADORNO ON ETHICAL DEPTH

§ 1. Introduction: On the Importance of Reflective Judgment

Take the last two chapters to have presented, in broad terms, a structural understanding of human agency, wherein the world—subject either to inquisitive awe (Maimonides) or to moral critique (Adorno)—underwrites a basic understanding of what it means to be human and free. In either case, our freedom is a worldly freedom that requires anachronism within and toward the world as it presently stands. Any human world, however, has a history, which is a fact with which any anachronism must contend. Human judgment is therefore essential. For example, could a proper understanding of the historical density of the world affect which mood toward the world—wonder or outrage—is or ought to be primary? If history is progressive, then perhaps our moral outrage always ought to be tempered, if not outright shifted to awe. This may be one way to contextualize within my unfolding account the fact that Maimonides has generally been seen as "unhistorical."[1] When scholars have opposed this view of Maimonides,[2] claiming that he did have some sense of history, they have nonetheless maintained that he had no particular philosophy of history,[3] if that's understood as implying some way of conceptualizing the thought that humans could grasp a pattern or logic to history. This may be true, but such a debate about Maimonides's views of history doesn't settle the question of what sort of understanding of history Maimonides's phenomenological views commit him to, especially not when his thought is juxtaposed with Adorno's views.

One way to understand the question that's emerging and that animates this chapter is to return to an earlier analogy that I drew between Maimonides and Kant. In chapter 1, I noted that Maimonides's orientation toward the world suggests a view analogous to the view Kant develops in *Critique of the Power of Judgment*, in which something about the world (natural beauty) demands judgment from our subjective capacities. Let me return to Kant's views in more depth. Sometime in 1787,[4] Kant realized that the faculty of

1. For the classic claim, see Salo Baron, "The Historical Outlook of Maimonides," *Proceedings of the American Academy for Jewish Research* 6 (1934): 5–113.

2. See Kenneth Seeskin, "Maimonides' Sense of History," *Jewish History* 18, nos. 2–3 (2004): 129–45; Shubert Spero, "Maimonides and the Sense of History," *Tradition* 24, no. 2 (1989): 128–37.

3. Seeskin explicitly draws a contrast with Hegel in Seeskin, "Maimonides' Sense of History," 142. Spero also acknowledges that Maimonides "did not articulate a systematic 'progress theory' of history" but claims that "there is every reason to believe that had he been able to catch a glimpse of human development up to our times, he would have had no difficulty in . . . fashion[ing] a recognizable progress theory of history" (Spero, "Maimonides and the Sense of History," 136).

4. See Kant's letter to Reinhold in December 28 and 31, 1787, where he notes that he is "now at work on the critique of taste, and I have discovered a kind of a priori principle different from those heretofore observed" (Immanuel Kant, *Philosophical Correspondence, 1759–1799*, trans. Arnulf Zweig [Chicago: University of Chicago Press, 1967], 127). For a concise overview of types of judgment in Kant, see Angelica Nuzzo, "Reflective Judgment, Determinative Judgment, and the Problem

judgment itself has an a priori principle, which is that there is something that might be known about the parameters of judgment that does not depend solely on empirical claims or concerns. What Kant claims to have discovered is that there is a class of judgments that concern cases in which a subject experiences a free play between the understanding (which generally supplies the concept for a judgment) and the imagination (which exhibits representations). During such a free play, the understanding and imagination vivify one another, creating a possibly endless process wherein judgment appears bound by no particular conceptual determination: the phenomenon in question exceeds any particular conceptual determination.[5] The concept involved in the judgment must be found or invented, for it presently does not exist. Nonetheless, such judgments demand universal agreement because they depend on shared human characteristics (the possession of the faculty of understanding, imagination, and judgment); we might say they are reflective of a common humanity.[6] Kant associates such judgments with judgments of beauty. A judgment of beauty about nature, Kant believes, reveals another a priori principle: the formal purposiveness of nature. As Kant puts it, "the self-sufficient beauty of nature reveals to us a technique of nature, which makes it possible to represent it as a system in accordance with laws the principle of which we do not encounter anywhere in our entire faculty of understanding."[7] In the first chapter, I suggested that Maimonides's conception of world commits him to some version of Kant's idea: the world is saturated and hangs

of Particularity," *Washington University Jurisprudence Review* 6, no. 1 (2013): 7–25.

5. See Kant, *Critique of the Power of Judgment*, trans. Paul Geyer and Eric Matthews (Cambridge: Cambridge University Press, 2000), 5: 316.

6. The political significance of such an idea is taken up in Hannah Arendt, *Lectures on Kant's Political Philosophy* (Chicago: University of Chicago Press, 1982); Stanley Cavell, *Conditions Handsome and Unhandsome* (Chicago: University of Chicago Press, 1990).

7. Kant, *Critique of the Power of Judgment*, 5: 246.

together in such a way as to allow for the perpetual multiplication of judgments about it. Maimonides's negative theology commits him to the idea that our claims about the world and the ways in which elements of it hang together are inexhaustible (our claims about what God is not are thereby also equally inexhaustible). Adorno's thought correspondingly relies on reflective judgment,[8] wherein judgements about suffering in the world, and any demands that such suffering ought not to exist, often are the "expression of a conviction whose grounding remains subjective . . . but which expects or claims justification from the (universal) concurrence of other subjectivities."[9] Forms of suffering themselves evolve, and present norms may be incapable of properly registering cases of suffering (for an example, think of how the evil of sexual harassment was understood and experienced prior to the legal introduction of the term "sexual harassment").[10]

For both Maimonides and Adorno, the world—when it is understood as composed of particular, historical occurrences—appears only from particular (worldly) contexts and subjective capacities; and the same is true the other way around: certain subjective capacities and contexts are possible only

---

8. A point I have argued for in Shuster, *Autonomy after Auschwitz: Adorno, German Idealism, and Modernity* (Chicago: University of Chicago Press, 2014), 111–12. A similar point was made earlier in María Pía Lara, *Narrating Evil: A Postmetaphysical Theory of Reflective Judgment* (New York: Columbia University Press, 2007).

9. Cavell, *Conditions Handsome and Unhandsome*, xxvi.

10. The potential disconnect between then current norms and particular experiences not captured by those norms has led contemporary scholars to speak of "hermeneutical injustice" and "epistemic injustice," the former denoting injustice related to how people may interpret their experience and the latter denoting injustice as it arises according to how people may possess knowledge. See Miranda Fricker, *Epistemic Injustice: Power and the Ethics of Knowing* (Oxford: Oxford University Press, 2007); Vivian M. May, "'Speaking into the Void'? Intersectionality Critiques and Epistemic Backlash," *Hypatia* 29, no. 1 (2014): 94–112; José Medina, *The Epistemology of Resistance: Gender and Racial Oppression, Epistemic Injustice, and the Social Imagination* (Oxford: Oxford University Press, 2013).

in light of particular views of history (for example, germane to the US context, think of how segments of US society tell the story of Reconstruction, either as a dismal failure or a dismal betrayal, and what such views propose for what—and importantly who—can be seen in the world [and not], and what might be done [and not]). The question with which this chapter is concerned, then, is not exclusively the question of whether history is regressive or progressive (although this is, of course, important), but is rather the question of how best to understand the ontological structure of any conception of history that underwrites the relationship between human agency and the world. Because the world unfolds in history, and because human judgment is able to engage that world, how is the historical dimension—the historical density—of the world best understood? Although Maimonides himself did not think much about this question, it is implicit in his view of the world; strikingly, Adorno, and especially his colleague, Walter Benjamin, spent significant time thinking about exactly this question, and, it is around them that this chapter is oriented.

§ 2. On the Importance of Universal History

Adorno's conception of history is animated, above all, by an objection to and modification of constructions of "universal history" (the idea of composing a history of humanity), especially as histories are found in Hegel and Marx. Adorno's alternative conception of history incorporates universal history but melds with it a principle of historical discontinuity, thereby producing a dialectical conception of history wherein continuity and discontinuity are animated by the ethical disposition sketched in chapter 2. All this requires significantly more detail, and for that reason, much of this chapter is engaged with sketching conceptions of universal history in Hegel and Marx in order to foreground Adorno's own conception of history, which points beyond this tradition even as it is indebted to it.

Three themes are central to what follows. First, this tradition, starting especially with Hegel, but continuing through Marx and Adorno, is intimately concerned with human freedom,[11] as is *How to Measure a World?* The construction of history is therefore part of the project of conceptualizing and actualizing human freedom, and, as the last section has suggested, of understanding human freedom as involving anachronism. Second, and intimately related to the first theme, is the importance of elucidating the exact relationship between nature and history. For much of this tradition, nature is fundamentally conceived as the antithesis of history,[12] which is properly the only site of human freedom. As might be obvious from my suggestions thus far, the phenomenological view of world that has emerged sees the two as inseparable (although they may, of course, be distinguishable): it just is the case that human freedom affects (what we see and can see and therefore do in) the world, and vice versa. And as I had already noted in the introduction, to the extent that this entire book is indebted to an entire German philosophical tradition, this tradition conceives being free not as fundamentally actualizing some natural fact about ourselves,[13] but rather as achieving a sort of

---

11. For ways of understanding Hegel's connection to conceptualizations of freedom, see especially Paul Franco, *Hegel's Philosophy of Freedom* (New Haven, CT: Yale University Press, 2002); Frederick Neuhouser, *Foundations of Hegel's Social Theory: Actualizing Freedom* (Cambridge, MA: Harvard University Press, 2003); Alan Patten, *Hegel's Idea of Freedom* (Oxford: Oxford University Press, 1999); Christopher Yeomans, *Freedom and Reflection: Hegel and the Logic of Agency* (Oxford: Oxford University Press, 2011). For Marx, see James J. O'Rourke, *The Problem of Freedom in Marxist Thought* (Dordrecht, Neth.: D. Reidel, 2012), 11–50. And for Adorno, see Shuster, *Autonomy after Auschwitz*.

12. Robert B. Pippin, "Naturalness and Mindedness: Hegel's Compatibilism," *European Journal of Philosophy* 7, no. 2 (1999); Robert B. Pippin, "What Is the Question for Which Hegel's Theory of Recognition Is the Answer?," *European Journal of Philosophy* 8, no. 2 (2000): 155–72.

13. Wilfrid Sellars, *Empiricism and the Philosophy of Mind* (Cambridge, MA: Harvard University Press, 1997), 76.

self-relation,[14] one that is historically constructed and mediated and that therefore intimately involves questions of recognition and sociality.[15] This point about freedom raises the third theme that animates much of this tradition and my discussion, namely the idea of alienation (*Entfremdung*). If themes like self-relation and mutual recognition are crucial to a conception of human freedom, then alienation becomes central to the extent that it serves both to prohibit the achievement of freedom and to make conspicuous its absence. At a very high-altitude view of things, note that something like alienation animates both Maimonides's and Adorno's accounts as I've presented them: any view that sees in the world more than what presently is might be said to be alienated from that world; the German sense of "ent-fremd," as the suggestion of the causation of alien-ness or strangeness captures quite well this high-altitude view.

In order to give more depth to the discussion that follows, let me situate it by giving a sense of how philosophy of history is approached in German philosophy from Kant onward, because, like the philosophy of action, the German tradition approaches things differently from other traditions. The term "philosophy of history" was coined by Voltaire to apply to what he hoped to accomplish in his mammoth *Essai sur les mœurs et l'esprit des nations* (An essay on the manners and spirit of nations),[16] which was twofold: an examination of

14. Robert B. Brandom, *Tales of the Mighty Dead: Historical Essays in the Metaphysics of Intentionality* (Cambridge: Cambridge University Press, 2002), 21; Brandom, "Freedom and Constraint by Norms," *American Philosophical Quarterly* 16, no. 3 (1979): 187–96; Christine M. Korsgaard, *Self-Consitution: Agency, Identity, and Integrity* (Oxford: Oxford University Press, 2009).

15. Axel Honneth and Hans Joas, *Social Action and Human Nature*, trans. Raymond Meyer (Cambridge: Cambridge University Press, 1988); Robert B. Pippin, *Hegel's Practical Philosophy: Rational Agency as Ethical Life* (Cambridge: Cambridge University Press, 2008).

16. For more on this point, see Karl Löwith, *Meaning in History: The Theological Implications of the Philosophy of History* (Chicago: University

the facts of history and an assessment of the ways in which those facts (and others) had been valued by prior generations of humans. Voltaire's procedure was related to but quite distinct from the way in which Jean-Jacques Rousseau tackled history in his famous second Discourse, the 1755 Discourse on the Origin and Basis of Inequality among Men.[17] And it is Rousseau, more than Voltaire, who had a profound influence on the German philosophical tradition.[18] According to Rousseau, when one looks at how history has unfolded, both from a systematic perspective (that is, what is it that drives history to unfold in the way that it does?) and from a moral one (that is, how do we assess the way in which history has unfolded?), one must conclude that human civilization has been responsible for the general ruination of humanity. Rousseau's answer to the Academy of Dijon's competition on the origins of inequality is one that continued to resonate in the German tradition:[19] namely that the origins of human inequality are to be found exactly in human society—although, importantly, for Rousseau, as well as for these later traditions, the emergence of human society is entirely natural.[20]

of Chicago Press, 2011), 1; Jerome Rosenthal, "Voltaire's Philosophy of History," *Journal of the History of Ideas* (1955): 151–78.

17. Jean-Jacques Rousseau, "Discourse on the Origin of Inequality," trans. Donald A. Cress, in *Basic Political Writings*, ed. Donald A. Cress, 25–81 (Indianapolis: Hackett, 1987).

18. On this point, see David James, *Rousseau and German Idealism* (Cambridge: Cambridge University Press, 2013); George Armstrong Kelly, *Idealism, Politics and History: Sources of Hegelian Thought* (Cambridge: Cambridge University Press, 2010).

19. Simon Jarvis, *Adorno: A Critical Introduction* (Cambridge, UK: Polity, 1998), 41.

20. Rousseau, "On the Social Contract," trans. Donald A. Cress, in *Basic Political Writings*, ed. Donald A. Cress, 141–227 (Indianapolis: Hackett, 1987).

§ 3. Alienation, Freedom, and Universal History: Hegel and Marx

With Rousseau's suggestion, the distinction between nature and history already looms large. If human society both is the origin of human misery and also is entirely natural, then there is here a question about the proper moral assessment of these two characteristics of human society. Indeed, is the moral status of human society even best understood as a moral question at all, because it appears unavoidable? The same issue arises with Kant's famous notion of an "unsocial sociability" (*ungesellige Geselligkeit*), wherein the idea is that every individual is naturally driven to be an egoist while pursuing interests that can be actualized only in society. For any individual, such a tension "awakens all his powers, brings him to conquer his inclination to laziness, and propelled by vainglory, lust for power, and avarice, to achieve a rank among his fellows whom he cannot tolerate but from whom he cannot withdraw."[21] Although for Kant this picture still implied certain theological commitments,[22] the basic idea might be entirely divorced of theological requirements and understood simply, as presented by Adam Smith, as an "invisible hand,"[23] or, later, in Hegel's words, as the "cunning of history."[24] With all such views, it is not too

---

21. Immanuel Kant, *On History*, ed. Lewis White Beck, trans. Lewis White Beck, Robert E. Anchor, and Emil L. Fackenheim (New York: Bobbs-Merrill, 1963), 15.

22. Shuster, *Autonomy after Auschwitz*, 42–71.

23. Adam Smith, *The Wealth of Nations* (New York: Modern Library, 1937), 485; Craig Smith, *Adam Smith's Political Philosophy: The Invisible Hand and Spontaneous Order* (London: Routledge, 2006).

24. Georg Wilhelm Friedrich Hegel, *Lectures on the Philosophy of World History*, trans. H. A. Nisbet (Cambridge: Cambridge University Press, 1975), 89; Steven B. Smith, *Modernity and Its Discontents: Making and Unmaking the Bourgeois from Machiavelli to Bellow* (New Haven, CT: Yale University Press, 2016), 145.

much to speak of "a history with a definite natural plan for creatures who have no plan of their own."[25]

Hegel's philosophy of history depends on a conception that equally trades on the relationship between the social and the natural.[26] As Hegel stresses in the *Phenomenology of Spirit* (written in 1806–7), the idea of freedom as an achievement—captured by his notion of spirit—makes its first appearance exactly at the point in his account where two distinct self-consciousnesses confront each other amid an otherwise ordinary existence in the natural world.[27] Human freedom appears as a concept and possible achievement with a struggle in the natural world that emerges between these two self-consciousnesses,[28] an account itself importantly influenced by history, in the form of the Haitian revolution.[29] Emerging is a distinct dialectical intertwining between nature and history. According to Hegel, with the emergence of self-consciousness and the encounter—and struggle—between two self-consciousnesses, recognition emerges as the locus where human freedom is understood and actualized. Hegel describes how through the struggle between the two, one self-consciousness looms as master—enslaver—and the other as a slave, and how the struggle between them engenders concrete historical actualizations and failures of recognition,

25. Kant, *On History*, 12.
26. See Sebastian Rand, "The Importance and Relevance of Hegel's Philosophy of Nature," *Review of Metaphysics* 61, no. 2 (2007), 379–400; Robert B. Pippin, *Hegel on Self-Consciousness: Desire and Death in the Phenomenology of Spirit* (Princeton, NJ: Princeton University Press, 2011).
27. Georg Wilhelm Friedrich Hegel, *Hegel's Phenomenology of Spirit*, trans. A. V. Miller (Oxford: Oxford University Press, 1977), 100.
28. The encounter between these two self-consciousnesses has captivated philosophical commentary and there are dozens upon dozens of works on this. One of the most recent and sophisticated (and which can, in turn, be mined for earlier references) is Pippin, *Hegel on Self-Consciousness*.
29. On this point, see Susan Buck-Morss, *Hegel, Haiti, and Universal History* (Pittsburgh, PA: University of Pittsburgh Press, 2009).

all dependent initially on the slave and the slave's forced investment in work and the sort of avenues for recognition that such work forces the slave toward.[30] The societal shapes eventually give way to more and more complex historical shapes and configurations, ones that require particular, and often large and complex, institutional structures—families and courts and police and nation-states—to enable and actualize recognition between subjects, and thereby human freedom.[31] Involved in this process is also the eventual historical emergence of the claim that all humans—because they are self-conscious—possess a standing within what might be termed a "space of reasons"[32] and might thereby appeal to such a standing in cases where they are otherwise denied their freedom and standing as a self-consciousness.[33]

In Hegel's words, though, such a new perspective—such a "new world is no more a complete actuality than is a newborn child."[34] Essential to any such normative claim about the universality of human self-consciousness and freedom is also a procedure wherein one must achieve freedom in what might be termed a "thick" sense, understood chiefly by means of several tasks. First, one must grasp how one came to possess such a notion of freedom; for Hegel, doing so amounts to being able to construct a history (as he does in the *Phenomenology* and in his lectures on history) that reveals how self-consciousness has passed "through a series of shapes [in order to] attain to a knowledge of itself."[35] The

---

30. Jon Stewart, "The Architectonic of Hegel's Phenomenology of Spirit," *Philosophy and Phenomenological Research* 55, no. 4 (1995): 138.

31. For two robust developments, see Georg Wilhelm Friedrich Hegel, *Elements of the Philosophy of Right* (Cambridge: Cambridge University Press, 1991); Neuhouser, *Foundations of Hegel's Social Theory*.

32. Sellars, *Empiricism*.

33. Terry Pinkard, *Does History Make Sense?: Hegel on the Historical Shapes of Justice* (Cambridge, MA: Harvard University Press, 2017), 29.

34. Hegel, *Hegel's Phenomenology of Spirit*, 7.

35. Ibid., 265.

shapes might be understood as particular shapes of spirit, that is, shapes of human society, whether Greek or Roman or whatever, where each is "more basic than an intersubjective unity among different agents," but rather "includes such intersubjective agreements" in addition to "a conception of the world as something to which those agreements are in tune or not."[36] They may equally well be understood as "forms of life,"[37] where that signifies all the various worldly "attunements" that individuals within a particular form of life share, both by upbringing (*Bildung*), personal reflection, explicit and implicit normative commitments and saliences, and the ways in which they share, interpret, and habitually actualize particular basic biological facts.[38] In short, Hegel is here also talking about a sense of world in the rich phenomenological sense I have been developing throughout *How to Measure a World?* Second, and falling directly out of the first general procedure, Hegel takes a particular conception and construction of history to be essential: one must understand and be able to tell a historical story about how one's present shape of spirit—and therefore one's present conception of freedom—rests on earlier actualizations and failures of self-consciousness activity. It is only out of the failures that there emerge the successes, and it is essential to Hegel's aims to grasp both of these "thick" senses of freedom as intimately bound up with history, because, as is famously denoted by his use of the German term *aufheben*, each subsequent shape

36. Terry Pinkard, "What Is a Shape of Spirit?," in *The Phenomenology of Spirit: A Critical Guide*, ed. Dean Moyar and Michael Quante (Cambridge: Cambridge University Press, 2008), 114–15.

37. Georg Wilhelm Friedrich Hegel, "The Spirit of Christianity and Its Fate," trans. Richard Kroner and Thomas Malcom Knox, in *Early Theological Writings* (University Park: University of Pennsylvania Press, 2011), 287; Pinkard, "What Is a Shape of Spirit?"

38. Stanley Cavell, *This New yet Unapproachable America: Lectures after Emerson after Wittgenstein* (Albuquerque, NM: Living Batch, 1989), 40–52.

both annuls and maintains elements of the prior shape.[39] It is not too much, then, also to speak here of alienation, as Hegel himself does in the preface to his *Phenomenology*, where he describes how consciousness "becomes alienated (*entfremdet*) from itself and then returns to itself from this alienation."[40] Furthermore, it is only through the construction of such an account that one might truly be able to feel at home inside a particular shape,[41] achieving thereby the sort of self-relation to oneself and to one's society—and therefore to one's possibilities and actions—that is required for human freedom. At the conclusion of one of his lectures on the history of philosophy, with a story about the historical movements from one shape to another, Hegel notes, "I have tried to exhibit their necessary procession out of one another, so that each philosophy necessarily presupposes the one preceding it."[42] Hegel's invocation of "necessity" raises all the chief questions aimed at his account, namely what sort of necessity is implied and especially whether it commits him to some sort of problematic fatalism or teleology, or theodicy, or even totalitarianism.[43] Implied in these tasks is also a third procedure, one that puts stress on the transitions from

---

39. This notion is notoriously difficult, but a good stab can be found in B. C. Birchall, "Hegel's Notion of Aufheben," *Inquiry* 24, no. 1 (1981): 75–103; Georg Wilhelm Friedrich Hegel, *Science of Logic*, trans. George Di Giovanni (Cambridge: Cambridge University Press, 2010), 81–82.

40. Hegel, *Hegel's Phenomenology of Spirit*, 21.

41. Hegel, *Elements of the Philosophy of Right*, 42.

42. Georg Wilhelm Friedrich Hegel, *Lectures on the History of Philosophy*, vol. 3, *Medieval and Modern Philosophy*, trans. Frances H. Simson and E. S. Haldane (Lincoln: University of Nebraska Press, 1995), 212.

43. On the problem of teleology, see Martin Heidegger, *Hegel's Phenomenology of Spirit* (Bloomington: Indiana University Press, 1994). On theodicy, see Theodor W. Adorno, *Negative Dialectics*, trans. E. B. Ashton (New York: Seabury, 1973), 140. On totalitarianism, see Hubert Kiesewetter, *Von Hegel zu Hitler die politische Verwirklichung einer totalitaren Machtstaatstheorie in Deutschland, 1815–1945* (Frankfurt: Lang, 1974); Karl Popper, *The Open Society and Its Enemies* (London: Routledge, 2006).

one shape to another,[44] asking us to acknowledge how in each of the foregoing procedures, one's self-conscious activity is implicated,[45] both in the understanding of one's past (how prior historical shapes fit together) and in the understanding of one's present (to what extent one's current shape reflects its own ideals, that is, makes sense to oneself, allows for freedom).

Essential to Hegel's account is a sort of two-stage process, wherein the first stage denotes the (self-)movement of the shapes of consciousness—their breakdown and subsequent reformation—and then a subsequent reconstruction of all this at a second stage, where the various breakdowns are arranged and understood through a unified narrative.[46] The former reveals the process by which a particular historical notion of human freedom was achieved and the latter actualizes it by means of a distinct historical justification, one that reveals a process of periodization and thereby constructs history as having moved toward such a notion of human freedom.[47] Practically, then, in the realm of history, "the failure of a way of life is expressed in the way in which it fails to sustain allegiance to itself, and in the dissolution of such a way of life, those living during its dissolution have to pick up the pieces that still seem to work, discard what is no longer of use or value, and fashion some new whole out of what remains, almost always without any overall plan for

---

44. The transitions were always of central importance to Hegel—as he noted in letters, everything hangs on the transitions. See Johannes Hoffmeister, ed., *Briefe von und an Hegel* (Hamburg: Felix Meiner, 1952), 1: 328–31. For a systematic approach to why this is the case, with reference to Goethe's work on transitions within biological life as an influence on Hegel, see Eckart Förster, *The Twenty-Five Years of Philosophy*, trans. Brady Bowman (Cambridge, MA: Harvard University Press, 2012).

45. William Bristow, *Hegel and the Transformation of Philosophical Critique* (Oxford: Oxford University Press, 2007).

46. See Förster, *Twenty-Five Years*, 306–73.

47. Shuster, *Autonomy after Auschwitz*, 134–68.

what they are doing."[48] Many of the aforementioned controversies surrounding Hegel's philosophy of history arise from a consideration of this process. What is the nature of the whole or totality that emerges here? Does it stand in a problematic relation to the past (the problem of theodicy), and does it suggest a problematic sort of totalization (the problems of teleology, fatalism, or even totalitarianism)? One recent suggestion is to see this task as a sort of "infinite end,"[49] where no one action or even set of actions—in other words, no single or even single set of rational reflections on or construction of history—exhausts the task. Instead, such an assessment of history is rather a "principle" or "generality"[50] by means of which one consistently—if one aims to be free—parses one's situation and its relationship to the past. With such a view, grounded in the emergence of a particular notion of human freedom as based on self-conscious mutual recognition, including importantly self-recognition (feeling "at home with oneself"—"*bei sich selbst*"), "the conception of what it ultimately means to lead a human life is an infinite end,"[51] that is, not something that is accomplished once and for all but one that must be performed time and time again, in perpetuity. Let me note that although this idea of "feeling at home" in one's world is central to Hegel's project, it ought profitably be seen as the linchpin that separates my approach from his. (This is another way to stress the importance

48. Pinkard, *Does History Make Sense?: Hegel on the Historical Shapes of Justice*, 79–80.
49. Ibid., 40–44. For Rödl's notion of an infinite end, which Pinkard draws on, see Sebastian Rödl, "The Form of the Will," in *Desire, Practical Reason, and the Good*, ed. Sergio Tenenbaum (Oxford: Oxford University Press, 2010), 147–49.
50. G. E. M. Anscombe, "Authority in Morals," in *Ethics, Politics and Religion*. Collected Philosophical Papers, vol. 3 (Minneapolis: University of Minnesota Press, 1981), 48.
51. Pinkard, *Does History Make Sense?*, 42.

and presence of anachronism in this book—more on all this shortly.)

It is in this context, in acknowledging that Hegel's procedure might be understood as retrograde, that one should take the early Marx's statement (seen already in chap. 2) that "philosophers have only interpreted the world[;] . . . the point, however, is to change it."[52] Implied in the statement is a sort of political-ethical sentiment—which is central to Adorno—that any such reconstruction rests on a historical account that suggests that the world ought to be different. Marx therefore accepts elements of Hegel's procedure. He agrees with Hegel that a consistent self-alienation of self-consciousness from a particular shape of spirit drives human history:[53] It just is the case that particular shapes break down, stop making sense to subjects, and thereby invite reflection on their breakdown.[54] What's at stake between them, though, is the nature of the alienation: is it the case that it arises from the living and concrete norms that animate a particular form of life (Hegel)?[55] Or does it have to do with the material (economic) conditions that allegedly actually give rise to those norms (Marx)? And these two senses of alienation are central for understanding the basis for alienation that animates Adorno's work.

According to Marx,[56] it is exactly because material conditions—modes of production (denoting both the actual

52. Karl Marx, "Theses on Feuerbach," in *The Marx-Engels Reader*, ed. Robert C. Tucker (New York: Norton, 1978), 145.

53. See Rainer Forst, "Noumenal Alienation: Rousseau, Kant and Marx on the Dialectics of Self-Determination," *Kantian Review* 22, no. 4 (2017): 523–51; Jean Hyppolite, *Studies on Marx and Hegel*, trans. John O'Neill (New York: Harper, 1969), 130–37.

54. Karl Marx, *Economic and Philosophical Manuscripts of 1844*, trans. Martin Milligan (New York: Prometheus, 1978).

55. Georg Wilhelm Friedrich Hegel, *The Encyclopædia Logic*, trans. Théodore F. Geraets, Wallis Arthur Suchting, Henry Silton Harris (Indianapolis: Hackett, 1991), 115.

56. Karl Marx, "The German Ideology, Part I," in *The Marx-Engels Reader*, ed. Robert C. Tucker (New York: Norton, 1978), 155.

forces of production and the relations of production)—drive conceptual activity (superstructure) that, in Marx's famous claim, Hegel's entire account must be stood "upon its head."[57] Marx's inheritance of Hegel's stress on alienation pushes him to employ Hegel's basic procedure—of an inherent, diagnosable crisis within a form of life—to specify four forms of alienation whose origins lie in material conditions: alienation from the products of one's labor, alienation from the processes of one's labor, and alienation from one's own natural and social existence as a human being.[58] And it is these forms of alienation and the ills connected with them—notably the production of a wide range of ideologies, whether religious, social, or political—that prohibit the achievement of human freedom.[59] If this is true, and if one can tell a seemingly causal story about the various ways in which material conditions can be arranged and the sorts of forms of alienation they will produce, then Marx, in distinction to Hegel, has allegedly produced a theory of history—dialectical materialism—as opposed to a mere philosophy of history, where the former implies a scientific account distinct from the allegedly merely "reflective construal" of the latter.[60] A lot more might be said here about both the relationship between Hegel and Marx and the best formulation of Marx's theory, as well as how and what best to assess when it comes to material conditions.[61] What is

57. Karl Marx, *The Marx-Engels Reader*, ed. Robert C. Tucker (New York: Norton, 1978), xxi.

58. Marx, *Economic and Philosophical Manuscripts*; Andreas Wildt, *Die Anthropologie des frühen Marx* (Hagen, Ger.: Kuirs der Fernuniversität, 1987).

59. See Jonathan Wolff, *Why Read Marx Today?* (Oxford: Oxford University Press, 2003); Karen Ng, "Ideology Critique from Hegel and Marx to Critical Theory," *Constellations* 22, no. 3 (2015): 393–404.

60. See Gerald Allan Cohen, *Karl Marx's Theory of History: A Defence* (Oxford: Oxford University Press, 2000), 27.

61. A debate that continues to the present day, as evidenced by the success of Thomas Piketty, *Capital in the 21st Century* (Cambridge, MA: Harvard University Press, 2014).

most conspicuous for the present discussion and for my aims here, however, is the extent to which both Marx and Hegel use an experience and understanding of alienation in order to present a universal history, an account that conceives of history as a whole that admits of periods that can be revealed on the world stage, thereby presenting a fundamental continuity to history. The distinctions between a theory and a philosophy of history ultimately materialize in what each conceives as the most salient feature of history (idealism versus materialism), not in what is the proper overarching method for doing so or the proper form of the historical account in question. Note also that each tradition is involved in reducing or doing away with this alienation: the alienation itself ought not to exist; this point forms the bridge to the notion of anachronism as I have been sketching it in this book, most notably in Adorno's work (which inherits this notion), but also, as I have argued, in Maimonides's work.

Furthermore, note also the extent to which Marx's account conceives of human labor and its organization as that which—and here the details will surely be important—can prohibit individuals from being free of alienation, that is, of being free. At an eagle's eye view of things, the central question is how to conceive of labor altogether,[62] both conceptually (as in what role does it play and ought it play human life?) and materially (what is the corresponding arrangement of actual society that corresponds to what role labor ought to play in human life?). These questions extend far beyond the scope of my discussion here, but they do reveal an important point: namely, that whatever story one tells about the evolution

---

62. On this point, in various ways, see Hannah Arendt, *The Human Condition* (Chicago: University of Chicago Press, 1958); Moishe Postone, *Time, Labor, and Domination: A Reinterpretation of Marx's Critical Theory* (Cambridge: Cambridge University Press, 1993); Tama Weisman, *Hannah Arendt and Karl Marx: On Totalitarianism and the Tradition of Western Political Thought* (Lanham, MD: Lexington, 2013).

of human labor and the modes of production, and therefore of human alienation, it is also a story about the production and possibility of human freedom, for it just is the case that "there comes a time when this alienation becomes a living contradiction."[63]

One way to understand the trajectory of Marxist thought as well as elements of Adorno's thinking is to see them as concerned with the conditions that allow for such critical consciousness, concerned with exactly when such a time materializes, when alienation becomes unlivable, practically unsustainable.[64] Although it did not turn out to be the proletariat that bore or induced the revolution—indeed, the status or necessity of the revolution out of the history of capitalism is itself a topic of debate[65]—it nonetheless remains true that any critical consciousness "cannot emancipate itself without transcending the conditions of its own life" and "cannot transcend the conditions of its own life without transcending all the inhuman conditions of present society."[66] And Marx's talk of transcendence here brings to the fore all the issues that opened this chapter: the relationship between nature and history (what is being transcended possibly?), the importance and status of alienation (what can move one toward such transcendence?), and the very construction of history itself (how exactly do we account for the conditions of present society, and especially in what sort of—genealogical or phenomenological—depth?). Note how implicated all these questions are with any conception of the world in

63. Hyppolite, *Studies on Marx and Hegel*, 103.
64. See Rahel Jaeggi, *Alienation*, trans. Alan E. Smith and Frederick Neuhouser (New York: Columbia University Press, 2014).
65. Cohen, *Karl Marx's Theory*, 202.
66. Karl Marx, "The Holy Family (Excerpts)," in *Writings of the Young Marx on Philosophy and Society*, ed. David L. Easton and Kurt H. Guddat (Indianapolis: Hackett, 1997), 368.

phenomenological terms: there are deep stakes involved in one's experience of the world with each of these questions.

The fundamental issue with universal history is not simply that it tells a progressive story about history, but rather that it presents history (and therefore temporality) as the sort of thing that can be divided up into distinct periods unified by a sort of similarity or homogeneity, allowing it to thereby be conjoined into a whole, a totality. This whole is then harnessed to provide a justification for the present. And this is true even if such a history aims to critique the present; in other words, all this is equally true of any regressive universal history. Yet although universal history is conceived as essentially linear, it need not be linear in a strict sense:[67] with the sort of nonmetaphysical readings of Hegel that have arisen recently, there may in fact be no predetermined telos, and the movement from one shape to another may admit of regressions and failures. Nonetheless, any such history is linear in the deeper sense that the construction of the overall picture of its movement is one where the various pieces are *able* to fit together into a broader whole. Notably, this whole need not be presupposed in the beginning, as many critics allege; rather, it may arise from the self-movement of the shapes in question, exactly in the way that Hegel suggests in the *Phenomenology*, where it runs along the "pathway of despair" according to an internal logic, and where it ends only when it arrives "at a point at which it gets rid of its semblance of being burdened with something alien."[68] But, nonetheless, in such a procedure the construction of such history is not itself made a problem.

What would it mean to make the construction of history itself a problem? It would not be sufficient merely to

---

67. Cf. Simon Clarke, *Marx's Theory of Crisis* (London: Palgrave Macmillan, 1993); Pinkard, *Does History Make Sense?*

68. Hegel, *Hegel's Phenomenology of Spirit*, 49, 56.

highlight the fact that, say, Hegel was Eurocentric,[69] which although true (and equally true of Marx), is irrelevant to the broader point. Even were Hegel "properly" (without racial bias and ignorance) to incorporate all the elements of world history that he overlooks or gets wrong, his historical account (and Marx's) would still see history as a continuous whole, a totality.[70] We are here entering the crux of these matters as they relate to anachronism and the great theme of the book at hand.

§ 4. Suffering and Dialectical History: Benjamin and Adorno

Adorno's alternative, following Walter Benjamin, is that any such construction of history ought to be rejected. On what grounds? Before answering, let me make clearer what Adorno has in mind. In lectures from 1964 to 1965, Adorno puts the significance of Benjamin's view of history as follows: "His idea is that, contrary to what traditional philosophy believed, facts do not simply disperse in the course of time, unlike immutable, eternal ideas."[71] Instead, according to Adorno, "while the traditional view inserts facts into the flow of time, they really possess a nucleus of time in themselves, they crystallize time in themselves. . . . In accordance with this,

69. Robert Bernasconi, "Hegel at the Court of the Ashanti," in *Hegel after Derrida*, ed. Stuart Barnett, 41–63 (London: Routledge, 1998); Bernasconi, "With What Must the Philosophy of World History Begin? On the Racial Basis of Hegel's Eurocentrism," *Nineteenth Century Contexts* 22, no. 2 (2000): 171–201; Bernasconi, "With What Must the History of Philosophy Begin?: Hegel's Role in the Debate on the Place of India within the History of Philosophy," *Proceedings of the Hegel Society of America* 16 (2003): 35–49.

70. Martin Jay, *Marxism and Totality: The Adventures of a Concept from Lukács to Habermas* (Berkeley: University of California Press, 1986); György Lukács, *History and Class Consciousness: Studies in Marxist Dialectics* (Cambridge, MA: MIT Press, 1972).

71. Theodor W. Adorno, *History and Freedom*, ed. Rolf Tiedemann, trans. Rodney Livingstone (Cambridge, UK: Polity, 2006), 91.

we might say that history is discontinuous in the sense that it represents life perennially disrupted."[72] What Adorno aims to develop, then, is a dialectical account of history wherein "discontinuity is posited as a feature of history, not as an alternative theory of history."[73] Adorno's point might be broached as follows, flowing from two main insights. First, any construction of history leaves out something. The history in question may be ambitious, and it may even be written from the perspective of the vanquished as opposed to the victors, the low opposed to the high, the ordinary opposed to the extraordinary, but all constructions of history fundamentally—always, irreducibly—leave out something. Yet, and this is the second point, the things left out happened and therefore "possess a nucleus of time in themselves," where that means essentially that they each have a self-standing and concrete determinacy that does not exclusively rely on being placed into a context. Nonetheless, particular pieces of history can appear to and for us only in particular contexts; this is what Adorno means when he notes that "what we can legitimately call ideas is this nucleus of time within the individual crystallized phenomena, which can only be decoded (*erschließen*) by interpretation."[74] The use of *decode* is important here because it stresses the fact that although these events are perpetually available, in order for them to be something for us, they must be decoded, that is, interpreted. We must do something to and with them, and that is always true, even as they have their own freestanding—concrete—existence that makes available and invites such procedures. Benjamin captures this idea in a characteristically natty metaphor when he notes that eternal truth, if such a thing might be said to exist, is more like "the

72. Adorno, *History and Freedom*, 91.
73. Brian O'Connor, "Philosophy of History," in *Theodor Adorno: Key Concepts*, ed. Deborah Cook (Stocksfield, UK: Acumen, 2008), 182.
74. Adorno, *History and Freedom*, 91.

ruffle on a dress than some idea."[75] A ruffle on a dress is oddly both everything and nothing: on one hand, it is inessential to what a dress is (a dress is just an item of clothing regardless of whether it has ruffles); on the other hand, a ruffle can make the dress, both for better and for worse: it is what makes the dress all the rage at a particular moment, gives it unique standing among other fashions, and also what dates it, what makes it ultimately unwearable—because no longer stylish—from the perspective of a later moment. What's eternal then is just the fact of the radical and freestanding uniqueness of every moment, which possesses a concrete, monadic existence that can nonetheless be revealed to us only by means of the intervention of human subjectivity. Any placement of an event into a particular history ultimately distorts its unique nucleus of time; at the same time, this uniqueness can only be expressed in particular moments, which are themselves subject to the same parameters and which are further embedded in other moments. Every moment thereby already dialectically makes itself a problem. Imagine now what it might mean to see the world, in its historical density, as composed of such unique nuclei of time.

One way we might understand the conception of history emerging here is to see history as imbued with a quasi-religious significance. As noted in chapter 2, Adorno sometimes calls it metaphysical, where that implies "more than what is." Minimally, we saw there that it suggests that with any historical account, lines of suggestiveness appear that point beyond the account in which the lines of salience are embedded, whether by means of what has been forgotten or overlooked or by means of what wasn't actualized or failed to appear but was nonetheless available or suggested. As Adorno notes that, in the construction of history, we always

75. Walter Benjamin, *The Arcades Project* (Cambridge, MA: Harvard University Press, 1999), 463.

detect "something hopeful that stands in precise opposition to what the totality appears to show."[76] It is for this reason that Adorno speaks of metaphysics arising "at the point where the empirical world is taken seriously."[77] An analogy might be drawn with the way in which the concept of a "saturated phenomenon" has emerged in contemporary phenomenology of religion.[78] One way to think about this notion, especially in this context, is that any particular part of history—any point—might be seen as a sort of "saturated phenomenon," where its concrete existence (and therefore its possibilities via interpretation) always overflow or exceed whatever account it is placed into. In this way, the necessity of human intervention in the interpretation of history and the unique "nucleus of time"—the deep materiality—of any particular historical point are both affirmed (and we might equally well say node, event, or whatever instead of point—the proper term itself must crucially be open to contestation). As Adorno puts it, "what would be beyond, appears only in the materials and categories inside."[79] The analogy with a saturated phenomenon might also, as my discussion at the beginning of this chapter suggests, alternatively be made out with reference to Kant's work.[80] Reflective judgments reveal phenomena that exceed our conceptual capacities, and it is these phenomena that themselves that demand such judgments. The understanding is unable to supply a proper concept for the particular representation and enters into a free play with

76. Adorno, *History and Freedom*, 91.

77. Theodor W. Adorno, *Metaphysics: Concept and Problems*, ed. Rolf Tiedemann, trans. Edmund F. N. Jephcott (Stanford, CA: Stanford University Press, 2000), 8.

78. Most notably Jean-Luc Marion, *Being Given: Toward a Phenomenology of Givenness* (Palo Alto, CA: Stanford University Press, 2002), 202; Marion, *In Excess: Studies of Saturated Phenomena* (New York: Fordham University Press, 2002).

79. Adorno, *Negative Dialectics*, 140.

80. Marion, *Being Given*.

our imagination, multiplying the range and possibilities of applicable concepts; our faculties are so vivified that no particular concept exhausts the representation in question. Our standing with respect to history is analogous: we construct histories, but they do not exhaust the historical record, which always exceeds any of our constructions. As Arendt puts the thought, every new event "illuminates its own past; it can never be deduced from it."[81] Analogous to the way in which beauty reveals something about our subjectivity according to Kant, the historical and the natural are interpenetrated in constructions of history: it is a natural fact about history—not about our subjectivity—that history exceeds our constructions, even as such a surplus is possible or diagnosable only by virtue of our subjective capacities.

What interests me most about this view of history is the sort of robust ethical commitment that appears to underwrite it. Bringing that commitment to the fore strikes me as central for completing this dialectical conception of history. To do that, it is worthwhile to attend to the ways in which similar themes appear in Benjamin's work. Let me quote a few passages from his paralipomena (notes) to "On the Concept of History":

> The notion of a universal history is bound up with the notion of progress and the notion of civilization [*Kultur*]. In order for all the moments in the history of humanity to be incorporated in the chain of history, they must be reduced to a common denominator—"civilization," "enlightenment," "the objective spirit," or whatever one wishes to call it.[82]

---

81. Arendt, "Understanding and Politics," in *Essays in Understanding, 1930–1954: Formation, Exile, and Totalitarianism*, ed. Jerome Kohn (New York: Schocken, 2011), 319.
82. Walter Benjamin, *Gesammelte Schriften*, ed. Rolf Tiedemann and Hermann Schweppenhäuser (Frankfurt: Suhrkamp, 1977), 1: 1233; Benjamin, "Paralipomena to 'On the Concept of History,'" in *Selected Writings*, ed. Howard Eiland and Michael W. Jennings (Cambridge, MA: Harvard University Press, 2002), 4: 403.

> Marx says that revolutions are the locomotive of world history. But perhaps it is wholly otherwise. Perhaps revolutions are an attempt by the passengers on this train—namely, humankind—to activate the emergency brake.[83]
>
> In the idea of a classless society, Marx secularized the idea of messianic time. And that was good. The disaster began when the Social Democrats elevated this idea to an "ideal." The ideal was defined . . . as an "infinite [*unendlich*] task." . . . Once the classless society had been defined as an infinite task, the empty and homogeneous time was transformed into an anteroom, so to speak, in which one could wait for the emergence of the revolutionary situation with more or less placidness.[84]

Immediately, note the extent to which Benjamin also attacks any version of universal history, whether progressive or regressive. According to Benjamin, the problem with such history is twofold. First, Benjamin takes it that such a conception, by conceptualizing temporality as homogeneous time, gets the history fundamentally wrong, a point that animates Benjamin's thinking from his earliest days.[85] Second, such a conception of history serves the practical function of pacifying subjects and obfuscating the origins and nature of their suffering, all while suggesting that the ideal toward which history moves is something measurable and merely currently absent.[86] Either of these points is a book-length topic in its own right, but a focus on the motive or impulse that animates

---

83. Benjamin, *Gesammelte Schriften*, 1: 1232; Benjamin, "Paralipomena," 4: 402.

84. Benjamin, *Gesammelte Schriften*, 1: 1231; Benjamin, "Paralipomena," 4: 401–2.

85. On this point, see Peter Fenves, *The Messianic Reduction: Walter Benjamin and the Shape of Time* (Palo Alto, CA: Stanford University Press, 2011).

86. See Idit Dobbs-Weinstein, *Spinoza's Critique of Religion and Its Heirs: Marx, Benjamin, Adorno* (Cambridge: Cambridge University Press, 2015), 129.

Benjamin's thinking is useful for understanding the broader view of history emerging here.

One can see an analogous ethical stance already in Adorno's 1932 lecture, "The Idea of Natural-History,"[87] a lecture that he presented to the Frankfurt Kant society, and which continued to influence Adorno's thinking until his death.[88] Although a general consensus around the text has not yet emerged,[89] and although there are many issues and interlocutors for Adorno in the text,[90] certain facts about the text are relatively uncontroversial. Historically, Adorno was likely responding to a debate over historicism, spurned by the work of Ernst Troeltsch, specifically Troeltsch's 1922 book,[91] *Der Historismus und seine Probleme* (Historicism and its problems).[92] One of Troeltsch's chief claims is that the periodization of history can be viewed from the perspective of an ideal—here also fundamentally religious—integration of the periods from the perspective of the present. In response, Adorno agrees with a historicist rejection of such an idealization. Thus he notes that Heidegger's ontological project does arrive at a plausible rejoinder to such a philosophy of history

---

87. Theodor W. Adorno, "The Idea of Natural-History," trans. Robert Hullot-Kentor, in *Things beyond Resemblance: Collected Essays on Theodor W. Adorno*, ed. Robert Hullot-Kentor, 252–70 (New York: Columbia University Press, 2006). Also available in Robert Hullot-Kentor, "The Idea of Natural History," *Telos* 60 (1984): 111–24.

88. On this point, see Susan Buck-Morss, *The Origin of Negative Dialectics: Theodor W. Adorno, Walter Benjamin, and the Frankfurt Insitute* (New York: Free Press, 1977), 52.

89. See Tom Whyman, "Understanding Adorno on 'Natural-History,'" *International Journal of Philosophical Studies* 24, no. 4 (2016): 452.

90. Robert Hullot-Kentor, "Introduction to T. W. Adorno's 'The Idea of Natural-History,'" in *Things beyond Resemblance: Collected Essays on Theodor W. Adorno*, 234–51 (New York: Columbia University Press, 2006).

91. Buck-Morss, *Origin of Negative Dialectics*, 53. See especially her note 70.

92. Ernst Troeltsch, *Der Historismus und seine Probleme* (Tübingen, Ger.: J. C. B Mohr, 1922).

by "eliminating the pure antithesis of history and being," since "history itself . . . has become the basic ontological structure."[93] For Heidegger, humans are fundamentally historical in their own existence, where their "possibilities of access and modes of interpretation" are always "diverse, varying in different historical circumstances."[94] The term Heidegger introduces to capture this is *historicity* (*Geschichtlichkeit*), a fundamental existential structure common to all human beings. The fact that every human is thrown into a particular locus of concern, a particular horizon and world of interpretation and possibility, means that one's projects for and possibilities in history are set by such a particular being-in-the-world, a particular historical horizon. The fact that one's world is so constituted is itself, however, according to Heidegger, an ontological fact of being human, a fact that admits of authentic and inauthentic modes of relation, that is, modes that do or do not acknowledge the ontological fact.[95]

Adorno agrees with Heidegger that it just is the case that particular circumstances determine one's access to history and one's possibilities for historical conceptualization and that there are serious issues with the sort of account Troeltsch offers. What Adorno alleges as a problem for Heidegger's account is the fact that, with any view of history, we need to be able to understand elements of it as necessary and other elements as contingent. Yet exactly such a view is impossible with Heidegger's rubric,[96] because all of history is of a

93. Hullot-Kentor, "Translation of T. W. Adorno's 'The Idea of Natural-History,'" 256.
94. Heidegger, *Basic Problems*, 21–22.
95. See *Being and Time*, §§12–18, 31–33, 35–42, 62, 64–65, 72–77.
96. On this point, see Samir Gandesha, "The 'Aesthetic Dignity of Words': Adorno's Philosophy of Language," *New German Critique*, no. 97 (2006): 148; Brian O'Connor, "Adorno, Heidegger and the Critique of Epistemology," *Philosophy and Social Criticism* 24, no. 4 (1998): 58; Peter E. Gordon, *Adorno and Existence* (Cambridge, MA: Harvard University Press, 2016), 49–54.

kind: contingent. We might ask at this point whether this is a convincing reading of Heidegger,[97] because what Heidegger is driving at is that there just are ontological, formal qualities inherent in being human, that is, to being a creature who possesses a past, present, and future and who therefore (potentially) relates to them in affective and value-laden ways that ultimately disclose temporal possibilities and realities in particular, heterogeneous (i.e., *non*homogeneous) experiences of time. It just is the case that such a creature is confronted with the possibility of nothingness, of death.[98] On one hand, this fact certainly seems to undermine Adorno's charge that Heidegger's ontology somehow prohibits us from understanding history in its specificity, that it makes mysterious actual history with its necessities and contingencies. On the other hand, Adorno's critique appears to diagnose a real problem when we realize that Adorno is really stressing the conception of history presented here, as modeled on a sort of "saturated phenomenon." The point might be developed as follows. Adorno's charge is not the merely or solely, say, historical-critical point that breakdowns of agency are just fundamentally not understandable by means of formal qualities about being and nonbeing—that is, an attack on the Heideggerian claim that such breakdowns are really variations on the fact that at the core of every human existence is the nullity of death.[99]

---

97. This point is well raised in Iain Macdonald, "Truth and Authentication: Heidegger and Adorno in Reverse," in *Adorno and Heidegger*, ed. Iain Macdonald and Krzysztof Ziarek, 6–22 (Stanford, CA: Stanford University Press, 2008).

98. Heidegger, *Being and Time*, §58.

99. See Robert B. Pippin, "On Being Anti-Cartesian: Hegel, Heidegger, Subjectivity, and Sociality," in *Idealism as Modernism: Hegelian Variations* (Cambridge: Cambridge University Press, 1997), 385; Pippin, "Necessary Conditions for the Possibility of What Isn't: Heidegger on Failed Meaning," in *The Persistence of Subjectvity* (Cambridge: Cambridge University Press, 2005), 77.

Instead, Adorno's point, without denying the aforementioned historical-critical point, is the ethical charge that such a view of history—with its formalism—minimizes concrete sources of human suffering.[100] The suffering undergone by others throughout history can never be located fundamentally in any formal ontology[101] or in my experience of death, rather such suffering emerges only through someone else's death. Adorno's point is that to locate an explanation of concrete cases of suffering where Heidegger aims to locate it is to miss an important dimension of what it means to be human, of what it means to value other humans. Levinas puts this same point as the idea that being truly human "consists precisely in opening oneself to the death of the other, in being preoccupied with his or her death."[102] Although more detail is needed here,[103] a shared sense of such a critique of Heidegger brings Adorno close to someone like Levinas[104] (the overall critique is, to my mind, plausibly bolstered by Heidegger's own shocking suggestion, after the Nazi genocide, that agriculture as "a mechanized food industry" is "in essence the same as the production of corpses in the gas chambers and extermination camps").[105]

A rejection of the sort of conception of history present in Heidegger's ontology requires one to propose a philosophy

100. For a little more on Adorno's moral epistemology, see Shuster, "Nothing to Know: The Epistemology of Moral Perfectionism in Adorno and Cavell," *Idealistic Studies* 44, no. 1 (2015): 1–29.

101. Max Pensky, "Toward a Critical Theory of Death: Adorno on Dying Today," *Adorno Studies* 1, no. 1 (2017) :43–65.

102. Emmanuel Levinas, "The Philosopher and Death," in *Alterity and Transcendence* (New York: Columbia University Press, 1999), 157–58.

103. Richard A. Cohen, "Levinas: Thinking Least about Death—contra Heidegger," in *Self and Other: Essays in Continental Philosophy of Religion*, 21–39 (Dordrecht, Neth.: Springer, 2006).

104. On this point, see footnote 110 of chapter 2.

105. Martin Heidegger, "Insight into That Which Is: Bremen Lectures 1949," trans. Andrew J. Mitchell, in *Bremen and Freiburg Lectures: Insight into That Which Is and Basic Principles of Thinking* (Bloomington: Indiana University Press, 2012), 27.

of history that somehow acknowledges both the deeply historical nature of human agency and the deeply saturated materiality of every moment of history. Adorno finds the basis for such a conception of history in György Lukács's notion of second nature and quotes Lukács extensively in his lecture.[106] Lukács writes that such second nature is "a petrified estranged complex of meaning that is no longer able to awaken inwardness; it is a charnel house of rotted interiorities."[107] Lukács's suggestion throughout *The Theory of the Novel* (written in 1914–15) is the by-now-familiar claim that capitalism forms individuals whose natural comportment toward and within the world—indeed whose world, in a deep phenomenological sense—is always already shot through with conventions that reify people and things, alienate humans from each other and their activities, and fundamentally fail to offer a meaningful human existence. The "charnel house" metaphor should not be minimized—on this point, Adorno and Lukács have a common ethical sensibility. Where Adorno parts company with Lukács is in how meaning might be actualized in response to such a state of affairs. For Lukács, according to Adorno, meaning can reappear only by means of a "theological resurrection . . . an eschatological context."[108] Adorno's suggestion is that, in thinking that history can only be vivified by something beyond history, Lukács is in fact betraying his own ethical estimation of history as a sort of charnel house. Adorno's claim is that Lukács sees the history he describes not as a charnel house—concretely, with a full acknowledgment of the suffering it betrays—but instead as only a symbol, where "death and destruction . . .

---

106. Adorno, "Idea of Natural-History," 261.
107. György Lukács, *The Theory of the Novel: A Historico-Philosophical Essay on the Forms of Great Epic Literature*, trans. Anna Bostock (Boston: MIT Press, 1971), 64; Adorno, "Idea of Natural-History," 262.
108. Adorno, "Idea of Natural History," 262.

[are] idealized,"[109] as pointing to cosmic forces. Lukács fails to acknowledge the concrete nature of historical suffering. How exactly? Adorno invokes Benjamin's conception of allegory, which cannot be developed in the proper depth here,[110] but which can nonetheless be understood as—most minimally—aiming to present history as a site where "the observer is confronted with the facies hippocratia of history, a petrified primordial landscape."[111] And here Benjamin means "Hippocratic face" quite literally and clinically: it is the face that is produced by impending death. For Benjamin, nature can be understood only as perpetually bound up with its destruction, and thus the fundamental category for any construction of history is "transience" or "decay."[112] What I take Benjamin to be after with this claim, and Adorno also, is the idea that although we perpetually write history—that is, place its unique and individual points into a context, even though the most fundamental truth about all such points is that they are all entirely unique, all possessed of "a nucleus of time in themselves"—the only historical truth is that "history is discontinuous in the sense that it represents life perennially disrupted."[113] Every moment, even when placed into a historical account that makes it into some sense-making context, also fundamentally carries its own opposition to that context and potentially resists it. The only truth about history

---

109. Walter Benjamin, *The Origin of German Tragic Drama*, trans. John Osborne (London: New Left, 1977), 166; Adorno, "Idea of Natural History," 263, translation modified. Adorno explicitly quotes Benjamin.

110. See Howard Caygill, "Walter Benjamin's Concept of Allegory," in *The Cambridge Companion to Allegory*, ed. Rita Copeland and Peter T. Struck, 241–54 (Cambridge: Cambridge University Press, 2010); Bainard Cowan, "Walter Benjamin's Theory of Allegory," *New German Critique*, no. 22 (1981): 109–22.

111. Adorno, "Idea of Natural-History," 262; Benjamin, *Origin of German Tragic Drama*, 166. Again, Adorno is here quoting Benjamin explicitly.

112. Adorno, "Idea of Natural-History," 262.

113. Adorno, *History and Freedom*, 91.

is that it "constantly repeats this process of disruption."[114] For this reason, the fundamental category of history is transience or decay. Or, as Adorno puts it, we ought to say "history is highly continuous in discontinuity."[115] And the reason Benjamin's notion of allegory is central to this point is the simple fact that allegory—unlike symbolism, which merely invokes one thing to really mean something else—affirms the historical uniqueness and concreteness of the things that it allegorizes and the moment that allows any such allegory to work. This is why Benjamin calls for a "Copernican revolution in historical perception."[116] Benjamin notes that "formerly it was thought that a fixed point had been in 'what had been,' and one saw the present engaged in tentatively concentrating the forces of knowledge on this ground. Now this relation is to be overturned, and what has been is to become the dialectical reversal—the flash of awakened consciousness . . . the facts become something that just now first happened to us, first struck us; to establish them is the affair of memory."[117] All constructions of history—like allegories—always fail to exhaust the present context, always pointing beyond it, even as they also depend on that context, requiring it for any construction of history and meaning. Here again the process of decay emerges as an entirely natural fact about history—it just is the case that every historical event carries with it possibilities unrealized and that every historical view ignores or overlooks or hides them. Any such natural fact of decay, however, can be revealed only through human intervention, through an understanding of exactly what is decaying and how, or what failed to be actualized and how. This is the context in which we ought to read Adorno's pronouncement in *Negative Dialectics* that, "where Hegelian metaphysics

114. Ibid.
115. Ibid., 92.
116. Benjamin, *Arcades Project*, 388.
117. Ibid., 388–89.

transfigures the absolute by equating it with the total passing of all finite things, it simultaneously looks a little beyond the mythical spell it captures and reinforces."[118] It looks "a little beyond" it because Hegel's avowed impulse—to capture "the total passing of all finite things"—is in fact, exactly right; but Hegel fails—turns to mythology—exactly when he thinks that he can do it, even in a text as ambitious and powerful as the *Phenomenology*. True progress in this realm would bring to a halt all constructions of history that stress continuity and progress and instead apply the "emergency brake" that Benjamin suggests, reorienting our view of the entire historical record and its relationship to us, something that remains a possibility at every moment.[119]

§ 5. Conclusion: Not Being at Home

More weight can be given to the conception of history that's surfaced here by marshaling some other elements of its basis in Benjamin's thought. In "On the Concept of History," Benjamin notes that it is a truth that "nothing that has ever happened should be regarded as lost to history."[120] Benjamin continues, noting that only for a "redeemed mankind has its past become citable in all its moments."[121] I take this just to be the point about history as a sort of "saturated phenomenon." On one hand, Benjamin's point is the now relatively common point that history must be decolonialized;[122] on

---

118. Adorno, *Negative Dialectics*, 360.
119. On this point, see Theodor W. Adorno, "Progress," trans. Henry W. Pickford, in *Critical Models: Interventions and Catchwords* (New York: Columbia University Press, 1998).
120. Benjamin, "On the Concept of History," in *Selected Writings*, ed. Howard Eiland and Michael W. Jennings (Cambridge, MA: Harvard University Press, 2002), 4: 390.
121. Ibid.
122. Walter Mignolo, *The Darker Side of Western Modernity: Global Ftures, Decolonial Options* (Durham, NC: Duke University Press, 2011).

the other hand, Benjamin is adding even more depth to this point: every history, of whatever sort, will leave something out—indeed, more accurately—will leave someone out, a great deal many someones. The impetus to seeing history as a sort of "saturated phenomenon" is not merely, say, ontological, about the qualitative nature of history, but rather also ethical. This is the context in which we should read Benjamin's claim that "the only historian capable of fanning the spark of hope in the past is the one who is firmly convinced that even the dead will not be safe from the enemy if he is victorious."[123] And, as Benjamin points out, "this enemy has never ceased to be victorious."[124]

What might it mean to write history from this different perspective? In part, some honesty is required here: there is a reason that Benjamin's Arcades Project was never finished—it is an almost impossible task that requires seeking out all the refuge, everything that's been discarded, avoided, and lost. Writing such history is difficult, if not impossible. Nonetheless, it must be noted that what's at stake is not its completion but an understanding of what it might mean to be inspired and animated by such a conception of history. It would require rejecting all constructions of universal history. At the same time, it paradoxically also requires the construction of a limited sort of universal history: in order to acknowledge the suffering of prior generations—and here we must speak of generations upon generations—we must construct a minimal regressive universal history. As Adorno famously notes, "no universal history leads from savagery to humanitarianism, but there is one leading from the slingshot to the megaton bomb."[125] Such a history is constantly and increasingly regressive (so no nostalgia is implied here).

---

123. Benjamin, "On the Concept of History," 4: 391.
124. Ibid.
125. Adorno, *Negative Dialectics*, 320.

And Adorno implores us to acknowledge that history has largely been a series of catastrophes and that one can trace this sequence from our earliest days mastering nature.[126] Adorno summarizes all this as the idea that "the unity that cements the discontinuous, chaotically splintered moments and phases of history—the unity of the control of nature, progressing to rule over men, and finally to that over men's inner nature . . . it ends in the total menace which organized mankind poses to organized men, in the epitome of discontinuity."[127] At the same time, because of the same aforementioned ethical impulse and the view of nature it takes, even such a regressive universal history must be denied. As Adorno puts it, "universal history must be constructed and repudiated."[128] "Constructed" because to fail to do so is to fail to acknowledge the suffering of past generations, and any such acknowledgment rests on the quasi-religious understanding of every moment of history as unquantifiably full and every unique human life as sacred; and "repudiated" because to fail to do so is both (1) to fail to be ethically sensitive to the historical fact that history has reached a moment when its end "has become a real possibility,"[129] and (2) to fail to acknowledge the irreducible singularity of every moment and every life. This is what Adorno suggests when he writes that "philosophy interprets such [historical] coding, the always new Mene Tekel, in that which is smallest, the fragments struck loose through decay, but which carry objective meaning."[130] The reference to "mene tekel" here invokes the fifth chapter

---

126. See Horkheimer and Adorno, *Dialectic of Enlightenment, Philosophical Fragments*, trans. Edmund Jephcott, Cultural Memory in the Present Series, ed. Mieke Bal and Hent de Vries (Stanford, CA: Stanford University Press, 2002).

127. Ibid.

128. Ibid.; translation modified.

129. Marc Nicolas Sommer, *Das Konzept einer negativen Dialektik: Adorno und Hegel* (Tübingen, Ger.: Mohr Siebeck, 2016), 325.

130. Adorno, *Negative Dialectics*, 360.

of the biblical Book of Daniel, where these words appear as prophecy, signifying מנא (mene) and תקל (tekel). The former Near Eastern root signifies measurement (equally, discernment) and the latter signifies weighing (equally, finding insufficient, wanting). In Daniel, the idea is that God finds the days of the kingdom under discussion numbered and wanting; in Adorno's invocation, the "always new Mene Tekel" denotes both the fundamental saturated nature of history (something that might only be grasped in the moment of complete redemption), and the fundamental inadequacy of every moment, which perpetually disappears, and which is transient, decaying.

One might argue that the aims of such a view are to offer us a bit of therapy,[131] to allow us to counter a particular view of the philosophy of history, one that imputes some sort of greater meaning to the whole beyond the present moment. That is not incorrect, but it seems to me to miss the manifestly ethical—and therefore sociopolitical—import behind the project, an ethical import that fundamentally opposes any procedure that minimizes or overlooks any human life, with the particular experiences of suffering central to any human life, as well as the particular expectations of happiness that follow from any such procedure.[132] There is more to be said about this impulse than what was said in chapter 2, especially about its philosophical parameters and justifications,[133] but note the way in which it requires for its existence the construction of anachronism toward the world (with everything that I am claiming that requires). In this way, although sharing some points of commonality with a reading of Hegel that

---

131. Whyman, "Understanding Adorno on 'Natural-History.'"
132. Benjamin, "On the Concept of History," 4: 389–90.
133. For elaborations, see J. M. Bernstein, *Adorno: Disenchantment and Ethics* (Cambridge: Cambridge University Press, 2001); Freyenhagen, *Adorno's Practical Philosophy: Living Less Wrongly* (Cambridge: Cambridge University Press, 2013); Shuster, *Autonomy after Auschwitz*.

stresses his view of the construction of history as a sort of "infinite end," Adorno parts company from these Hegelians exactly in the way in which he rejects the desire to "be at home," even as a general aim. To do so is to betray an ethical imperative imposed on us by contemporary experience; as Adorno simply puts it: "today . . . it is part of morality not to be home."[134] We might thereby, as Levinas suggests, be able to leave Hegel's system "through the very door by which Hegel thinks we enter it,"[135] that is, by means of alienation.[136]

Returning to the broader themes of *How to Measure a World?*, note that wonder may produce alienation as deep as suffering does (albeit likely not as painful); this has been the theme developed in chapter 1 herein through Maimonides's thought. And although Adorno and Maimonides have radically divergent understandings of evil,[137] it is important

---

134. Theodor W. Adorno, *Minima Moralia: Reflections on a Damaged Life*, trans. Edmund F. N. Jephcott (London: Verso, 2005), 39.

135. Levinas, "Hegel and the Jews," trans. Seán Hand, in *Difficult Freedom: Essays on Judaism* (Baltimore, MD: Johns Hopkins University Press, 1960), 238.

136. Sarah Hammerschlag puts the point quite well when she writes that for Levinas, we are not speaking of "another form of Being-in-the-world but a kind of Being-in-resistance-to-the-world." Hammerschlag, "'A Splinter in the Flesh': Levinas and the Resignification of Jewish Suffering, 1928–1947," *International Journal of Philosophical Studies* 20, no. 3 (2012): 410. The same is true of Adorno and Benjamin.

137. In a deep sense, as I noted above (see footnote 63 of chap. 2), Maimonides subscribes exactly to the sort of view that denigrates matter as an obstacle to the comprehension of ultimate reality (this point is so ubiquitous as not to require citation, but some key passages are *The Guide of the Perplexed*, trans. Shlomo Pines (Chicago: University of Chicago Press, 1963) 3.8, 430; 3.9, 436; 3.10, 440, and so forth). Maimonides's entire "solution" to the problem of evil (the existence of evil in light of a monotheistic conception of God as omnipotent, omniscient, and omnibenevolent) is to argue that matter just is the sort of thing that inclines toward evil and it is not an abrogation of God's power that he could not create things otherwise (this doesn't, to me, solve the deeper issue that God could have refrained from creating anything at all). For a concise statement of Maimonides's views on evil, see Tamar M. Rudavsky, *Maimonides* (Oxford, UK: Blackwell, 2009), 138–49. There is also here a potential

to understand that, to the extent that the world with which they concern themselves is a human world, and to the extent that each requires an exploration of that world in the most minute and concrete of ways, both Adorno and Maimonides necessitate a commitment to viewing the world as materially and humanly "saturated" exactly in the ways outlined in this chapter; when we speak of a human world, we speak also of a history of that world. Whether we approach the world in awe or in outrage, there can ultimately be no feeling at home in it or with it. What is instead required is a constant vigilance and renewal of practical and theoretical capacities oriented around exploring the world in the context of our human agency; (human) judgment and world are made for one another, and only through them emerges what lies beyond.

---

tension between Maimonides's commitment to his negative theology and the very emergence of the problem of evil (which depends on God having certain attributes). For a classic statement of this point, see Norbert Samuelson, "On Knowing God: Maimonides, Gersonides, and the Philosophy of Religion," *Judaism* 18, no. 1 (1969): 64. For an argument against such a procedure, see Eliezer Berkovits, *God, Man and History* (Jerusalem: Shalem, 2004), 51–68; Shubert Spero, "Is the God of Maimonides Truly Unknowable?," *Judaism* 22, no. 1 (1973): 66. Spero and Berkovits raise especially interesting questions about the relation of the ethical to conceptions of God, and these questions take on a particular cast in light of the ethical sensitivity that's on display in Adorno's work in my reconstruction in these past two chapters. The core question is fundamentally about the scope of the negative theology, with Spero and Berkovits arguing that negative theology is not meant to range across an understanding of God's goodness. Maimonides's text seems to me ambiguous enough—most exemplified by the debates about any possible esoteric understanding of the text (see footnote 4 of chap. 1)—that it is hard to settle this question. And in a deep sense, Erich Fromm captures the stakes of this debate when he notes that "the 'negative theology' of Maimonides leads, in its ultimate consequence—though one not contemplated by Maimonides—to the end of theology. How can there be a 'science of God' when there is nothing one can say or think about God?" (Erich Fromm, *You Shall Be as Gods: A Radical Interpretation of the Old Testament and Its Tradition* [New York: Fawcett Premier, 2013], 32). My approach is simply to bracket these question in order to pursue the analysis of world that I have set as the task here.

4

LANGUAGE AND WORLD

LEVINAS AND CAVELL ON ETHICAL FOUNDATIONS

§ 1. Introduction: Discourse and World

Having placed priority on human judgment, note a simple fact: how we describe phenomena in the world matters. As George Carlin once noted, whether we describe something as "shell shock," "battle fatigue," "operational exhaustion," or "posttraumatic stress disorder" makes a difference for how we respond to that phenomenon (the same is true, say, whether we call something "torture" or "enhanced interrogation techniques"). This last chapter orients itself around a basic phenomenological point: having a world is impossible without discourse, which ought to be understood fundamentally as the idea that a world is a world of meaning and significance (and, important to note, neither is restricted to language understood in some narrow sense as speech only).[1]

---

1. One might think of the way Heidegger conceives of discourse as a fundamental structure of having a world (it is not the *only* such structure). See Martin Heidegger, *Being and Time*, trans. Joan Stambaugh (Albany: State University of New York, 1996), §34. On this point, see also the discussion throughout Steven Crowell, *Normativity and Phenomenology in*

A summary of the entire impulse behind this chapter is captured by a wonderful passage from Stanley Cavell's work: "A word has meaning against the context of a sentence. A sentence has meaning against the context of a language. A language has meaning against the context of a form of life. A form of life has meaning against the context of a world. A world has meaning against the context of a word."[2] Cavell's point might be unpacked as the idea that as soon as we are in a world we are implicitly and explicitly engaged in judgment and interpretation: because they locate us in an entire world, what *words* we use matters. If all that is the case, however, my subjectivity is never the sole arbiter of things, indeed it is not even the source of meaning, rather meaning is itself an *intersubjective* achievement, one that is accomplished only among others, through discourse;[3] what words *we* use matters.

§ 2. Knowing Myself Is Knowing the World Is Knowing Others

If discourse is central, and if our world is fundamentally an intersubjective world, then my relationship with an other must be a key point of interest (really, my relationship to a great many others, but any account of that begins with a single other).[4] One quick way to proceed is to start with a

---

Husserl and Heidegger (Cambridge: Cambridge University Press, 2013), beginning on 201. With respect to the first point in this footnote, note how Heidegger stresses that hearing and keeping silent are also central to discourse; that is, what is at stake is a relationship of and to meaning and significance and everything that implies, which far exceeds mere words or language conceived in narrow terms.

2. Stanley Cavell, *The Senses of Walden: An Expanded Edition* (Chicago: University of Chicago Press, 2013), 112.

3. In broad terms, an excellent elaboration of Hannah Arendt's phenomenology as stressing exactly the importance of this intersubjective dimension for any phenomenological project can be found in Sophie Loidolt, *Phenomenology of Plurality: Hannah Arendt on Political Intersubjectivity* (London: Routledge, 2017).

4. We might say we are always already an ethical agent. On this use of *ethical*, originating as it does in Levinas's work, see Diane Perpich,

picture of how our ordinary language practices work. Donald Davidson, a prominent twentieth-century philosopher of language, begins with the idea that, although any understanding of human subjectivity (knowledge of one's own mind) is bound up with objectivity (knowledge of the external world), it is also bound up with intersubjectivity (knowledge of other minds).[5] The three are inseparable and equally primordial. This tripartite relationship is such that none of the three can be lost without also losing the others; in short, all three are necessary for us to have a world in the phenomenological sense elaborated through the present book. For a subject to have any sort of desires or beliefs about the world, that subject must be able to distinguish between the way things *seem* and the way things actually *are* (I could not so much even believe that these books are in front of me if I could not be mistaken about that fact—if I could not get at, correctly or incorrectly, whether the books are or are not in front of me; truth requires the possibility of error). Notably, however, merely distinguishing between things or navigating the world—as plenty of nonlinguistic creatures (can) do—is not enough to produce a distinction between "mere seeming and being,"[6] for such a distinction is normative in nature.

Davidson stresses that "unless language is shared, there is no way to distinguish between using . . . language correctly

---

The Ethics of Emmanuel Levinas (Stanford, CA: Stanford University Press, 2008), 1–17. Perpich's response is especially relevant to worries like those of Richard Rorty, who take Levinas's notion of the ethical to be "gawky, awkward, and unenlightening" (Richard Rorty, "Response to Simon Critchley," in *Deconstruction and Pragmatism*, ed. Chantal Mouffe [London: Routledge, 1996], 41).

5. For a broader analysis of Davidson's philosophy of language, see James Pearson, "Distinguishing W. V. Quine and Donald Davidson," *Journal for the History of Analytical Philosophy* 1, no. 1 (2011): 1–22; Bjørn Ramberg, *Donald Davidson: Philosophy of Language* (Basel, Switz.: Wiley-Blackwell, 1991).

6. Donald Davidson, "Three Varieties of Knowledge," in *Subjective, Intersubjective, Objective* (Oxford, UK: Clarendon, 2001), 209.

and incorrectly; only communication with another can supply an objective check."[7] One way to put this point is to note that in order for me to have my "take" on the world, there has to be a world out there for me, but in order for that to be possible, I need to be able to conceive a possible distance between that world and my take on it, opening up the possibility of an alternative take on it (someone else's take). There is, in Davidson's term of art, a constant "triangulation" between self, other, and the world. Any potential knowledge of the world presupposes that I have beliefs about the world, which are either confirmed or disconfirmed amid others who are themselves orienting their own beliefs about a common, shared world. It is "essential to language that it enables us to make ourselves intelligible to others and to find others intelligible, that it enables us to make our own minds known to others and to know the minds of others."[8] And because all such procedures are normative in nature, interpretation is imperative.

Such a view is fundamentally opposed to any naive philosophical stance that begins with a subject's inner life in order then to move outward, building from that subjectivity the concepts of objectivity and intersubjectivity. Here is Davidson again:

> Now, my own view is that, until we have an idea of what's going on in the minds of other people, it doesn't make sense to say that we have the concept of objectivity, of something existing in the world quite independent of us. The empiricists have it exactly backwards, because they think that first one knows what's in his own mind, then, with luck, he finds out what is in the outside world, and, with even more luck, he

---

7. Ibid., 209–10.
8. John McDowell, "*Subjective, Intersubjective, Objective,*" in *The Engaged Intellect: Philosophical Essays* (Cambridge, MA: Harvard University Press, 2009), 153.

finds out what is in somebody else's mind. I think differently. First we find out what is in somebody else's mind, and by then we have got all the rest. Of course, I really think that it all comes at the same time.⁹

The notion of objectivity requires "the concept of intersubjective truth."¹⁰ That notion, in turn, requires that the subject in question have at least some sense of a common, external world, for it is by such a possibility that an alternative take on the world arises and is ultimately adjudicated.¹¹ The notion of *alternative takes*, however, makes sense only if a subject has her own take, and so forth. Conversation does not merely presuppose that, when speaking to someone, we are just checking to see whether their views match up to ours, but rather conversation suggests that we are both presupposing a common world between us that we allow to serve as the standard for judgment between us.¹² Communication makes possible the notion of my own mind as much as the mind of another.¹³

What's striking is that Davidson's view finds an almost entirely analogous expression in Levinas's philosophy, which, as I noted already in the introduction, is cultivated explicitly in the wake of the Nazi genocide.¹⁴ The remainder

---

9. Giovanna Borradori, *The American Philosopher: Conversations with Quine, Davidson, Putnam, Nozick, Danto, Rorty, Cavell, Macintyre, and Kuhn* (Chicago: University of Chicago Press, 1994), 50.

10. Donald Davidson, "Rational Animals," in *Subjective, Intersubjective, Objective* (Oxford, UK: Clarendon, 2001), 105.

11. On this point, especially see Bjørn Ramberg, "Post-ontological Philosophy of Mind: Rorty versus Davidson," in *Rorty and His Critics*, ed. Robert B. Brandom (Oxford, UK: Blackwell, 2000), 363.

12. On this point, see Donald Davidson, "A Nice Derangement of Epitaphs," in *Truth, Language, and History*, 89–107 (Oxford, UK: Clarendon, 2005).

13. See Donald Davidson, "Rational Animals"; Donald Davidson, "Thought and Talk," in *Inquiries into Truth and Interpretation*, 155–71 (Oxford, UK: Clarendon, 1973).

14. On this point, see Michael Morgan, *Discovering Levinas* (Cambridge: Cambridge University Press, 2007), 1–39.

of this chapter is concerned, therefore, with teasing out the seeming *ethical* significance of such a view of language and the world (in other words, Levinas somehow takes a discussion of language to be central to the explicitly ethical project he crafts in response to the Nazi genocide). In *Totality and Infinity*, Levinas's coins a term of art—*infinity*—that serves as an entry point both for his philosophy of language and for its significance in any discussion of ethics. Infinity, Levinas suggests, must be conceived in opposition to totality.[15] According to Levinas, infinity is excessive, exceeding various saliencies of demarcation. It is not a mere mathematical infinity, manipulable and hierarchically arranged in a calculable discourse of infinities, but rather a singularity distinct from whatever order it is exceeding. Often Levinas makes the point in the following ways:

> Infinity is not the object of contemplation, that is, is not proportionate to the thought that thinks it. The idea of infinity is a thought which at every moment thinks more than it thinks.[16]
>
> Contrary to the ideas which always remain on the scale of the "intentional object," or on that of their *ideatum*, and so exert a hold on it; contrary to the ideas by which thinking progressively grasps the world, the idea of the Infinite would contain more than it was able to do. It would contain more than its capacity as a *cogito*. Thought would think in some manner beyond what it thinks.[17]
>
> The idea of infinity is exceptional in that its *ideatum* surpasses its idea.[18]

---

15. For a discussion of the notion of infinity in Levinas, see Luc A. Anckaert, *A Critique of Infinity: Rosenzweig and Levinas* (Leuven, Belg.: Peeters, 2006).

16. Levinas, "Philosophy and the Idea of Infinity," trans. Alphonso Lingis, in *Collected Philosophical Papers* (Dordrecht, Neth.: Martinus Nijhoff, 1987), 56.

17. Emmanuel Levinas, *Of God Who Comes to Mind*, trans. Bettina Bergo (Stanford, CA: Stanford University Press, 1998), xii.

18. Emmanuel Levinas, *Totality and Infinity*, trans. Alphonso Lingis (Dordrecht, Neth.: Kluwer, 1961), 49.

Levinas harks back to Descartes's invocation of the notion of infinity in Descartes's third meditation in the *Meditations* as the model for his conception.[19] To be clear, especially with an eye toward how this term of art is relevant to a discussion of ethics, note that Levinas is not concerned with infinity as a metaphysical or merely ontological category; rather, he is highlighting the possibility of infinity understood as a sort of logical place marker—potentially actualized in a wide array of discursive undertakings—for something that overflows what is presently available.

With language explicitly in mind, Levinas suggests that discourse or language is a category of the idea of infinity.[20] What might that mean? Note that the use of *category* here simply highlights that this notion can be actualized in a range of domains, whether, say, epistemological, linguistic, or ontological (just to name a few). Language, as another such domain, therefore somehow formally instantiates the notion of infinity. Suggestions that may otherwise seem cryptic, such as the idea that "language is perhaps to be defined as the very power to break the continuity of being or of history,"[21] or that "language presupposes interlocutors, a plurality,"[22] ought to be understood as the relatively straightforward idea that an essential attribute of language or discourse is that it can serve as a medium that is capable of presenting and representing novelty. As J. L. Austin puts it, "even if some language is now purely descriptive, language was not in origin so, and much of it is still not so."[23] When Levinas suggests

---

19. See René Descartes, *Discourse on Method and Meditations on First Philosophy*, trans. Donald A. Cress (Cambridge, MA: Hackett, 1998), 23–34.

20. "Separation and interiority, truth and language, constitute the categories of the idea of infinity (*constituent les catégories de l'idée de l'infini*)" (Levinas, *Totality and Infinity*, 62).

21. Levinas, *Totality and Infinity*, 195.

22. Ibid., 73.

23. James Langshaw Austin, "Other Minds," in *Philosophical Papers*, 3rd ed., ed. James Opie Urmson and Geoffrey James Warnock (Oxford: Oxford University Press, 1979), 103.

that language is a category of the idea of infinity, he means exactly that language is a site where infinity is instantiated: where through discourse one agent can present to another something that is entirely new to the second agent. Someone may say something to me that entirely turns my world upside down, breaks it wholly, destroys it, or upends it in redemption or wonder or unforeseeable novelty.

Before turning explicitly to the ethical significance of the use of infinity in this context, let me note that, like Davidson, Levinas sees language as central to allowing for my own take on the world,[24] which ultimately makes sense only amid others, and within a common world. As Levinas puts it, "things acquire a rational signification . . . because an other is associated with my relations with them."[25] Designating something "to the Other" is an act of placing "things in the perspective of the Other."[26] Only through the plurality of perspectives does a common world emerge. Intersubjectivity ("plurality" in Levinas's terminology) allows for objectivity ("commonality" in Levinas's words). A common world Levinas often terms simply a shared "theme." Note the following

---

24. *Take* may imply an entirely conceptual relationship. I should note here that Levinas acknowledges the possibility of nonconceptual content, what he terms "living from" and "enjoyment" (*jouissance*) (Levinas, *Totality and Infinity*, 109–87). Levinas's strategy is to derive nonconceptual content from nonrepresentationalism. See Robert Bernasconi, "Re-reading *Totality and Infinity*," in *The Question of the Other*, ed. Charles Scott and Arlene Dallery (Buffalo, NY: State University of New York Press, 1989), 28. This is a novel strategy whose elaboration is far beyond my scope here. I can note that I am tempted to agree with Christopher Peacocke when he suggests that "it is a conceptual truth that no-one can have an experience with a given representational content unless he possesses the concepts from which the content is built up" (Christopher R. Peacocke, *Sense and Content: Experience, Thought, and Their Relations* [Oxford, UK: Clarendon, 1983], 19). In this case, unlike Levinas, the arguments for nonconceptual content that I am aware of still maintain that such content is representational. For example, Gareth Evans, *The Varieties of Reference* (Oxford: Oxford University Press, 1982).
25. Levinas, *Totality and Infinity*, 209.
26. Ibid.

examples: "To speak is to make the world common, to create commonplaces."[27] "Language does not refer to the generality of concepts, but lays the foundations for a possession in common."[28] "Language makes possible the objectivity of objects and their thematization."[29]

Just as Davidson suggests, common language makes possible a common world.

Common language and a common world allow for the possibility of objectivity. Levinas puts it as the idea that "to know objectively would . . . be to constitute my thought in such a way that it already contained a reference to the thought of . . . others."[30] Levinas elaborates this idea with the suggestion that in "speaking I do not transmit to the Other what is objective for me," rather "the objective becomes objective only through [our] communication."[31] Again, as in Davidson, the possibility of error is intimately linked to truth: "objectivity results from language, which permits the putting into question of possession."[32] *Possession* here denotes the idea that a subject could come to "possess" an object conceptually: the subject makes something conform or fall under a concept (the German philosophical context that animates Levinas's philosophy sheds light on this point, where "grasping" [*greifen*] is intimately related to the notion of "conceptualization" [*begreifen*] and to the idea of a "concept" [*Begriff*]).[33] With and amid others, agents realize that their "possession" of something, by means of concepts, may

27. Ibid., 76.
28. Ibid.
29. Ibid., 210.
30. Ibid., 210.
31. Ibid.
32. Ibid., 209.
33. For more on this context, see Martin Shuster, "Levinas and German Idealism: Fichte and Hegel," in *The Oxford Handbook of Emmanuel Levinas*, ed. Michael Morgan, 195–219 (Oxford: Oxford University Press, 2019).

come to be contested: we may be accused of applying the wholly wrong concept, or of applying the right one incorrectly. Central to discourse is the possibility of disagreement, for "truth arises where a being separated from the Other is not engulfed in him, but speaks to him."[34] Levinas's term of art for such a possibility is *distance*: there must be a possible distance between my perspective and the perspective of the interlocutor; truth both "spans and does not span" such a distance.[35] As already noted in Davidson's thought, truth does *not* span this distance because this distance is a prerequisite to the very possibility of truth, while truth *does* span this distance because to come to agree, we must bridge it. More accurately, Levinas might have said that such spanning is possible but by no means required or guaranteed. Every linguistic agent just is an authority unto her or himself, but none more authoritative than another (and with respect to certain things, some less so). The distance between us—the authority that we each possess and instantiate—ultimately rests on language, which is fundamentally "a relation in which" agents "absolve themselves from the relation, [and] remain absolute within the relation."[36]

Davidson and Levinas thereby evince a shared view of language; it is this view that ultimately grounds Levinas's claims about ethics. To see this, note that such a view, as Levinas points out, commits us to the rejection of any notion of universal reason as something that is already out there, waiting to be discovered; instead, reason is itself a sort of conversation or task. Levinas puts this idea as the suggestion that "language is not limited to the maieutic awakening of thoughts common to beings. It does not accelerate the inward maturation of a reason common to all; it teaches and introduces

---

34. Levinas, *Totality and Infinity*, 62.
35. Ibid., 64.
36. Ibid.

the new into a thought."[37] For Levinas, the idea of universal reason as something always already available "out there," waiting for any particular agent to grasp, allegedly undermines discourse, individuality, and alterity. Levinas puts all this as the idea that "reason makes human society possible; but a society whose members would be only reasons would vanish as a society. What could a being entirely rational speak of with another entirely rational being? Reason has no plural; how could numerous reasons be distinguished?"[38] The vision of language emerging here requires the possibility of distinct *reasons* as opposed to a universal reason.[39] In this way, Levinas suggests that truth is thereby finite.[40] Let me be clear that Levinas is not glorifying irrationalism, or is somehow against human reason. Levinas's point is instead that any such reason does not come premade; universal reason—if it is to exist—must be achieved. The existence of reason presupposes language and discourse, not the other way around; and to the extent that reason exists, it must be established, and that time and time again. Only language can create universal reason (it equally well may not, shamefully, dangerously, or even simply by chance). Davidson proposes an entirely analogous idea when he notes that the "truth of sentences remains relative to language, *but that is as objective as can be.*"[41]

37. Ibid., 219.
38. Ibid., 119.
39. Levinas and Rorty therefore are much closer than Rorty anticipated. See Rorty's claim that "Nobody likes either human or divine tyrants. But the specifically Kantian sense of autonomy—having one's moral decisions made by reason rather than by anything capable of being influenced by experience—is quite a different matter." See footnote 4 in this chapter and Richard Rorty, "Kant vs. Dewey: The Current Situation of Moral Philosophy," in *Philosophy as Cultural Politics: Philosophical Papers* (Cambridge: Cambridge University Press, 2007), 4: 187–88.
40. Levinas, "Philosophy and the Idea of Infinity," 115.
41. Donald Davidson, "On the Very Idea of a Conceptual Scheme," *Proceedings and Addresses of the American Philosophical Association* 47 (1973): 198; emphasis added.

As a caveat, it might be noted, of course, that properly interpreting someone else "necessarily invests the person interpreted with basic rationality."[42] According to Davidson, such a basic rationality rests on two principles: the principle of coherence and the principle of correspondence (and taking these together, we might term the two simply the "principle of charity"). The former requires that a level of internal, logical consistency of beliefs is attributed to any speaker. The latter requires that the speaker is responding to the same world as I am. What falls under either principle—what is coherence or correspondence—is not determined a priori, in advance. Together, as the principle of charity, there just "are many ways of assigning our own sentences to the sentences and thoughts of someone else that capture everything of significance."[43] Inherent in such procedures is therefore a sense of indeterminacy,[44] which exactly drives conversation and understanding.[45] Or we might say simply that "understanding is a matter of degree: others may know things we do not, *or even perhaps cannot*. What is certain is that the clarity and effectiveness of our concepts grows with the growth of our understanding of others. There are no definite limits to how far dialogue can or will take us."[46] And all this is again just a way of reiterating

42. Donald Davidson, "Three Varieties of Knowledge," 211.
43. Ibid., 214.
44. As Davidson explicitly points out in a footnote (ibid., 215), he accepts Quine's thesis of the indeterminacy of translation. See Quine's classic "gavagai" example in William Van Orman Quine, *Word and Object* (Cambridge, MA: MIT Press, 1960).
45. It should be noted that Levinas also subscribes to this thesis. See especially Emmanuel Levinas, *Otherwise Than Being; or, Beyond Essence*, trans. Alphonso Lingis (Dordrecht, Neth.: Kluwer, 1991), 49–50. For a discussion of Levinas and Quine on this point, see Aryeh Botwinick, "Emmanuel Levinas's *Otherwise Than Being*, the Phenomenology Project, and Skepticism," *Telos* 2006, no. 134 (2006): 107–8.
46. Donald Davidson, "Three Varieties of Knowledge," 219; emphasis added. I here only want to suggest that the principle of charity does not require a *preestablished* universal reason that is somehow already out there to be grasped (the position Levinas opposes). I don't believe either

that the "truth of sentences remains relative to language, but that is as objective as can be."[47]

If conversation and an other are central to rationality, and therefore to having a self and world, then the ethical realm—initially understood as the relationship between Self and Other—emerges as a site of further investigation. One way really to bring the point into focus is to note that in order for me to be a linguistic agent, I must see myself as being a master of language (with both the positive and negative connotations of that term, even to the point of violence—more on this shortly). At the same time, because I am never the sole arbiter in discourse, the Other also is such a master; the possibility of disagreement now clearly comes into focus as a locus for investigation. This is a point another twentieth-century philosopher of language, Stanley Cavell, captures well when he notes that if there is disagreement about something, and "if the disagreement persists, there is no appeal beyond us, or if beyond us two, then not beyond some eventual us."[48] In Levinas's words, language both "announces a society" and "permits the maintenance of a separated I."[49]

Because we are each masters of language, and because no one more than anyone else (at least not in the sense of having any inherent authority), our learning in language is never over. Cavell presents this aspect of language in dramatic terms when he writes,

> If what can be said in a language is not everywhere determined by rules, nor its understanding anywhere secured

---

thinker is opposed to universal reason as such (say, as an achievement). A relevant idea here is Ian Hacking's notion of "styles of reasoning" (Ian Hacking, *Historical Ontology* [Cambridge, MA: Harvard University Press, 2004], 159–99).

47. Donald Davidson, "On the Very Idea," 198.

48. Stanley Cavell, *The Claim of Reason: Wittgenstein, Skepticism, Morality, and Tragedy* (Oxford: Oxford University Press, 1979), 19.

49. Levinas, *Totality and Infinity*, 68.

through universals, and if there are always new contexts to be met, new needs, new relationships, new objects, new perceptions to be recorded and shared, then perhaps it is as true of a master of a language as of his apprentice that though "in a sense" we learn the meaning of words and what objects are, the learning is never over, and we keep finding new potencies in words and new ways in which objects are disclosed.[50]

A noteworthy part of having such authority, and part of being a master of language, is possessing the ability to put words to new uses. Cavell terms this ability "word projection."[51] To illustrate the phenomenon, we might think of a simple expression like "give me the rock." The range of things this utterance might signify is vast—whether in the context of the drug trade (crack cocaine), the context of sports (basketball or football), the context of romance (engagement ring), the context of geology (the stone), or other contexts beyond (say, a rock and roll concert or murder or a variety of as yet unimagined contexts). It just is the case that words can perpetually be projected into novel contexts. Remarkably, such projections, even though they might be entirely novel, appear to be understood and (often easily) understandable by others. In this way, "learning is never over, and we keep finding new potencies in words and new ways in which objects are disclosed."[52]

Possibilities for word projection, however, are not infinite. As Cavell points out, "what will *count* as a legitimate projection is deeply controlled. . . . An object or activity or event onto or into which a concept is projected, must *invite* or *allow* that projection."[53] Projections are possible by virtue of being initiated into a particular form of life: "you cannot

50. Cavell, *Claim of Reason*, 180.
51. Davidson also spends some time discussing this phenomenon; see Davidson's discussion of malapropism in D. Davidson, "Nice Derangement of Epitaphs."
52. Cavell, *Claim of Reason*, 180.
53. Ibid., 183.

use words to do what we do with them until you are initiate of the forms of life which gives those words the point and shape they have in our lives."[54] Initiation is not simply learning the meanings of words,[55] but rather learning the complex "background" that allows for those words.[56] I quote Cavell at length here:

> When you say "I love my love" the child learns the meaning of the word "love" and what love is. *That (what you do)* will *be* love in the child's world; and if it is mixed with resentment and intimidation, then love is a mixture of resentment and intimidation, and when love is sought *that* will be sought. When you say "I'll take you tomorrow, I promise," the child begins to learn what temporal durations are, and what *trust* is, and what you do will show what trust is worth. When you say "Put on your sweater," the child learns what commands are and what *authority* is, and if giving orders is something that creates anxiety for you, then authorities are anxious, authority itself uncertain. Of course, the person, growing, will learn other things about these concepts and "objects" also. They will grow gradually as the child's world grows. But all he or she knows about them is what he or she has learned and *all* they have learned will be part of what they are. And what will the day be like when the person "realizes" what he "believed" about what love and trust and authority are? And how will he stop believing it? What we learn is not just what we have studied; and what we have been taught is not just what we were intended to learn. What we have in our memories is not just what we have memorized.[57]

---

54. Ibid., 184.

55. As in way in which Augustine is presented in the opening of Ludwig Wittgenstein, *Philosophical Investigations*, trans. G. E. M. Anscombe (Upper Saddle River, NJ: Prentice Hall, 1958).

56. For a very different reading of the idea of this background than I am about to give, see John Searle, *The Construction of Social Reality* (New York: Free Press, 1995), 127–49.

57. Cavell, *Claim of Reason*, 177.

What is true of children is true also of adults—learning is never over. Language forms an inheritance, continually subject to interpretation, and therefore to (re)inheritance and (re)interpretation, time and time again. Which is why Levinas is led to frame the encounter with the Other in terms of teaching.[58] He claims that "the relation with the Other, or Conversation . . . is a teaching (*enseignement*)."[59] Being initiated into speech is being initiated into a world, and vice versa. Levinas puts all this forcefully as the idea that "speech is thus the origin of all signification—of tools and all human works—for through it the referential system from which every signification arises receives the very principle of its functioning, its key . . . speech first founds community by *giving*."[60] But neither language nor being initiated into language can be understood simply as the transfer of information. Cavell, in a famous and oft-cited passage, puts the point as follows:

> We learn and teach words in certain contexts, and then we are expected and expect others, to be able to project them in further contexts. Nothing insures that this projection will take place (in particular, not the grasping of universals nor the grasping of books of rules), just as nothing insures that we will make, and understand, the same projections. That on the whole we do is a matter of our sharing routes of interest and feeling, modes of response, senses of humor and of significance and of fulfillment, of what is outrageous, of what is similar to what else, what a rebuke, what forgiveness, of when an utterance is an assertion, when an appeal, when an explanation—all the whirl of organism Wittgenstein calls "forms of life." Human speech

---

58. Two excellent discussions of Levinas and teaching and education are Anna Strhan, *Levinas, Subjectivity, Education: Towards an Ethics of Radical Responsibility* (London: Blackwell, 2012); Sharon Todd, *Learning from the Other: Levinas, Psychoanalysis, and Ethical Possibilities in Education* (Buffalo, NY: SUNY Press, 2003). See also Claire Katz, *Levinas and the Crisis of Humanism* (Bloomington: Indiana University Press, 2012).
59. Levinas, *Totality and Infinity*, 51.
60. Ibid., 98.

and activity, sanity and community, rest upon nothing, but nothing less, than this. It is a vision as simple as it is difficult, and as difficult as it is (and because it is) terrifying.[61]

Scenes of instruction might end in uncertainty; this just is the nature of language and the human relationship(s) on which it rests. Always there is a possible worry about whether teacher and student "will [be able to] go on together."[62] Any "authority in these matters of grounding is based on nothing substantive in me, nothing particular about me.... There is no fact about me that constitutes the justification of what I say and do over against what the other, say the child, says and does."[63] Any linguistic agent, then, is a master of language,[64]

---

61. Stanley Cavell, "The Availability of Wittgenstein's Later Philosophy," in *Must We Mean What We Say?* (Cambridge, MA: Harvard University Press, 2002), 52.

62. Cavell, *Conditions Handsome and Unhandsome* (Chicago: University of Chicago Press, 1990), 76.

63. Ibid. As seen earlier, this doesn't mean a rejection of the notion of "truth." The point is that what counts or might come to count as true is itself part of the conversation.

64. Much more can be said here about the sort of naturalism that is or is not shared between Cavell and Levinas. For example, it might be objected that Levinas would oppose any such naturalism, because (1) not only would such naturalism imply a determinism in tension with the account I've sketched here, but also that (2) such a naturalism threatens to undermine the priority of the Other. Mixed in with these concerns are also more complex exegetical concerns about the relationship between teaching, fecundity, and paternity and the relationship between these and the encounter with the Other. On this latter point, an excellent discussion is Claire Katz, "Turning toward the Other: Ethics, Fecundity, and the Primacy of Education," in *Totality and Infinity at 50*, ed. Diane Perpich and Scott Davidson (Pittsburgh, PA: Duquesne University Press, 2012). On the former point, Cavell is clearly opposed to any sort of naturalistic determinism. As he states, "most people do descend from apes into authorities, but it is not inevitable" (*Claim of Reason*, 178). As Cavell's discussion shows, such initiation is natural to the extent that it requires nothing more than the natural, but this doesn't mean that it's inevitable or determined. For an excellent discussion of Levinas and Wittgenstein on the point of naturalism, see Bob Plant, *Wittgenstein and Levinas: Ethical and Religious Thought* (London: Routledge, 2005), 148–80.

but such mastery, especially in its importance to both agreement and disagreement, raises fundamental questions about how to understand community. As Cavell highlights, if all linguistic agents are masters, and if so frequently there is agreement in conversation, then "the feeling that the fact of language is like a miracle" might arise.[65]

§ 3. *Expression and Others, and the Possibility of Violence*

Earlier I noted that the idea of being a master invokes also far more vicious possibilities than teaching. It is important to understand that the possibility of violence is also inherent in being a linguistic agent, and that, shockingly, it is exactly this fact that underlines the ethical import of being a linguistic agent. To begin to develop this point, note how Cavell broaches the relationship between community, reason, and language. He claims that our linguistic claims, as Levinas already noted, are claims to and for reason. (At the most extreme point, we might be said to be trying to establish potentially universal reason.) Such claims, then, ought to be equally well understood as claims to community. Cavell writes, "I do not know in advance how deep my agreement with myself is, how far responsibility for the language may run. But if I am to have my own voice in it, I must be speaking for others and allow others to speak for me. The alternative to speaking for myself representatively (for *someone* else's consent) is not: speaking for myself privately. The alternative is having nothing to say, being voiceless, not even mute."[66] A claim is always my claim for and to another. For this reason, it is impossible to develop a language that would

---

65. Stanley Cavell, "What Is the Scandal of Skepticism?," in *Philosophy the Day after Tomorrow* (Cambridge, MA: Harvard University Press, 2005), 139.
66. Cavell, *Claim of Reason*, 28.

be entirely private, for *any* language, even one that hasn't yet been learned by anyone else, must be—because dependent on a public world and a potential Other—one that is *capable* of being learned by someone else (the suggestion is importantly not that one *couldn't* invent a language others wouldn't know but that one couldn't invent a language that others could *never* know, and this again, because of any language's dependence on self, world, and other in equal parts).[67] Any claim is a claim to community. We speak for others, but also for ourselves, amid others.[68] As Cavell puts it, "the philosophical appeal to what we say, and the search for our criteria on the basis of which we say what we say, are claims to community." In turn, the "wish and search for community are the wish and search for reason."[69]

Language is such that claims do not exist in a vacuum; claims are always interpreted by others as much as by me amid others. In speaking, I might come to speak for others. Similarly, when others speak, their speech is expressive. I cannot but take stock of it (even if only to ignore it or reject it or oppose it). Levinas captures this point when he compares language to a battering ram.[70] One of Wittgenstein's students, Rush Rhees, once called it a grappling iron.[71] Exactly because it is expressive, language *gets through to*

---

67. For Cavell's rejection of the private language argument, see Hilary Putnam, "Philosophy as the Education of Grownups: Stanley Cavell and Skepticism," in *Reading Cavell*, ed. Alice Crary and Sanford Shieh (London: Routledge, 2006). For Levinas's rejection of the private-language argument, see Adriaan Peperzak, *Beyond: The Philosophy of Emmanuel Levinas* (Evanston, IL: Northwestern University Press, 1997), 62.

68. For more on this, see Richard Eldridge, "The Normal and the Normative: Wittgenstein's Legacy, Kripke, and Cavell," *Philosophy and Phenomenological Research* 46, no. 4 (1986): 571.

69. Cavell, *Claim of Reason*, 20.

70. Levinas, "Language and Proximity," 122.

71. Rush Rhees, "What Is Language?," in *Wittgenstein and the Possibility of Discourse*, ed. D. Z. Phillips (Cambridge: Cambridge University Press, 1998), 27.

others: sometimes whether it is desired or desirable to do so. Levinas and Cavell both stress that language is expressive.[72] Through words, agents express themselves. The difference between being a subject and being an object is categorical and insurmountable. To speak with Levinas, the face of a subject expresses itself—it has its own "light," whereas "objects have no light of their own; they receive a borrowed light."[73] In other words, a subject is significant in and of herself, but an object gains significance generally through subjects (when, say, we place them into a web of signification; the same, of course, is true of subjects, but the crucial point is that any subject can always oppose such placement, even to the point of death). Levinas and Cavell (through his reading of the philosopher Ludwig Wittgenstein),[74] stress this fact of expressivity.[75] Some typical formulations include the following:

72. This is central to their rejection of what has come to be termed the private-language argument. For Cavell, the locus of discussion on this point is Wittgenstein. With Wittgenstein, there is some debate about where the private-language argument explicitly occurs. I agree with Kripke that it occurs as early as §202 and as late as §265 in Wittgenstein, *Philosophical Investigations*. On this point, see Saul Kripke, *Wittgenstein on Rules and Private Language* (Cambridge, MA: Harvard University Press, 1982), 3. The bulk of Cavell's discussion of the argument occurs at *Claim of Reason*, 343–54. For a discussion of the private-language argument in a context similar to mine, and also with Levinas in mind, see Søren Overgaard, *Wittgenstein and Other Minds: Rethinking Subjectivity and Intersubjectivity with Wittgenstein, Levinas, and Husserl* (London: Routledge, 2007), 63–82.

73. Levinas, *Totality and Infinity*, 74. Compare with Wittgenstein's suggestion of the impossibility of looking at a stone and imagining it as having sensations in Wittgenstein, *Philosophical Investigations*, §284.

74. Throughout, my elaborations of Wittgenstein's thought can be read as shorthand for Cavell's Wittgenstein—due to restrictions of space, I am not here able to defend this reading of Wittgenstein in the context of other readings in any robust sense.

75. On this comparison to Wittgenstein, I am indebted to Søren Overgaard, "Rethinking Other Minds: Wittgenstein and Levinas on Expression," *Inquiry* 48, no. 3 (2005): 249–74; Overgaard, "The Problem of Other Minds: Wittgenstein's Phenomenological Perspective," *Phenomenology*

> The face of the Other at each moment destroys and overflows the plastic image it leaves me, the idea existing to my own measure and to the measure of its *ideatum*—the adequate idea. It does not manifest itself by these qualities . . . it *expresses itself.*[76]

> The light in other people's faces. Do you look into *yourself* in order to recognize the fury in *his* face? It is there as clearly as in your own breast.[77]

> In general I do not surmise fear in him—I *see* it. I do not feel that I am deducing the probable existence of something inside from something outside; rather it is as if the human face were in a way translucent and that I were seeing it not in reflected light but rather in its own.[78]

> The human body is the best picture of the human soul—not, I feel like adding, primarily because it represents the soul but because it expresses it.[79]

In a slight modification of the existentialist philosopher Jean-Paul Sartre's point about freedom, we might say we are doomed to expressiveness. Furthermore, in understanding someone, we are not discovering some private, already existent inner state, but rather interpreting, from a shared linguistic source, the expression(s) of another subject.

Cavell notes that such expressivity presents the perpetual temptation of a fantasy of inexpressiveness; the first-person perspective makes this fantasy most apparent. Conceiving

---

and the Cognitive Sciences 5, no. 1 (2006): 53–73. He initially drew my attention to the similarities and especially to some of the passages I am about to reference. Although Overgaard makes no reference to Cavell, I think it will be obvious how Cavell's thought naturally fits here.

76. Levinas, *Totality and Infinity*, 51.

77. Ludwig Wittgenstein, *Zettel*, ed. G. E. M. Anscombe and Georg Henrik von Wright, trans. G. E. M. Anscombe (Berkeley: University of California Press, 1967), §220.

78. Ludwig Wittgenstein, *Remarks on the Philosophy of Psychology*, 2 vols. (Chicago: University of Chicago Press, 1988), 2: §170.

79. Cavell, *Claim of Reason*, 356.

of my inner life as somehow radically private—as forever inaccessible to others—appears really to guarantee that my inner life is therefore perpetually available to me. And the same is true if I substitute another for myself; in that case, the fantasy is meant to guarantee that the Other is forever inaccessible to me. In either case, the fantastical desire is to avoid interpretation, whether of my own (complex) inner life or of the (equally complex) inner life of someone else. Pursuing such a fantasy is to avoid acknowledging the lack of transparency in either realm, and the importance of interpretation in each; we are through and through linguistic creatures, whether speaking solely to someone else or to ourselves. What such a fantasy ultimately aims to do is to soothe the pressure of being such a linguistic agent (of being ourselves only among others): with every word, every bit of discourse and language, there are potential tensions and points of disagreement, if not outright rejection. We can and often do fail to connect, sometimes even with ourselves, and do so often in dangerous or disturbing ways. Nothing is guaranteed, not with me or with someone else, for discourse saturates everything.

The very distinction between inner and outer, between what's public and what's private, does not operate in the way in which this fantasy suggests.[80] My inner life is, in many respects, what it is by virtue of the particular stance I have or have not taken toward it. Our inner lives are an achievement, not a given.[81] The fantasy, Cavell claims, is not "skeptical *enough*: the Other is still left, along with his knowledge of himself: so am I, with mine."[82] Levinas makes this same point about an inner life, when he points out that "the primordial

80. See Terry Pinkard, "Innen, Aussen und Lebensformen: Hegel und Wittgenstein," in *Hegels Erbe*, 254–92 (Frankfurt: Suhrkamp, 2004).

81. In Richard Moran's words, I "avow" attitudes, I do not merely discover them (Moran, *Authority and Estrangement: An Essay on Self-Knowledge* [Princeton, NJ: Princeton University Press, 2001]).

82. Cavell, *Claim of Reason*, 353.

essence of expression and discourse does not reside in the information they would supply concerning an interior and hidden world."[83] Much more might be said here about the sort of psychoanalytic commitments that are emerging. What is central to my purposes, however, is just the relatively basic point—inherent in any understanding of psychoanalysis—that interpretation is a central feature of our lives.[84] Whether I acknowledge it or not, I may be an angry person, but whether and how I acknowledge it also makes me something else: perhaps an angry person and a repentant or remorseful one, or an angry person and a self-loathing or destructive one. This is even more the case when we interpret others; expression—whether my own or someone else's—always requires interpretation, and neither such expression nor such interpretation occurs merely or wholly in public or in private, rather it perpetually moves between the two. Cavell stresses the importance of interpretation in a powerful way when he notes that "the wish underlying this fantasy covers a wish ... for the connection between my claims of knowledge and the objects upon which the claims are to fall to occur without my intervention, apart from my agreements [i.e., apart from interpretation]," something that Cavell ultimately and rightly notes is "unappeasable."[85]

My knowledge of the world—of others as much as of myself—occurs in the context of discourse. Discourse is always public; I may have private thoughts, but there is nothing in those thoughts that makes them potentially inaccessible to others, except my refusing the Other access (and likewise for anyone else's private thoughts). Interpretation

---

83. Levinas, *Totality and Infinity*, 200.
84. The centrality of psychoanalysis for the conception of language being developed here is captured compactly and well in Andrew Norris, *Becoming Who We Are: Politics and Practical Philosophy in the Work of Stanley Cavell* (Oxford: Oxford University Press, 2017), 44–47.
85. Cavell, *Claim of Reason*, 352.

implies authority, even if only for myself.[86] The fantasy of inexpressiveness is the fantasy of complete transparency. It is the wish to see everything as determined immediately, without interpretation.[87] And it is therefore an abdication of our powers as agents and of our world as one constituted by agents. Such a fantasy trades on the idea that uncertainty in one area necessitates or arises only because of certainty in another (the certainty of an inner life requires an uncertainty about the lives of others, or vice versa). The fantasy, in short, assumes that there are areas of our life that might not be subject to interpretation, that could somehow be immediately or baldly read by, say, an omniscient (and perhaps thereby omnipotent) observer.[88] In stressing the importance of interpretation, certainty is not thereby refused, rather it—as reason was seen to be earlier—is understood as an achievement, and one not arrived at simply by some fact about our epistemic access, about the immediacy of that certainty.[89]

Cavell's elaboration on the fantasy of inexpressiveness refers again to the importance of Levinas's distinction between totality and infinity. When Levinas speaks of everything being "reunited under one gaze,"[90] the fantasy of inexpressiveness captures elements of Levinas's worry: he is explicitly setting infinity against any stance that would understand human existence and our being in the world in

86. Ibid., 383.
87. In this way, there is here also an argument against "the given," but pursued along different lines than in, say, Wilfrid Sellars, *Empiricism and the Philosophy of Mind* (Cambridge: Cambridge University Press, 1997).
88. An option that is in fact impossible because such inner lives are fundamentally *relational*, exist only in relation to someone else or between myself and myself. For more on this point, see Shuster, "Nothing to Know: The Epistemology of Moral Perfectionism in Adorno and Cavell," *Idealistic Studies* 44, no. 1 (2015): 1–29.
89. In opposition to this, I think both Cavell and Levinas propose what's been termed an "ethics of suspicion." See Robert Bernasconi, "The Ethics of Suspicion," *Research in Phenomenology* 20 (1990): 3–18.
90. Levinas, *Totality and Infinity*, 36.

static terms, where the Other "would vanish at the end of [such a] history."[91] It is striking that both Cavell and Levinas understand such a fantasy as expressing a fundamental isolation.[92] As noted already in the introduction, the importance of interpretation is already present in Levinas's earliest writings, especially, for example, in "The Philosophy of Hitlerism" (1934).[93] There, Levinas is suspicious of any philosophy that immediately accords "a feeling of identity between our bodies and ourselves."[94] In that essay,[95] Levinas already suggests that even when we start with the identity of "our bodies and ourselves," we will already discover, "in the depths of this unity, the duality of a free spirit that struggles against the body to which it is chained."[96] Where, in this early essay, Levinas locates the potential disjunction between self and body and self and world in the ordeal of pain and the recognition of a bodily self that lags behind, Levinas later, like Cavell, locates this potential disjunction in the fact of expression, in my experience with an Other. Interpretation, expression, and the encounter with the Other

---

91. Ibid., 52.

92. Emmanuel Levinas, *Ethics and Infinity*, trans. Richard A. Cohen (Pittsburgh, PA: Duquesne University Press, 1985), 58.

93. A related objection might be that this post–World War II context is foreign to Cavell's work. For an argument against this point, see Martin Shuster, "Language and Loneliness: Arendt, Cavell, and Modernity," *International Journal of Philosophical Studies* 20, no. 4 (2012): 473–97; Shuster, *Autonomy after Auschwitz: Adorno, German Idealism, and Modernity* (Chicago: University of Chicago Press, 2014). In this context, see also Cavell's remark that "we have in some way to miss the particular experience of Nazism in order to go on with our lives" in Stanley Cavell, *Little Did I Know: Excerpts from Memory* (Stanford, CA: Stanford University Press, 2010), 61.

94. Levinas and Hand, "Reflections on the Philosophy of Hitlerism," *Critical Inquiry* 17, no. 1 (1990): 68.

95. The problem of this essay is one that Levinas carries well into his mature work. On this point, see Robert Bernasconi, "No Exit: Levinas' Aporetic Account of Transcendence," *Research in Phenomenology* 35, no. 1 (2005): 101–17.

96. Levinas and Hand, "Reflections on the Philosophy of Hitlerism," 68.

reveal a "rebellion or refusal to remain" within the bounds of the fantasy of transparency. Interpretation presupposes the Other, and the standing possibility of disunity, both from the Other and possibly even from myself. As Levinas simply puts it: "the social is beyond ontology."[97]

Our social realm is therefore an achievement. To be a user of language is always to recognize that my use of language may isolate me: discourse never guarantees community but only makes it possible. Our claim may isolate us, and my words might never reach anyone, if there is simply no one to be reached by my claims, by *these* claims. In such a case, it is not that consensus is not reached (as if all it needed was a little more work), but rather that it may be impossible to speak of a consensus between *us*; there just is no us. We simply do not—and may never—speak for each other. Cavell highlights such a possibility when he labels the potential persistence of disagreement an "intellectual tragedy." He writes, "The only source of confirmation here is ourselves. And each of us is fully authoritative in this struggle. . . . But if the disagreement persists, there is no appeal beyond us, or if beyond us two, then not beyond some eventual us. There is such a thing as intellectual tragedy. It is not a matter of saying something false. Nor is it an inability or refusal to say something or to hear something from which other tragedies may spring."[98] Part of the power of language is that there is never a guarantee of agreement. As Cavell highlights, we might rebuke someone, or be rebuked. In many such cases, matters are not to be settled by reference to truth or falsity, because the Other "hasn't said something false about 'us'; he has learned that there is no us (yet, maybe never) to say anything about. What is wrong with his statement is that he made it to the wrong party."[99]

97. Levinas, *Ethics and Infinity*, 58.
98. Cavell, *Claim of Reason*, 19–20.
99. Ibid., 20.

Our interactions can always come to an end; we just might not be able to go on together. Following one of Wittgenstein's images, we might describe the situation as us having reached bedrock during digging, where the gesture between us is one of turning one's spade and saying, "This is simply what I do." In doing so, I "cannot then say I am right."[100] To do so would be to initiate a "violence" that would seek "to represent a community that does not exist."[101] One deep consequence of the philosophy of language that's emerged here is that the notion of truth, central to any language, is no guarantee of agreement (about what's true or about anything else). And it is this possibility—the perpetual possibility of disagreement—that ought to be understood as the most basic ethical problem. With Cavell, we might say that I may "already know everything skepticism concludes" while realizing that "my ignorance of the existence of others is not the fate of my natural condition as a human knower, but *my way of inhabiting that condition.*"[102]

§ 4. Ethics, Knowledge, and Acknowledgment

To really bring into focus the extent to which language is saturated by a basic ethical concern, let me turn for a moment to an issue that Davidson recognizes but ultimately ignores in his philosophy of language. He writes that "before anyone can speak a language, there must be another creature interacting with the speaker. Of course this cannot be enough, since mere interaction *does not show how* the interaction *matters* to the creatures involved."[103] This remark is notoriously suggestive. What does it mean for an interaction

---

100. Cavell, *Conditions Handsome and Unhandsome*, 95–96.
101. Ibid.
102. Cavell, *Claim of Reason*, 432; emphasis added.
103. Donald Davidson, "The Second Person," in *Subjective, Intersubjective, Objective* (Oxford, UK: Clarendon, 2001), 120; emphasis added.

to *matter*? Could I not interact with others—make claims, respond to them, and so forth, and all about a common world—even as I take others simply not to matter? In fact, isn't one of the ills of the contemporary world that we do this day in and day out (usually attached to our smartphones) as we go about the various tasks that late capitalism proposes for us? What Davidson ignores except in this passing remark is the basic fact that discourse is not an end in itself, but rather the relationship that animates it or makes it possible or visible is the end; that end is precarious, indeed may even remain unachieved. Philosophers have termed this problem a skeptical problem: a skepticism about other minds. Even as we may converse with others, we may fundamentally fail to acknowledge their humanity, seeing them formally as no different from "automata, zombies, [or] androids."[104] Cavell comes to call such events skeptical "recitals," which is meant to emphasize their formalized nature, where there are distinct, formal ways of failing to acknowledge another; such recitals are an instantiation both of our metaphysical condition (the fact of our separation) and of the "practical difficulty ... of coming to know another person, and how little we can reveal of ourselves to another's gaze, or bear of it."[105] Wittgenstein describes an analogous situation where he imagines seeing nearby children as automata. He points out that such an example produces in us "some kind of uncanny feeling."[106] What Cavell, Wittgenstein, and Levinas all stress, however, is that life often just *is* uncanny; such is our condition, our fate.

Unlike Davidson, Cavell and Levinas see how and whether interactions come to matter (or fail to do so) as an urgent philosophical issue. (This is so much the case that Levinas calls

104. Cavell, *Claim of Reason*, 425.
105. Ibid., 90.
106. Wittgenstein, *Philosophical Investigations*, §420.

ethics in this register "first philosophy.") In understanding the possibility of isolation as a basic feature of being a user of language,[107] Cavell emphasizes the extent to which such isolation is not a failure of knowledge, but rather a failure of acknowledgment. The skeptical problem of other minds is not a problem of knowledge therefore, so much so that Cavell notes that "skepticism concerning other minds is not a skepticism but a tragedy."[108] While this point receives its sharpest elaboration in Cavell's Shakespeare writings,[109] it can provisionally be developed here as a point about our relations to ourselves and to others. Skepticism occurs with "the insinuation of absence, of a line, or limitation."[110] Such limits do not, however, reveal the absence of something, a lack of knowledge, but rather the presence of something, a particular way we have comported ourselves toward the Other.

In suggesting that the Other might fail to matter (or register) because of the limits of acknowledgment as opposed to knowledge, Cavell's suggestion is that the question of our relationship to others is not to be solved through knowledge. When I have taken a particular stance toward the Other, I will not be swayed by some knowledge claim about them. ("Look, he's a Jew and *not* vermin!" or "He is a human, and not an ape" or "She is not up to something.") It is in this tenor that we should understand Cavell's various analyses of Shakespearean tragedy: it is not that characters such as Othello and Lear illustrate a failure to recognize certain

107. For Levinas's notion of separation, see footnote 20 in this chapter and the surrounding discussion and also Elif Çirakman, "Levinas' Disruptive Imagination: Time, Self and the Other," *Analecta Husserliana* 83 (2004): 100. Probably the most forceful argument for the importance of separation for Levinas is Leora Batnitzky, "Encountering the Modern Subject in Levinas," *Yale French Studies*, no. 104 (2004): 6–21.

108. Cavell, *Claim of Reason*, xxiii.

109. See Stanley Cavell, *Disowning Knowledge in Seven Plays of Shakespeare* (Cambridge: Cambridge University Press, 2003).

110. Stanley Cavell, *In Quest of the Ordinary: Lines of Skepticism and Romanticism* (Chicago: University of Chicago Press, 1994), 51.

cognitive limits, perhaps demanding knowledge where none can be had, but rather that they fail to acknowledge particular individuals, justifying the actions that go with such a failure in intellectual terms. It is also for this reason that neither Cavell nor Levinas engages in any serious fashion with the more traditional way in which the problem of other minds might be conceived as a merely epistemological problem of knowledge (as in scenarios involving brains in vats or philosophical zombies).[111] To speak of minds, as opposed to others—*other people*—is already to reveal a particular orientation toward the Other (one that implies a potentially dangerous abstraction). As Cavell puts the point:

> If one says that this is a *failure* to acknowledge another's suffering, surely this would not mean that we fail, in such cases, to *know* that he is suffering? It may or it may not. The point, however, is that the concept of acknowledgment is evidenced equally by its failure as by its success. It is not a description of a given response but a category in terms of which a given response is evaluated. (It is the sort of concept Heidegger calls *existentiale*.) A "failure to know" might just mean a piece of ignorance, an absence of something, a blank. A "failure to acknowledge" is the presence of something, a confusion, an indifference, a callousness, an exhaustion, a coldness.[112]

In another context, Cavell makes the same point by suggesting that "if something separates us, comes between us, that

---

111. David J. Chalmers, *The Conscious Mind: In Search of a Fundamental Theory* (Oxford: Oxford University Press, 1996); Hilary Putnam, *Reason, Truth and History* (Cambridge: Cambridge University Press, 1981), 1–22.

112. Stanley Cavell, "Knowing and Acknowledging," in *Must We Mean What We Say?* (Cambridge, MA: Harvard University Press, 2002), 263–64. I take Marie McGinn's otherwise excellent article to misrepresent Cavell on this point. McGinn seems to miss the ethical as opposed to metaphysical nature of Cavell's claims. See Marie McGinn, "The Real Problem of Others: Cavell, Merleau-Ponty and Wittgenstein on Scepticism about Other Minds," *European Journal of Philosophy* 6, no. 1 (1998): 45–58.

can only be a particular aspect or stance of the mind itself, a particular *way* in which we relate, or are related (by birth, by law, by force, in love) to one another—our positions, our attitudes, with reference to one another. Call this our history. It is our present."[113]

Levinas pursues a related position in *Totality and Infinity* when he claims that "the expression the face introduces into the world does not defy the feebleness of my power, but my power for power (*mon pouvoir de pouvoir*)."[114] Because the Other can always contest my knowledge—indeed can ultimately contest even the *existence* of any "us" whatsoever. Our relation is not determined by the possession or lack of possession of some knowledge between us. This is why Levinas notes that the Other disrupts my "power for power." Even if I imagine that the Other might be unable to resist the force of my might, the Other can always cancel this might or force; indeed, the Other can cancel *any* of my possible power by rejecting every justification of such power or might. Even if the Other is subjected to murder, that murder can never compel agreement about the murder, its justness, or our relationship. When it comes to the perspective of the Other, that perspective is irreducible to mine, and I am wholly powerless (and this remains true even with the possibility of a variety of methods of persuasion, bloody and otherwise). The Other is never "grasped" conceptually (understood) without allowing herself or himself to be grasped (that is, by playing a part in that understanding). Any account involving the Other is always a *relational* account consisting of more than my understanding of the Other; it is not entirely up to me (the German context

---

113. Cavell, *Claim of Reason*, 369.
114. Levinas, *Totality and Infinity*, 198; translation modified. In a different context, both Gerald Bruns and James Conant have also drawn such a connection. See Gerald L. Bruns, "Stanley Cavell's Shakespeare," *Critical Inquiry* 16, no. 3 (1990): 620; James Conant, "On Bruns, on Cavell," *Critical Inquiry* 17, no. 3 (1991): 629.

is again instructive, with the relationship between "*greifen*" and "*begreifen*," grasping and knowing).[115] The "problem" of my relationship with an Other is not a problem of knowledge. And the *question* of my relationship with another (of how I take the Other) could never be settled by more knowledge (Cavell) or more power (Levinas).

Levinas makes this point in a variety of places, but one of the most suggestive occurs in a late essay for the Belgian philosopher and psychoanalyst, Alphonse de Waelhens, called simply "In Memory of Alphonse de Waelhens" (1984).[116] There, discussing the phenomenology of Maurice Merleau-Ponty, Levinas suggests that Merleau-Ponty remains wed to a model of intersubjectivity conceived as a species of knowledge. This leads Levinas to ask whether intersubjectivity is based simply on "a 'taking cognizance,' and a sort of coinciding of two thoughts in the mutual knowledge of one by the other."[117]

---

115. See Levinas, *Totality and Infinity*, 198. See also Shuster, "Nothing to Know."

116. There is much more that can be said about de Waelhens and Levinas (and Cavell, for that matter). Levinas also invokes de Waelhens at *Otherwise Than Being*, 120, where he speaks of the ethical relationship being a "non-philosophical experience." In de Waelhens's own *La philosophie et les expériences naturelles* (1961), there is a demarcation between philosophy and nonphilosophical experience that may profitably be put into conversation with the distinction between the ordinary/everyday and philosophy in Cavell. So much so that de Waelhens often writes things like "The world, as constitutive of the non-philosophical experience which philosophy must define, achieves its meaning in language—not explicitly philosophical—but from which philosophical language is inseparable, because man is inseparable from such language, since man *is* language" and "Philosophy is reflection on a non-philosophical experience" (Alphonse de Waelhens, *La philosophie et les expériences naturelles* [The Hague: Martinus Nijhoff, 1961]), at 117 and 2, respectively. For a thought about Levinas as a philosopher of the ordinary (without reference to de Waelhens), see Michael Morgan, "Emmanuel Levinas as a Philosopher of the Ordinary," in *Totality and Infinity at 50*, ed. Diane Perpich and Scott Davidson (Pittsburgh, PA: Duquesne University Press, 2012).

117. Emmanuel Levinas, "In Memory of Alphonse de Waelhens," trans. Barbara Harshav and Michael B. Smith, in *Outside the Subject* (Stanford, CA: Stanford University Press, 1994), 111.

Answering negatively, Levinas instead claims that what is crucial is "proximity to one's neighbor."[118] In the course of discussion, he suggests that any relation to the Other is about "*attuning oneself to the other*," stressing that we must "conceive of the cognitive accession to the objectivity of the other person on the basis of his or her proximity as neighbor."[119] Talk of proximity here should be understood in light of an earlier Levinas essay, "Language and Proximity," where Levinas proposes a striking picture of language best understood as akin to touch, modeled on direct contact, that is, on proximity (compare this to the suggestion of language as a sort of battering ram noted earlier).[120] Levinas elsewhere wrote that "language is the possibility of entering into relationship independently of every system of signs common to the interlocutors. Like a battering-ram, it is the power to break through the limits of culture, body, and race."[121] Such a formulation might sound peculiar, especially if language is frequently seen exactly as the manifestation of culture. Levinas's point, however, is that (the transmission and maintenance of) culture is not the sole or even main function of language. Instead, in conceiving language on the model of contact, we should understand language as a constitutive element of our world: it literally underwrites what we do and how we do anything, and similarly for what we feel and how we feel. Sharing a language is sharing a world, and neither language nor world is a merely cognitive matter.[122] Both language and world involve saliencies, affordances, paths of action, and lines of exploration and agreements about the possibilities of

118. Ibid.
119. Ibid., 112. The analogy to the idea of attunement (*Übereinstimmung*) in Wittgenstein should not be overlooked. See Cavell, *Claim of Reason*, 32.
120. For a discussion of the evolution of this concept for Levinas, see Craig R. Vasey, "Emmanuel Levinas: From Intentionality to Proximity," *Philosophy Today* 25, no. 3 (1981): 178–95.
121. Levinas, "Language and Proximity," 122.
122. On this point of language being contact, see ibid., 116, 123.

each of them and many more things besides. Language instantiates, maintains, and sometimes disrupts a common world, which is why "our relation to the world as a whole, or to others ... is not one of knowing."[123] When Levinas speaks of proximity, he does not mean "spatial contiguity"[124] but rather aims to indicate the experience of being drawn together to the Other. The Other matters. In this context, compare again with Austin's remark, cited earlier, that "even if some language is now purely descriptive, language was not in origin so, and much of it is still not so."[125] When Levinas stresses that with the Other we have "a relation not with a very great resistance, but with something absolutely *other*: the resistance of what has no resistance—the ethical resistance," he is highlighting that the relation with the Other is fundamentally not one where we might resist or discover something *about* the Other (although these too are possibilities), but rather that in speaking to, with, or even against the Other we are always already related, close, *in proximity* to that Other.[126] Such is the power of language; Levinas's metaphor of a battering ram suggests that language can enter anywhere (everywhere). This relation within and through language—acknowledgment—is "evidenced equally by its failure as by its success."[127]

Knowledge and acknowledgment, grasping and neighboring, reveal two distinct planes or axes. As Levinas puts the point, "the movement of separation [of the I as a distinct Ego that grasps the world] is not on the same plane as

123. Cavell, *Claim of Reason*, 45.
124. Levinas, "Language and Proximity," 116.
125. James Langshaw Austin, "Other Minds," in *Philosophical Papers*, 3rd ed., ed. James Opie Urmson and Geoffrey James Warnock (Oxford: Oxford University Press, 1979), 103.
126. Levinas, *Totality and Infinity*, 199.
127. Cavell, "Knowing and Acknowledging," 263. For a different suggestion that links Cavell with Levinas on acknowledgment, see Simon Critchley, "Cavell's 'Romanticism' and Cavell's Romanticism," in *Contending with Stanley Cavell*, ed. Russel B. Goodman (Oxford: Oxford University Press, 2005), 54.

the movement of transcendence";[128] that is, the face-to-face relationship with the Other. I take Cavell to be suggesting an analogous point when he writes, "We are endlessly separate, for *no* reason. But then we are answerable for everything that comes between us; if not for causing it then for continuing it; if not for denying it then for affirming it; if not for it then to it. The idea of privacy expressed in the fantasy of a private language fails to express how private we are, metaphysically and practically."[129] It is not knowledge that separates me from the Other, but something else. Nor is it the case that more knowledge could bring us together. In language, I am always already beset by others.[130] In being beset, however, there are no guarantees of togetherness—our relations are fragile (and that fragility is what makes relation possible in the first place). In Cavell's words, "we may mistake someone's cares and commitments, or they may suddenly deny us. But what then breaks down is not moral argument but moral *relationship*."[131] In breaking down, however, such relationship does not disappear, no more than a marriage or friendship disappears in the face of an argument, or a deep hatred in the face of momentary cooperation. Proximity and acknowledgment make communication, relationship, and language possible.[132] In short, they make a world.

Part of such a world and its existence and maintenance is the standing possibility of refusal (Cavell) or murder (Levinas). Such possibilities, however, already show the extent to

128. Levinas, *Totality and Infinity*, 148.
129. Cavell, *Claim of Reason*, 369–70.
130. Levinas, "Language and Proximity," 123.
131. Cavell, *Claim of Reason*, 326; emphasis added.
132. This is the answer to the questions raised in Barry Stroud, *Understanding Human Knowledge: Philosophical Essays* (Oxford: Oxford University Press, 2002), 67. Stroud seems to misunderstand the level at which such explanations are pitched. As Cavell suggests, using a distinction of Heidegger's, it is an *existentiale*, as opposed to *existentiell* (the level at which Stroud's questions seem to operate). For more on this distinction, see Heidegger, *Being and Time*, Stambaugh trans., §12.

which the Other always already *matters*. Furthermore, the way in which this world is fashioned and maintained, and the way in which such a world matters, cannot be grounded exclusively in any sort of cognitive relation. As in Adorno and Maimonides, our relationship with the world is instead not one of knowledge: rather, it is at all points dependent on what is better understood as a practical standing toward that world, where that practical standing—either as wonder or moral outrage—is underwritten by an ethical relationship to an other, without which no such world could ever exist.

§ 5. Skepticism in Cavell and Levinas

It is striking how, for both Levinas and Cavell, skepticism emerges as a crucial site for exploring ethics. In *Otherwise Than Being*, Levinas writes that "language is already skepticism,"[133] and in a variety of places Cavell speaks of the "truth of skepticism."[134] Drawing out points of connection between Levinas and Cavell on skepticism offers the opportunity to return to the broader themes of *How to Measure a World?*,

---

133. Levinas, *Otherwise Than Being*, 170. For discussions of Levinas and skepticism, see Scott F. Aikin and J. Aaron Simmons, "Levinasian Otherism, Skepticism, and the Problem of Self-Refutation," *Philosophical Forum* 40, no. 1 (2009): 29–54; Robert Bernasconi, "Skepticism in the Face of Philosophy," in *Re-reading Levinas*, ed. Robert Bernasconi and Simon Critchley, 149–62 (London: Athlone, 1991); Paul Davies, "Asymmetry and Transcendence: On Scepticism and First Philosophy," *Research in Phenomenology* 35, no. 1 (2005): 118–40; Jan de Greef, "Skepticism and Reason," in *Face to Face with Levinas*, ed. Richard A. Cohen, 159–81 (Buffalo: State University of New York Press, 1986). My approach, in broad strokes, is akin to Bernasconi's and de Greef's but agrees with Aikin and Simmons on the crucial point that skepticism is not self-refuting. Although disagreeing with them on a particular point, I take Aikin and Simmons's move of introducing a "trust operator" (50) exactly to parallel the way that I've tried to draw Levinas close to Cavell on the point of acknowledgment. For Cavell on skepticism, see Espen Hammer, *Stanley Cavell: Skepticism, Subjectivity, and the Ordinary* (Cambridge, UK: Polity, 2002), 30–59.
134. Cavell, *Claim of Reason*, 7.

especially the relationship between world and what's beyond the world. Very quickly, Cavell's position might be glossed as the idea that "skepticism with respect to the other is not a generalized *intellectual* lack, but a stance I take in the face of the other's opacity and the demand the other's expression places upon me; I call skepticism my denial or *annihilation* of the other."[135] In this way, "I am the scandal" of skepticism "with respect to the existence of others."[136] Levinas's invocation of skepticism is best understood by registering the shift in Levinas's thinking from *Totality and Infinity* to *Otherwise Than Being*. Much can be said about this shift,[137] to the point even of asking whether there is any shift.[138] Indisputable,

---

135. Cavell, "What Is the Scandal of Skepticism?," 150; emphasis added. This essay is also the only place that Cavell discusses Levinas's work. For discussions of Cavell and Levinas and Cavell's essay, see Hent de Vries, "From 'Ghost in the Machine' to 'Spiritual Automaton': Philosophical Meditation in Wittgenstein, Cavell, and Levinas," *Self and Other: Essays in Continental Philosophy of Religion* 60 (2007): 77–97; Michael Morgan, "Levinas on God and the Trace of the Other," in *The Oxford Handbook of Emmanuel Levinas*, ed. Michael Morgan (Oxford: Oxford University Press, 2019), 321–43. A shorter discussion also occurs in Paul Standish, "Education for Grown-ups, a Religion for Adults: Scepticism and Alterity in Cavell and Levinas," *Ethics and Education* 2, no. 1 (2007): 73–91.

136. Cavell, "What Is the Scandal of Skepticism?," 151. Cavell also explicitly cites Levinas, *Ethics and Infinity*, 8.

137. Invariably, the story must begin with Derrida's lengthy essay about Levinas and *Totality and Infinity*: Jacques Derrida, "Violence and Metaphysics," trans. Alan Bass, in *Writing and Difference* (Baltimore, MD: Johns Hopkins University Press, 1978), 79–154.

138. For an argument that there is no shift, see Batnitzky, "Encountering the Modern Subject." For other discussions on the nature of the shift, I've found useful Robert Bernasconi, "The Alterity of the Stranger and the Experience of the Alien," in *In the Face of the Other and the Trace of God: Essays on the Philosophy of Emmanuel Levinas*, 62–89 (New York: Fordham University Press, 2000); Robert Bernasconi, "What Is the Question to Which 'Substitution' Is the Answer?," in *The Cambridge Companion to Levinas*, ed. Simon Critchley and Robert Bernasconi, 234–51 (Cambridge: Cambridge University Press, 2002); Simon Critchley, *The Ethics of Deconstruction: Derrida and Levinas* (Delhi, India: Motilal Banarsidass, 2007), 4–13, 156–69, 225–37; Adriaan Peperzak, *To the Other: An Introduction to the Philosophy of Emmanuel Levinas* (West Lafayette, IN: Purdue

however, is that Levinas's vocabulary becomes more forceful, invoking, at its most dramatic points, images of "being hostage" to the Other. This change in vocabulary (and any shift that it reveals) is occasioned by Derrida's "Violence and Metaphysics," where, among many other points, Derrida stresses the inherent tension in using language to describe something that appears to be precognitive and prelinguistic (that is, the face-to-face relationship, or, equally, as I've suggested, our acknowledgment of an Other). As Derrida puts it, "by making the origin of language, meaning, and difference the relation to the . . . other, Levinas is resigned to betraying his own intentions in his philosophical discourse."[139]

In response to Derrida, Levinas stresses that even as our relationship to the Other precedes language and is therefore not exclusively cognitive, such a relationship can nonetheless be described through language. In *Otherwise Than Being*, Levinas pursues a distinction between the saying (*le dire*) and the said (*le dit*)[140] in order to achieve such a description. The former designates the (primordial) encounter with the Other and the latter describes that encounter. The two are forever separate. "The saying" is outside the realm of representation and knowledge, outside everything we might term "the said." The encounter with the Other always remains distinct from the description of that encounter. Levinas stresses that "proximity is a difference, a non-coinciding, an arrhythmia in time, a diachrony refractory to thematization, refractory to the reminiscence that synchronizes the phases of a past. The unnarratable other loses his face as a neighbor in

---

University Press, 1993), 209–35; Peperzak, "Beyond Being," *Research in Phenomenology* 8, no. 1 (1978): 239–61; Vasey, "Emmanuel Levinas."

139. Derrida, "Violence and Metaphysics," 151. In a sense, Stroud's objection to Cavell (see footnote 132 in this chapter) trades on a very similar point: the question of how we can *know* about a relationship that fundamentally is not one of knowledge.

140. For an concise discussion of these terms, see Critchley, *Ethics of Deconstruction*, 7–9.

narration. The relationship with him is indescribable in the literal sense of the term, unconvertible into a history, irreducible to the simultaneousness of writing, the eternal present of a writing that records or presents results."[141] "The saying" and "the said," then, might also be conceived as two alternate planes or axes (and one cannot even say planes of existence or nonexistence because "the saying" exactly is "otherwise than being," in other words, other than representation, knowledge, and so forth).

With this distinction, Levinas's invocation of skepticism comes into focus. He claims that "to conceive the *other than being* requires, perhaps, as much audacity as skepticism shows, when it does not hesitate to affirm the impossibility of statement while venturing to *realize* that impossibility by the very statement of this impossibility. . . . [If] skepticism has the gall to return (and it always returns as philosophy's legitimate child), it is because in the contradiction which logic sees in it the 'at the same time' of the contradictories is missing . . . because in general signification signifies beyond synchrony, beyond essence."[142] Levinas will ultimately say that "it is as though skepticism were sensitive to the difference between any exposure without reserve to the other, which is saying, and the exposition or statement of the said."[143] Levinas's point is then quite similar to Cavell's: skepticism is true to the extent that it captures something about being human, it represents the experience of alterity within language,[144]

---

141. Levinas, *Otherwise Than Being*, 166.

142. Levinas, *Otherwise Than Being*, 7; translation modified. See also Emmanuel Levinas, "Wholly Otherwise," in *Re-reading Levinas*, ed. Robert Bernasconi and Simon Critchley (London: Athlone, 1991), 5.

143. Levinas, *Otherwise Than Being*, 168.

144. Thus, the significance of Levinas's claim that "the skeptical discourse . . . *would be* self-contradictory *if* the saying and the said were only correlative" (Levinas, *Otherwise Than Being*, 168; emphasis added). Contrary to most interpreters, I do not believe that Levinas thinks skepticism is *self*-contradictory or *self*-refuting (this does not mean, however, that it cannot be refuted).

much in the same way that the fantasy of an inexpressive or an all-too-expressive language attempts to rationalize or to gloss over the fact of my relation to the Other. As Levinas puts it, "the permanent return of skepticism does not so much signify the possible breakup of structures *as the fact that they are not the ultimate framework of meaning*, that for their accord repression can already be necessary."[145] Both Levinas and Cavell therefore highlight the extent to which skepticism just is a standing possibility for any user of language.

A prelinguistic plane therefore underwrites the existence of any linguistic plane. Such a plane is established, "slips in" (to speak with Levinas) "like a thief." This plane is not therefore incapable of conceptualization; in fact, at its most basic, it just reveals the fact that language is inherited—as Levinas puts it, with language, "it is the possibility of being the author of what had been breathed in unbeknownst to me, of having received, one knows not from where, that of which I am author."[146] At some point, we learn to speak with words that are and are not our own (ours, because we speak them, but not solely ours—neither causally, because learned, nor conceptually, because forever open to contestation and interpretation). In language, we are both master and hostage to others. Yet any inheritance of language cannot be located in time—it doesn't correspond to a first word or sentence, because it is not a word or collection of words, it is an entire form of life, "all the whirl of organism,"[147] an "attuning" of ourselves,[148] irreducible to a

---

145. Levinas, *Otherwise Than Being*, 171; emphasis added. In this sense, the analogy between skepticism and Levinas's project is not as weak as in Aikin and Simmons, and this is so exactly because I agree with them, that the skeptic need not concede that skepticism is self-refuting. See Aikin and Simmons, "Levinasian Otherism," 46.

146. Levinas, *Otherwise Than Being*, 148–49.

147. Cavell, "Availability of Wittgenstein's Later Philosophy," 52.

148. For Levinas's use of this Wittgensteinian locution, see Levinas, "In Memory of Alphonse de Waelhens," 112. See also footnote 116 in this chapter.

collection of words or facts. Such an inheritance is, once we are among others, not something we might avoid or exempt ourselves from (although we might ultimately refuse the others who bestow it on us, or refuse ourselves from them or from ourselves). This inescapability of the inheritance of language is what Levinas highlights when he points out that the space of what he terms "proximity" is "impassive." As he puts it, "the impassiveness of space refers to the absolute coexistence, to the conjunction of all the points, being together at all points without any privilege, characteristic of the words of a language before the mouth opens."[149] As in Cavell, this position rejects any "fantasy of [a] voice that precedes language, that as it were gives itself language."[150] Our relationship within and to language is such that language is always "a resignation (prior to any decision, in passivity) at the risk of misunderstanding (like in love, where, unless one does not love with love, one has to resign oneself to not being loved), at the risk of lack of and refusal of communication."[151] Or, as Cavell puts it, "language puts us in bonds, that with each word we utter we emit stipulation, agreements we do not know and do not want to know we have entered, agreements we were always in, that were in effect before our participation in them. Our relation to our language—to the fact that we are subject to expression, victims of meaning—is accordingly a key to our sense of our distance from our lives, of our sense of the alien, of ourselves as alien to ourselves, thus alienated."[152]

To be a language user is to be subject to others, incapable of stability—forever exposed. At the same time, it is to

---

149. Levinas, *Otherwise Than Being*, 81.
150. Stanley Cavell, *A Pitch of Philosophy: Autobiographical Exercises* (Cambridge, MA: Harvard University Press, 1996), 69.
151. Levinas, *Otherwise Than Being*, 120.
152. Stanley Cavell, *In Quest of the Ordinary* (Chicago: University of Chicago, 1988), 40.

be someone—to make claims, to exist, to substitute oneself as an authority—a speaker, for all others (who collectively maintain the forever flowing boundaries of language). My linguistic existence is a fact of and within a language, and language is what it is only because of others apart from me. Words depend on their standing for me, but never solely on me. I am responsible for them, but in doing so, I am also responsible for and to the Other, ultimately hostage in meaning to the Other. My words originate from the Other and are spoken to and for the Other, and in fact, they gain any existence only because of the Other.[153] With language, then, we bear witness to the dual planes of knowing and acknowledging, saying and said, understanding thereby the very fact of language as itself already suggesting a commitment to ethics, if not to something even older and more robust (it would not be too much to say religious). Language here reveals the barest and simplest of prescriptions: "you shall not kill."

§ 6. Conclusion: Trace and World

Levinas and Cavell both draw striking conclusions about ultimate reality from the "truth" of skepticism as it pertains to the Other. Levinas, for example, stresses the "indetermination" at the heart of our precognitive and preexperiential encounter with the Other, an indetermination "that is not an appeal to form" or to "materiality."[154] Language thereby

---

153. It is in this sense that I think Cavell's worries about Levinas's "infinite responsibility" are misplaced. What Levinas terms "infinite responsibility for myself" and what Levinas terms "infinite responsibility for the other" are just two sides of the same coin: language. See Cavell, "What Is the Scandal of Skepticism?," 144.

154. Emmanuel Levinas, "God and Philosophy," in *Of God Who Comes to Mind*, trans. Bettina Bergo (Stanford, CA: Stanford University Press, 1998), 59.

"loses its function as luxury,"[155] exactly because it is commonplace, at the core of who we are, no more luxurious than the air we breathe. (Of course, in late capitalism, both the air we breathe and the Other who forms us are increasingly a luxury, exactly because each is overlooked or not properly understood or increasingly destroyed.) One commentator puts it well when she notes that "the idea of the infinite becomes a barrier and checkpoint for consciousness which cannot be evaded."[156] Cavell captures a related point with his suggestion that "the philosophical problem of the other" is "the trace or scar of the departure of God."[157] Cavell does not here mean departure in literal terms, as if God or the Infinite were a being that simply departed, but rather in conceptual and practical terms: it just is the case that once we begin talking *about* the infinite, then it has vanished.[158] For this reason, Levinas frequently deploys the notion of a "trace,"[159] capturing with that term the idea that, with our encounter with the Other, there is—in a deep sense—nothing there to capture, for it is what makes encounter—indeed, anything—possible in the first place. In this way, the encounter with the Other,

155. Ibid., 75.
156. Edith Wyschogrod, "God and 'Being's Move' in the Philosophy of Emmanuel Levinas," *Journal of Religion* 62, no. 2 (1982): 153.
157. Cavell, *Claim of Reason*, 470.
158. Another way to put this point is just to highlight—as Cavell himself does—that although Levinas and Cavell share much philosophically, they do not have the same religious disposition. As Cavell notes, elements of Levinas's thought propose to him "religious responsibilities I do not know are mine" (Cavell, "What Is the Scandal of Skepticism?," 151). For a discussion, see Morgan, "Levinas on God and the Trace of the Other."
159. For an excellent discussion of how this term appears in Levinas, see Bettina Bergo, "The Trace in Derrida and Levinas," Canadian Philosophical Association, London, Ontario, May 2005, https://www.academia.edu/1705190/The_Trace_in_Derrida_and_Levinas. See also Morgan, "Levinas on God and the Trace of the Other."

even as it underwrites the existence of a world, also already points beyond that world, making plausible the sort of apophasis that both Maimonides and Adorno instantiate in differing ways.[160]

160. This makes possible a potential connection—only flagged here—to mystical forms of Judaism, as in the sixteenth-century Jewish mystic Meir ben Ezekiel ibn Gabbai, who captures a formally analogous point when he conceives of God as "the great foundation, the divine voice, in which all new words that might be said are found" (היסוד שהוא הקול העליון ההוא הושמו בו כל הדברים העתידים להתחדש) (Meir Ibn Gabbai, *Avodat Hakodesh* [Jerusalem: Shivlei Orchot Hachaim, 1992], 3: 23). My attention was drawn to Gabbai in Gershom Scholem's fascinating essay, "Revelation in Tradition as Religious Categories," in Gershom Scholem, "Revelation and Tradition as Religious Categories," in *The Messianic Idea in Judaism and Other Essays on Jewish Spirituality*, trans. Michael A. Meyer (New York: Schocken, 2011), 299. For more on Gabbai, see Roland Goetschel, *Meir ibn Gabbay: le discours de la kabbale espagnole* (Leuven, Belg.: Peters, 1981).

CONCLUSION

In conclusion, it is worth pausing for a moment in order to consider the argumentative structure of *How to Measure a World?* In broad strokes, the first two chapters elaborated, in quite different ways, what it means to be in a world, ultimately suggesting two primordial possibilities (awed wonder and moral outrage). The last two chapters have revolved around the conditions of possibility for having a world in the first place, namely the dynamism and depth of a history that always already requires elaboration and the existence of language and (therefore) of others in order to make a world and history possible in the first place. The indeterminacy at the heart of language also underwrites and is formally analogous to the anachronism that's been sketched in *How to Measure a World?* Where the first half of the book shows how the aforementioned primordial ways of being the world prohibit feeling at home, the second half highlights how not feeling at home means acknowledging the sense of history that emerges through a deep consideration of those others who occupy the world with me, and who—also with me—construct and deconstruct the horizon and boundaries of that world. To the extent that we all have a world and can come to feel not at home in it, we are all "a little bit Jewish."[1]

---

1. Emmanuel Levinas, "Reality Has Weight," trans. Alin Cristian and Bettina Bergo, in *Is It Righteous to Be?: Interviews with Emmanuel Levinas*, ed. Jill Robbins (Palo Alto, CA: Stanford University Press, 2001), 164.

In *An Introduction to Metaphysics*, Heidegger notes that anyone for whom the Bible is "divine revelation and truth already has the answer to the question 'Why are there beings at all rather than nothing?'"[2] Heidegger continues, noting that such a person can never "authentically question without giving himself up as a believer" and can therefore never ask *the* philosophical question (the question of why there are beings rather than nothing). He concludes by mocking the very idea of a "Christian philosophy" as a sort of category mistake; in his estimation, it is "a round square and a misunderstanding."[3] One imagines that Heidegger would think the same about "Jewish philosophy" . . . or perhaps even worse.[4]

Yet we now know that Heidegger—as a philosopher—also pursued a phenomenological analysis of Judaism, albeit in terms quite different from those pursued here, alleging in quite grim and troubling terms that "the question of the role of *world Jewry* (*Weltjudentum*) is not a race-related one (*rassische*), but the *metaphysical* (*metaphysische*) question of the kind of humanity that can take over the uprooting of all beings from being as a world-historical task, and to do so in a way that is absolutely unbounded (*schlechthin ungebunden*), that can assume the world-historical task of uprooting (*Entwurzelung*) all beings from beyng."[5] Although the exact parameters of Heidegger's antisemitism and concomitant analysis of Jewry and Judaism is beyond my scope here,[6] it is

---

2. Martin Heidegger, *Introduction to Metaphysics*, trans. Gregory Fried and Richard Polt, 2nd ed. (New Haven, CT: Yale University Press, 2014), 8.

3. Ibid.

4. On the point of the latter, and on Heidegger's virulent and largely uninformed attitudes toward Judaism, see Elliot R. Wolfson, *The Duplicity of Philosophy's Shadow: Heidegger, Nazism, and the Jewish Other* (New York: Columbia University Press, 2018).

5. Martin Heidegger, *Heidegger Gesamtausgabe*, ed. Vittorio Klostermann (Frankfurt: Vittorio Klosterman, 1976), 96: 243.

6. On this point, see Donatella Di Cesare, *Heidegger and the Jews: The Black Notebooks* (London: Polity, 2018); Andrew J. Mitchell and Peter Trawny, eds., *Heidegger's Black Notebooks: Responses to Anti-Semitism*

obvious even from this short quote that Heidegger conceives of "world Jewry" in ontological terms, alleging that Judaism has a *metaphysical* significance, making a great deal of the "worldlessness of Jewry" (*Weltlosigkeit des Judentums*).[7] One immediate response to Heidegger is that, as Levinas had already suggested,[8] Heidegger's obsession with place has caused his phenomenological analysis to go awry.[9] *How to Measure a World?* shows that although Judaism ought to be closely linked to anachronism, such an anachronism in fact intimately requires a world; indeed, it makes sense only in the context of a world.[10] Such a response, however, might justify a phenomenological or philosophical approach to Judaism, but it does not yet capture the exact significance of the present analysis.

What exactly is the significance of claiming that "to be Jewish is not a particularity," and that "Jewish philosophy" is not merely some sociological subset of philosophy, but rather a "modality"[11] of being human? Such a claim brings

---

(New York: Columbia University Press, 2017); Ingo Farin and Jeff Malpas, eds., *Reading Heidegger's Black Notebooks 1931–1941* (Cambridge, MA: MIT Press, 2016); Philippe Lacoue-Labarthe, *Heidegger, Art, and Politics: The Fiction of the Political*, trans. Chris Turner (London: Basil Blackwell, 1990); Jean-Luc Nancy, *The Banality of Heidegger*, trans. Jeff Fort (New York: Fordham University Press, 2017); Wolfson, *The Duplicity of Philosophy's Shadow: Heidegger, Nazism, and the Jewish Other*.

7. Martin Heidegger, *Ponderings VII–XI: Black Notebooks 1938–1939*, trans. Richard Rocjewicz (Bloomington: Indiana University Press, 2017), 76.

8. See Emmanuel Levinas, "Heidegger, Gagarin and Us," in *Difficult Freedom: Essays on Judaism* (Baltimore, MD: Johns Hopkins University Press, 1990).

9. See footnote 24 of the Introduction.

10. And the same is true of language and other elements that Heidegger accuses Judaism of lacking. On Heidegger's basic lack of understanding about Judaism and even the Western Jewish inheritance, see Wolfson, *The Duplicity of Philosophy's Shadow: Heidegger, Nazism, and the Jewish Other*, 87; Marlène Zarader, *The Unthought Debt: Heidegger and the Hebraic Heritage*, trans. Bettina Bergo (Palo Alto: Stanford University Press, 2006).

11. Levinas, "Reality Has Weight," 164.

the fore some of the questions raised in the Introduction. What's ultimately at stake in linking Judaism to such a philosophical approach? And furthermore, why deploy "Judaism" when "monotheism" might be more apt (as the site of something like ontological difference, that is, the basic distinction between particular beings and how those beings are possible)?[12] As Levinas puts it, "I always thought that the invisible God of monotheism is not only a God who is not visible to the eyes. It is a nonthematizable God."[13]

At a very high-altitude view, one way to locate a response to such questions is to recall how Sigmund Freud, in *Moses and Monotheism* (written in 1939), locates Judaism in the history of the world. Without entering into or affirming one way or the other all the various psychoanalytic details of Freud's account, note an interesting remark that Freud makes toward the conclusion of the book, explicitly discussing the "prohibition against making an image of God—the compulsion to worship a God whom one cannot see."[14] Freud notes that such a prohibition must have had profound consequences, for "it meant that a sensory perception was given second place to what may be called an abstract idea," and that this ought to be understood as, "a triumph of intellectuality over sensuality."[15] Freud is quick to link such an approach to his own psychoanalytic theories and to the process of "an instinctual renunciation, with all its necessary psychological consequences."[16] For Freud, this renunciation underwrites the

---

12. In this context, see again footnote 79 in chapter 1.

13. Emmanuel Levinas, "Interview with Salomon Malka," trans. Alin Cristian and Bettina Bergo, in *Is It Righteous to Be?: Interviews with Emmanuel Levinas*, ed. Jill Robbins, 93–105 (Palo Alto, CA: Stanford University Press, 2001), 101.

14. Sigmund Freud, *The Standard Edition of the Complete Psychological Works of Sigmund Freud*, trans. James Strachey, Anna Freud, and Alan Tyson (London: Hogarth, 2001), 23: 112–13.

15. Ibid., 23: 113.

16. Ibid.

glories of human civilization and accomplishment ("one of the most important stages on the path to *hominization*," that is, becoming human).[17] Levinas invokes a similar, related sentiment when discussing Jewish ritual; he notes the way in which it was able to separate the practicing Jew from nature even "while itself remaining completely natural."[18] Remarking on this natural separation from nature, Levinas muses that "perhaps for that very reason, Jewish existence maintains a presence to the Most High God."[19] In broad contours, emerging here in different vocabulary and different guise, are once again questions about our fundamental comportment toward the world. Levinas's suggestion—similar to Freud's in form, albeit not in content—is the idea that the historical standing of Judaism amid world history somehow testifies to a fundamental anachronism toward that history and that world (this point about a relationship to the world is the tenor in which Levinas's remark that "Jews are a people who doubt themselves, who in a certain sense, belong to a religion of unbelievers,"[20] ought to be understood). Such an anachronism is available—indeed likely experienced at some point—by everyone, but it is not equally or at all times prioritized or recognized by all traditions or all segments of human cultural expression (including historical expressions of Judaism itself). Nonetheless, the possibility of a gap between self and world—anachronism—is central to human (ethical) accomplishment. One way to manifest such doubt is through moral critique (a position exemplified by Adorno), another way is through awed wonder (a position exemplified by Maimonides). In either case, because any such anachronism always

17. Ibid.
18. Emmanuel Levinas, "Judaism," trans. Sean Hand, in *Difficult Freedom: Essays on Judaism* (Baltimore, MD: Jons Hopkins University Press, 1960), 26. One finds analogous thoughts in Horkheimer and Adorno.
19. Ibid.
20. Levinas, "Reality Has Weight," 164.

only expresses itself in worldly terms, it may be the case that the most authentic expression of anachronism at a particular moment may turn out to be silence (think here of the idea that perhaps saying anything at all will be already to betray the impulse that animates a sense of not feeling at home. I think here of the idea touched on by Ralph Waldo Emerson and Stanley Cavell that at certain points "every word" that is said may "chagrin . . . us").[21]

Of course, this does not solve the historical questions raised here, something Levinas himself recognizes when he notes that he claims these things even while "knowing nothing of Buddhism."[22] Such an admission, although commendable (in that Levinas realizes the importance of Buddhism to this story), is also an invitation for future work (other such sites and traditions must be made explicit in this project); for that reason Levinas can claim that "there is not a single thing in a great spirituality that would be absent from another great spirituality."[23] There are also consequences for how we understand the evolution of Judaism and Jewish history itself. They would not be essentially Diasporist nor essentially Zionist; indeed, they would not be *essentially* anything (except perhaps expressive of a fundamental anachronism). Most immediately, such an approach would mean "decolonizing" Levinas's story,[24] and understanding monotheism robustly, not just as a historical phenomenon, and not solely as about Judaism, but as a phenomenological category that

---

21. Ralph Waldo Emerson, *The Essential Writings of Ralph Waldo Emerson* (New York: Modern Library, 2009), 137. See Cavell's references throughout Cavell, *Conditions Handsome and Unhandsome*, 28, 32, 37, 109.

22. Levinas, "Reality Has Weight," 164.

23. Emmanuel Levinas, *Of God Who Comes to Mind*, trans. Bettina Bergo (Stanford, CA: Stanford University Press), 93.

24. For such projects, see John Drabinski, *Levinas and the Postcolonial: Race, Nation, Other* (Edinburgh: Edinburgh University Press, 2011); Peter Atterton and Matthew Calarco, eds., *Radicalizing Levinas* (Buffalo: SUNY Press, 2010). See also footnote 11 of chapter 3.

denotes the sort of anachronism that's been presented in this book, one that is perpetually susceptible to violence but one that by no means requires it; indeed, one that also carries the most supreme peace as a native possibility.[25]

More proximally, however, would be understanding that bound up with such an anachronism is always an elaboration of potential sites and expressions of opposition to it (from the most scholastic to the most brutal). The most intense expression of this point would bring to the fore the importance of antisemitism to Western history,[26] suggesting ultimately that such antisemitism is also a modality of being human, standing opposed to the fundamental anachronism of the human and being bound up therefore with "the millions on millions of all confessions and all nations, victims of the same hatred of the other man, the same antisemitism."[27]

---

25. This would be to push back against claims that monotheism is inherently violent. For such a view, see Regina M. Schwartz, *The Curse of Cain: The Violent Legacy of Monotheism* (Chicago: University of Chicago Press, 1998).

26. For such a claim, see David Nirenberg, *Anti-Judaism: The Western Tradition* (New York: W. W. Norton, 2013). Notably, Freud had also already mused on telling a similar story about the West's relationship with antisemitism in *Moses and Monotheism*. See, for example, Freud, *The Standard Edition of the Complete Psychological Works of Sigmund Freud*, 23: 91–92.

27. This is Levinas's famous French epigraph to *Otherwise Than Being; or, Beyond Essence*, trans. Alphonso Lingis (Dordrecht, Neth.: Kluwer, 1991). Highly relevant here is Santiago Slabodsky, *Decolonial Judaism: Triumphal Failures of Barbaric Thinking* (London: Palgrave-Macmillan, 2014).

WORKS CITED

Adorno, Theodor W. *Critical Models: Interventions and Catchwords*. Translated by Henry W. Pickford. New York: Columbia University Press, 1998.

———. "Critique." Translated by Henry W. Pickford. In *Critical Models: Interventions and Catchwords*, 281–88. New York: Columbia University Press, 1998.

———. *History and Freedom*, edited by Rolf Tiedemann. Translated by Rodney Livingstone. Cambridge, UK: Polity, 2006.

———. "The Idea of Natural-History." Translated by Robert Hullot-Kentor. In *Things beyond Resemblance: Collected Essays on Theodor W. Adorno*, edited by Robert Hullot-Kentor, 252–70. New York: Columbia University Press, 2006.

———. *Lectures on Negative Dialectics*. Edited by Rolf Tiedemann. Translated by Rodney Livingstone. Cambridge, UK: Polity, 2008.

———. *Metaphysics: Concept and Problems*. Edited by Rolf Tiedemann. Translated by Edmund F. N. Jephcott. Stanford, CA: Stanford University Press, 2000.

———. *Minima Moralia: Reflections on a Damaged Life*. Translated by Edmund F. N. Jephcott. London: Verso, 2005.

———. *Negative Dialectics*. Translated by E. B. Ashton. New York: Seabury, 1973.

———. "Notes on Kafka." In *Prisms*, 243–71. Cambridge, MA: MIT Press, 1981.

———. "On Tradition." *Telos* 94 (1992): 75–82.

———. *Problems of Moral Philosophy*. Translated by Rodney Livingstone. Stanford, CA: Stanford University Press, 2000.

———. "Progress." Translated by Henry W. Pickford. In *Critical Models: Interventions and Catchwords*, 143–61. New York: Columbia University Press, 1998.

———. "Reason and Revelation." Translated by Henry W. Pickford. In *Critical Models: Interventions and Catchwords*, 135–43. New York: Columbia University Press, 1998.

Adorno, Theodor W., and Walter Benjamin. *The Complete Correspondence, 1928–1940*. Cambridge, MA: Harvard University Press, 2001.

Aikin, Scott F., and J. Aaron Simmons. "Levinasian Otherism, Skepticism, and the Problem of Self-Refutation." *Philosophical Forum* 40, no. 1 (2009): 29–54.

Al-Ghazālī. *The Alchemy of Happiness*. Translated by Claud Field. Lahore, Pak.: Sh. M. Ashraf, 1991.

———. *Mi'Yar al-'Ilm*. Cairo: Dar al-ma'arif, 1965.

Ali Khalidi, Muhammad. *Medieval Islamic Philosophical Writings*. Cambridge: Cambridge University Press, 2005.

Anckaert, Luc A. *A Critique of Infinity: Rosenzweig and Levinas*. Leuven, Belg.: Peeters, 2006.

Anidjar, Gil. *"Our Place in al-Andalus": Kabbalah, Philosophy, Literature in Arab Jewish Letters*. Palo Alto, CA: Stanford University Press, 2002.

Anscombe, G. E. M. "Authority in Morals." In *Ethics, Politics and Religion*, 43–50. Collected Philosophical Papers, vol. 3. Minneapolis: University of Minnesota Press, 1981.

Arendt, Hannah. "The Crisis in Education." In *Between Past and Future: Eight Exercises in Political Thought*, 170–93. New York: Penguin, 2006.

———. *Denktagebuch: 1950 bis 1973*. 2 vols. Edited by Ursula Ludz and Ingeborg Nordmann. Munich: Piper, 2002.

———. *The Human Condition*. Chicago: University of Chicago Press, 1958.

———. *Lectures on Kant's Political Philosophy*. Chicago: University of Chicago Press, 1982.

———. *The Origins of Totalitarianism*. London: André Deutsch, 1986.

———. *Thinking without a Banister: Essays in Understanding, 1953–1975*. New York: Schocken, 2018.

———. "Understanding and Politics." In *Essays in Understanding, 1930–1954: Formation, Exile, and Totalitarianism*, edited by Jerome Kohn, 307–28. New York: Schocken, 2011.

Aristotle. *Complete Works of Aristotle*. 2 vols. Edited by Jonathan Barnes. Princeton, NJ: Princeton University Press, 2014.

Assmann, Jan. *Of God and Gods: Egypt, Israel, and the Rise of Monotheism*. Madison: University of Wisconsin Press, 2008.

Atterton, Peter, and Matthew Calarco, eds. *Radicalizing Levinas*. Buffalo, NY: SUNY Press, 2010.

Auer, Dirk, Lars Rensmann, and Julia Schulze Wessel, eds. *Arendt und Adorno*. Frankfurt: Suhrkamp, 2003.

Austin, John Langshaw. "Other Minds." In *Philosophical Papers*, 3rd ed., edited by James Opie Urmson and Geoffrey James Warnock, 76–117. Oxford: Oxford University Press, 1979.

Baron, Salo. "The Historical Outlook of Maimonides." *Proceedings of the American Academy for Jewish Research* 6 (1934): 5–113.

Batnitzky, Leora. "Encountering the Modern Subject in Levinas." *Yale French Studies* 104 (2004): 6–21.

Benjamin, Walter. *The Arcades Project*. Cambridge, MA: Harvard University Press, 1999.

———. *Gesammelte Schriften*. Edited by Rolf Tiedemann and Hermann Schweppenhäuser. Frankfurt: Suhrkamp, 1977.

———. "On the Concept of History." In *Selected Writings*, edited by Howard Eiland and Michael W. Jennings, 4: 389–400. Cambridge, MA: Harvard University Press, 2002.

———. *The Origin of German Tragic Drama*. Translated by John Osborne. London: New Left, 1977.

———. "Paralipomena to 'On the Concept of History.'" In *Selected Writings*, edited by Howard Eiland and Michael W. Jennings, 4: 401–11. Cambridge, MA: Harvard University Press, 2002.

Bergo, Bettina. "The Trace in Derrida and Levinas." Canadian Philosophical Association, London, Ontario, May 2005. https://www.academia.edu/1705190/The_Trace_in_Derrida_and_Levinas.

Berkovits, Eliezer. *God, Man and History*. Jerusalem: Shalem, 2004.

Berlant, Lauren. "The Subject of True Feeling: Pain, Privacy, and Politics." In *Cultural Studies and Political Theory*, edited by Thomas R. Kearns and Austin Sarat, 49–84. Ann Arbor: University of Michigan Press, 1999.

Bernasconi, Robert. "The Alterity of the Stranger and the Experience of the Alien." In *In the Face of the Other and the Trace of God: Essays on the Philosophy of Emmanuel Levinas*, 62–89. New York: Fordham University Press, 2000.

———. "The Ethics of Suspicion." *Research in Phenomenology* 20 (1990): 3–18.

———. "Hegel at the Court of the Ashanti." In *Hegel after Derrida*, edited by Stuart Barnett, 41–63. London: Routledge, 1998.

———. "No Exit: Levinas' Aporetic Account of Transcendence." *Research in Phenomenology* 35, no. 1 (2005): 101–17.

———. *The Question of Language in Heidegger's History of Being*. New York: Springer, 2016.

———. "Re-reading *Totality and Infinity*." In *The Question of the Other*, edited by Charles Scott and Arlene Dallery, 23–34. Buffalo: State University of New York Press, 1989.

———. "Skepticism in the Face of Philosophy." In *Re-reading Levinas*, edited by Robert Bernasconi and Simon Critchley, 149–62. London: Athlone, 1991.

———. "What Is the Question to Which 'Substitution' Is the Answer?" In *The Cambridge Companion to Levinas*, edited by Simon Critchley and Robert Bernasconi, 234–51. Cambridge: Cambridge University Press, 2002.

———. "With What Must the History of Philosophy Begin?: Hegel's Role in the Debate on the Place of India within the History of Philosophy." *Proceedings of the Hegel Society of America* 16 (2003): 35–49.

———. "With What Must the Philosophy of World History Begin? On the Racial Basis of Hegel's Eurocentrism." *Nineteenth Century Contexts* 22, no. 2 (2000): 171–201.

Bernauer, James William, ed. *Amor Mundi: Explorations in the Faith and Thought of Hannah Arendt*. Dordrecht, Neth.: Springer, 2012.

Bernstein, Jay M. *Adorno: Disenchantment and Ethics*. Cambridge: Cambridge University Press, 2001.

Bielik-Robson, Agata. *Jewish Cryptotheologies of Late Modernity: Philosophical Marranos*. London: Routledge, 2014.

———. "Marrano Universalism: Benjamin, Derrida, and Buck-Morss on the Condition of Universal Exile." *Telos* 186 (2019): 25–44.

Birchall, B. C. "Hegel's Notion of Aufheben." *Inquiry* 24, no. 1 (1981): 75–103.

Bloch, Ernst. *The Utopian Function of Art and Literature: Selected Essays*. Translated by Jack Zipes and Frank Mecklenburg. Cambridge, MA: MIT Press, 1988.

Borradori, Giovanna. *The American Philosopher: Conversations with Quine, Davidson, Putnam, Nozick, Danto, Rorty, Cavell, Macintyre, and Kuhn*. Chicago: University of Chicago Press, 1994.

Botwinick, Aryeh. "Emmanuel Levinas's *Otherwise Than Being*, the Phenomenology Project, and Skepticism." *Telos* 134 (2006): 95–117.

Braiterman, Zachary. "Maimonides and the Visual Image after Kant and Cohen." *Journal of Jewish Thought and Philosophy* 20, no. 2 (2012): 217–30.

Brandom, Robert B. "Freedom and Constraint by Norms." *American Philosophical Quarterly* 16, no. 3 (1979): 187–96.

———. *Tales of the Mighty Dead: Historical Essays in the Metaphysics of Intentionality*. Cambridge: Cambridge University Press, 2002.

Bristow, William. *Hegel and the Transformation of Philosophical Critique*. Oxford: Oxford University Press, 2007.

Brittain, Christopher Craig. *Adorno and Theology*. London: Bloomsbury, 2010.

Brogan, Walter. *Heidegger and Aristotle: The Twofoldness of Being*. Buffalo, NY: SUNY Press, 2012.

Brown, Wendy, Peter E. Gordon, and Max Pensky. *Authoritarianism: Three Inquiries in Critical Theory*. Chicago: University of Chicago Press, 2018.

Broyde, Michael J. "Defilement of the Hands, Canonization of the Bible, and the Special Status of *Esther*, *Ecclesiastes*, and *Song of Songs*." *Judaism* 44, no. 1 (1995): 65–79.

Bruns, G. L. "Stanley Cavell's Shakespeare." *Critical Inquiry* 16, no. 3 (1990): 612–32.

Buck-Morss, Susan. *Hegel, Haiti, and Universal History*. Pittsburgh, PA: University of Pittsburgh Press, 2009.

———. *The Origin of Negative Dialectics: Theodor W. Adorno, Walter Benjamin, and the Frankfurt Insitute*. New York: Free Press, 1977.

Buijs, Joseph A. "The Philosophical Character of Maimonides' 'Guide'—a Critique of Strauss' Interpretation." *Judaism* 27, no. 4 (1978): 448–57.

Burrell, David B. *Knowing the Unknowable God: Ibn-Sina, Maimonides, Aquinas*. South Bend, IN: University of Notre Dame Press, 1992.

Camus, Albert. *Notebooks: 1935–1942*. Translated by Philip Thody. New York: Modern Library, 1963.

Caputo, John. *The Mystical Element in Heidegger's Thought*. New York: Fordham University Press, 1986.

Casey, Edward S. "Literary Description and Phenomenological Method." *Yale French Studies* no. 61 (1981): 176–201.

Cavell, Stanley. "The Availability of Wittgenstein's Later Philosophy." In *Must We Mean What We Say?*, 44–73. Cambridge, MA: Harvard University Press, 2002.

———. "The Avoidance of Love." In *Disowning Knowledge in Seven Plays of Shakespeare*, 39–125: Cambridge: Cambridge University Press, 2003.

———. *The Claim of Reason: Wittgenstein, Skepticism, Morality, and Tragedy*. Oxford: Oxford University Press, 1979.

———. *Conditions Handsome and Unhandsome*. Chicago: University of Chicago Press, 1990.

———. *Disowning Knowledge in Seven Plays of Shakespeare*. Cambridge: Cambridge University Press, 2003.

———. *In Quest of the Ordinary: Lines of Skepticism and Romanticism*. Chicago: University of Chicago Press, 1994.

———. "Knowing and Acknowledging." In *Must We Mean What We Say?*, 238–66. Cambridge, MA: Harvard University Press, 2002.

———. *Little Did I Know: Excerpts from Memory*. Stanford, CA: Stanford University Press, 2010.

———. *A Pitch of Philosophy: Autobiographical Exercises*. Cambridge, MA: Harvard University Press, 1996.

———. *The Senses of Walden: An Expanded Edition*. Chicago: University of Chicago Press, 2013.

———. *This New yet Unapproachable America: Lectures after Emerson after Wittgenstein*. Albuquerque, NM: Living Batch, 1989.

———. "What Is the Scandal of Skepticism?" In *Philosophy the Day after Tomorrow*, 132–55. Cambridge, MA: Harvard University Press, 2005.

Caygill, Howard. "Levinas's Prison Notebooks." *Radical Philosophy* 160 (2010): 27–35.

———. "Walter Benjamin's Concept of Allegory." In *The Cambridge Companion to Allegory*, edited by Rita Copeland and Peter T. Struck, 241–54. Cambridge: Cambridge University Press, 2010.

Césaire, Aimé. *Discourse on Colonialism*. Translated by Joan Pinkbaum. New York: Monthly Review Press, 2000.

Chalmers, David J. *The Conscious Mind: In Search of a Fundamental Theory*. Oxford: Oxford University Press, 1996.

Chin, Eliza Lo. *This Side of Doctoring: Reflections from Women in Medicine*. Oxford: Oxford University Press, 2002.

Çirakman, Elif. "Levinas' Disruptive Imagination: Time, Self and the Other." *Analecta Husserliana* 83 (2004): 91–115.

Clarke, Simon. *Marx's Theory of Crisis*. London: Palgrave Macmillan, 1993.

Cohen, Gerald Allan. *Karl Marx's Theory of History: A Defence*. Oxford: Oxford University Press, 2000.

Cohen, Hermann. *Religion of Reason: Out of the Sources of Judaism*. Translated by Simon Kaplan. New York: Frederick Ungar, 1972.

Cohen, Richard A. "Levinas: Thinking Least about Death—contra Heidegger." In *Self and Other: Essays in Continental Philosophy of Religion*, 21–39. Dordrecht, Neth.: Springer, 2006.

Cohen, S. Marc. "Alternation and Persistence: Form and Matter in *The Physics* and *De Generatione et Corruptione*." In *The Oxford Handbook of Aristotle*, edited by Christopher Shields, 205–27. Oxford: Oxford University Press, 2012.

Collins, Michael J. *Blue Collar, Blue Scrubs: The Making of a Surgeon*. New York: St. Martin's Griffin, 2009.

Conant, James. "On Bruns, on Cavell." *Critical Inquiry* 17, no. 3 (1991): 616–34.

Cook, Deborah. *Adorno on Nature*. London: Routledge, 2014.

———. "Through a Glass Darkly: Adorno's Inverse Theology." *Adorno Studies* 1, no. 1 (2017): 66–78.

Cowan, Bainard. "Walter Benjamin's Theory of Allegory." *New German Critique*, no. 22, special issue on Modernism (1981): 109–22.

Cristin, Renato. *Heidegger and Leibniz: Reason and Faith*. Dordrecht, Neth.: Kluwer Academic, 1998.

Critchley, Simon. "Cavell's 'Romanticism' and Cavell's Romanticism." In *Contending with Stanley Cavell*, edited by Russel B. Goodman, 37–54. Oxford: Oxford University Press, 2005.

———. *The Ethics of Deconstruction: Derrida and Levinas*. Delhi, India: Motilal Banarsidass, 2007.

Crowell, Steven. "Measure-Taking: Meaning and Normativity in Heidegger's Philosophy." *Continental Philosophy Review* 41, no. 3 (2008): 261–76.

———. *Normativity and Phenomenology in Husserl and Heidegger*. Cambridge: Cambridge University Press, 2013.

Dagli, Caner K. *Ibn al-'Arabī and Islamic Intellectual Culture: From Mysticism to Philosophy*. London: Routledge, 2016.

Davidson, Donald. "A Nice Derangement of Epitaphs." In *Truth, Language, and History*, 89–107. Oxford, UK: Clarendon, 2005.

———. "On the Very Idea of a Conceptual Scheme." In *Inquiries into Truth and Interpretation*, 183–199. Oxford, UK: Clarendon, 1973.

———. "Rational Animals." In *Subjective, Intersubjective, Objective*, 95–105.

———. *Subjective, Intersubjective, Objective*. Oxford, UK: Clarendon, 2001.

———. "The Second Person." In *Subjective, Intersubjective, Objective*, 107–21.

———. "Thought and Talk." In *Inquiries into Truth and Interpretation*, 155–71. Oxford, UK: Clarendon, 1973.

———. "Three Varieties of Knowledge." In *Subjective, Intersubjective, Objective*, 205–20.

Davidson, Herbert A. *Alfarabi, Avicenna, and Averroes on Intellect: Their Cosmologies, Theories of the Active Intellect, and Theories of Human Intellect*. Oxford: Oxford University Press, 1992.

———. *Moses Maimonides: The Man and His Works*. Oxford: Oxford University Press, 2010.

Davies, Paul. "Asymmetry and Transcendence: On Scepticism and First Philosophy." *Research in Phenomenology* 35, no. 1 (2005): 118–40.

De Boer, Karin. *Thinking in the Light of Time: Heidegger's Encounter with Hegel*. Translated by Karin de Boer and Janet Taylor. Buffalo, NY: SUNY Press, 2000.

De Greef, Jan. "Skepticism and Reason." In *Face to Face with Levinas*, edited by Richard A. Cohen, 159–81. Buffalo: State University of New York Press, 1986.

Derrida, Jacques. *Adieu to Emmanuel Levinas*. Palo Alto, CA: Stanford University Press, 1999.

———. "Violence and Metaphysics." Translated by Alan Bass. In *Writing and Difference*, 79–154. Baltimore, MD: Johns Hopkins University Press, 1978.

Descartes, René. *Discourse on Method and Meditations on First Philosophy*. Translated by Donald A. Cress. Cambridge, UK: Hackett, 1998.

De Vries, Hent. "From 'Ghost in the Machine' to 'Spiritual Automaton': Philosophical Meditation in Wittgenstein, Cavell, and Levinas." *Self and Other* 60 (2007): 77–97.

———. *Minimal Theologies: Critiques of Secular Reason in Adorno and Levinas*. Translated by Geoffrey Hale. Baltimore, MD: Johns Hopkins University Press, 2005.

De Waelhens, Alphonse. *La philosophie et les expériences naturelles*. The Hague: Martinus Nijhoff, 1961.

Di Cesare, Donatella. *Heidegger and the Jews: The Black Notebooks*. Cambridge: Polity, 2018.

Dobbs-Weinstein, Idit. *Spinoza's Critique of Religion and Its Heirs: Marx, Benjamin, Adorno*. Cambridge: Cambridge University Press, 2015.

Drabinski, John. *Levinas and the Postcolonial: Race, Nation, Other*. Edinburgh: Edinburgh University Press, 2011.

Dreyfus, Hubert. *Being-in-the-World: A Commentary on Heidegger's "Being and Time," Division I*. Cambridge, MA: MIT Press, 1991.

Ekstrom, Laura. *Free Will: A Philosophical Study*. London: Routledge, 1999.

El-Bizri, Nader. "Being and Necessity: A Phenomenological Investigation of Avicenna's Metaphysics and Cosmology." In *Islamic Philosophy and Occidental Phenomenology on the Perennial Issue of Microcosm and Macrocosm*, edited by Anna-Teresa Tymieniecka, 243–61. Dordrecht, Neth.: Springer, 2006.

———. *The Phenomenological Quest between Avicenna and Heidegger*. Buffalo, NY: SUNY Press, 2000.

Eldridge, Richard. "The Normal and the Normative: Wittgenstein's Legacy, Kripke, and Cavell." *Philosophy and Phenomenological Research* 46, no. 4 (1986): 555–75.

Emerson, Ralph Waldo. *The Essential Writings of Ralph Waldo Emerson*. New York: Modern Library, 2009.

Eran, Amira. "Al-Ghazālī and Maimonides on the World to Come and Spiritual Pleasures." *Jewish Studies Quarterly* 8, no. 2 (2001): 137–66.

Evans, Gareth. *The Varieties of Reference*. Oxford: Oxford University Press, 1982.

Fackenheim, Emil L. *To Mend the World*. Bloomington: Indiana University Press, 1994.

Fagenblat, Michael. *A Covenant of Creatures: Levinas's Philosophy of Judaism*. Stanford, CA: Stanford University Press, 2010.

———. "Levinas and Maimonides: From Metaphysics to Ethical Negative Theology." *Journal of Jewish Thought and Philosophy* 16, no. 1 (2008): 95–147.

———. "'The Passion of Israel': The True Israel according to Levinas, or Judaism 'as a Category of Being.'" *Sophia* 54, no. 3 (2015): 297–320.

Farin, Ingo, and Jeff Malpas, eds. *Reading Heidegger's Black Notebooks, 1931–1941*. Cambridge, MA: MIT Press, 2016.

Fenves, Peter. *The Messianic Reduction: Walter Benjamin and the Shape of Time*. Palo Alto, CA: Stanford University Press, 2011.

Finlayson, James Gordon. "On Not Being Silent in the Darkness: Adorno's Singular Apophaticism." *Harvard Theological Review* 105, no. 1 (2011): 1–32.

Forst, Rainer. "Noumenal Alienation: Rousseau, Kant and Marx on the Dialectics of Self-Determination." *Kantian Review* 22, no. 4 (2017): 523–51.

Förster, Eckart. *The Twenty-Five Years of Philosophy*. Translated by Brady Bowman. Cambridge, MA: Harvard University Press, 2012.

Förster, Eckart, and Yitzhak Y. Melamed. *Spinoza and German Idealism*. Cambridge: Cambridge University Press, 2012.

Foster, Roger. *Adorno: The Recovery of Experience*. Albany, MY: SUNY Press, 2007.

Foucher de Careil, Louis-Alexandre. *Leibniz, la Philosophie Juive et la Cabale: Trois Lectures à l'Académie des Sciences Morales et Politiques avec les Manuscrits Inédits de Leibniz*. Paris: Durand, 1861.

Fox, Marvin. *Interpreting Maimonides: Studies in Methodology, Metaphysics, and Moral Philosophy*. Chicago: University of Chicago Press, 1995.

Franco, Paul. *Hegel's Philosophy of Freedom*. New Haven, CT: Yale University Press, 2002.

Frank, Daniel, and Oliver Leaman. "What Is Jewish Philosophy?" In *History of Jewish Philosophy*, edited by Daniel Frank and Oliver Leaman, 1–13. London: Routledge, 1997.

Franke, William. *On What Cannot Be Said: Apophatic Discourses in Philosophy, Religion, Literature, and the Arts*. South Bend, IN: University of Notre Dame, 2007.

———. *A Philosophy of the Unsayable*. South Bend, IN: University of Notre Dame Press, 2014.

Freud, Sigmund. *The Standard Edition of the Complete Psychological Works of Sigmund Freud*. Translated by James Strachey, Anna Freud, and Alan Tyson. 24 vols. London: Hogarth, 2001.

Freudenthal, Gad. "Maimonides on the Knowability of the Heavens and of Their Mover (*Guide* 2: 24)." *Aleph* 8, no. 1 (2008): 151–57.

Frey, Hans-Jost. *Interruptions*. Translated by Georgia Albert. Buffalo, NY: SUNY Press, 1996.

Freyenhagen, Fabian. "Adorno's Politics Theory and Praxis in Germany's 1960s." *Philosophy and Social Criticism* 40, no. 9 (2014): 867–93.

———. *Adorno's Practical Philosophy: Living Less Wrongly*. Cambridge: Cambridge University Press, 2013.

———. "Critical Theory and Social Pathology." In *The Routledge Companion to the Frankfurt School*, edited by Axel Honneth, Espen Hammer, and Peter Gordon, 410–24. London: Routledge, 2018.

Fricker, Miranda. *Epistemic Injustice: Power and the Ethics of Knowing*. Oxford: Oxford University Press, 2007.

Fromm, Erich. *You Shall Be as Gods: A Radical Interpretation of the Old Testament and Its Tradition*. New York: Fawcett Premier, 2013.

Funkhouser, Eric. "On Privileging God's Moral Goodness." *Faith and Philosophy* 23, no. 4 (2006): 409–22.

Gallagher, Shaun. *How the Body Shapes the Mind*. Oxford: Oxford University Press, 2006.

Gandesha, Samir. "The 'Aesthetic Dignity of Words': Adorno's Philosophy of Language." *New German Critique*, no. 97 (2006): 137–58.

Geroulanos, Stefanos. *An Atheism That Is Not Humanist Emerges in French Thought*. Palo Alto, CA: Stanford University Press, 2010.

Gerson, Lloyd. *Aristotle and Other Platonists: Ancient Commentators on Aristotle*. Ithaca, NY: Cornell University Press, 2005.

Gil'adi, Avner. "A Short Note on the Possible Origin of the Title *Moreh ha-Nevuchim* (Hebrew)." *Tarbiz* 48 (1979): 346–47.

Goetschel, Roland. *Meir ibn Gabbay: Le discours de la kabbale espagnole*. Leuven, Belg.: Peeters, 1981.

Goetschel, Willi. *The Discipline of Philosophy and the Invention of Modern Jewish Thought*. New York: Fordham University Press, 2013.

Goodman, Lenn E. *Avicenna*. Ithaca, NY: Cornell University Press, 2006.

———. "Did al-Ghazali Deny Causality?" *Studia Islamica*, no. 47 (1978): 83–120.

———. "Maimonides and Leibniz." *Journal of Jewish Studies* 31, no. 2 (1980): 214–36.

Gordon, Ḥayim and Rivca. *Heidegger on Truth and Myth: A Rejection of Postmodernism*. Bern: Peter Lang, 2006.

Gordon, Peter E. *Adorno and Existence*. Cambridge, MA: Harvard University Press, 2016.

———. *Rosenzweig and Heidegger: Between Judaism and German Philosophy*. Berkeley: University of California Press, 2003.

Green, Arthur. *Radical Judaism: Rethinking God and Tradition*. New Haven, CT: Yale University Press, 2010.

Green, Kenneth Hart. *Jew and Philosopher: The Return to Maimonides in the Jewish Thought of Leo Strauss*. Buffalo, NY: SUNY Press, 2012.

———. *Leo Strauss and the Rediscovery of Maimonides*. Chicago: University of Chicago Press, 2013.

Grimm, Stephen. "The Value of Understanding." *Philosophy Compass* 7, no. 2 (2012): 103–17.

Guenther, Lisa. *Solitary Confinement: Social Death and Its Afterlives*. Minneapolis: University of Minnesota Press, 2013.

Guttmann, Julius. *Philosophies of Judaism: The History of Jewish Philosophy from Biblical Times to Franz Rosenzweig*. Translated by David Silverman. New York: Schocken, 1973.

Hacking, Ian. *Historical Ontology*. Cambridge, MA: Harvard University Press, 2004.

Hadot, Pierre, ed. *Philosophy as a Way of Life: Spiritual Exercises from Socrates to Foucault*, edited by Arnold I. Davidson. Oxford, UK: Wiley-Blackwell, 1995.

———. *The Present Alone Is Our Happiness: Conversations with Jeannie Carlier and Arnold I. Davidson*. Translated by Marc Djaballah and Michael Chase. Palo Alto, CA: Stanford University Press, 2009.

Hall, Timothy. "Reification, Materialism, and Praxis: Adorno's Critique of Lukács." *Telos* 155 (2011): 61–82.

Halper, Yehuda. "Does Maimonides's *Mishneh Torah* Forbid Reading the *Guide of the Perplexed*? On Platonic Punishments for Freethinkers." *AJS Review* 42, no. 2 (2018): 351–79.

Hammer, Espen. *Stanley Cavell: Skepticism, Subjectivity, and the Ordinary*. Cambridge, UK: Polity, 2002.

Hammerschlag, Sarah. "Another, Other Abraham: Derrida's Figuring of Levinas's Judaism." *Shofar* 26, no. 4 (2008): 74–96.

———. *Broken Tablets: Levinas, Derrida, and the Literary Afterlife of Religion*. New York: Columbia University Press, 2016.

———. "Levinas's Prison Notebooks." In *The Oxford Handbook of Levinas*, 21–35, edited by Michael Morgan. Oxford: Oxford University Press, 2018.

———. "'A Splinter in the Flesh': Levinas and the Resignification of Jewish Suffering, 1928–1947." *International Journal of Philosophical Studies* 20, no. 3 (2012): 389–419.

Harney, Stefano, and Fred Moten. *The Undercommons: Fugitive Planning and Black Study*. London: Minor Compositions, 2013.

Harries, Karsten. *Art Matters: A Critical Commentary on Heidegger's "The Origin of the Work of Art."* Dordrecht, Neth.: Springer, 2009.

Harvey, Steven. "Alghazali and Maimonides and Their Books of Knowledge." In *Be'erot Yitzhak: Studies in Memory of Isadore Twersky*, edited by Jay M. Harris, 99–117. Cambridge, MA: Harvard University Press, 2005.

Harvey, Warren Zev. "Maimonides' Critical Epistemology and *Guide* 2: 24." *Aleph* 8, no. 1 (2008): 213–35.

———. "Maimonides' First Commandment, Physics, and Doubt." In *Hazon Nahum: Studies in Jewish Law, Thought, and History Presented to Dr. Norman Lamm on the Occasion of His Seventieth Birthday*, edited by Jeffrey S. Gurock and Yaakov Elman, 149–62. New York: Yeshiva University Press, 1998.

Hegel, Georg Wilhelm Friedrich. *Elements of the Philosophy of Right*. Cambridge: Cambridge University Press, 1991.

———. *The Encyclopædia Logic*. Translated by Théodore F. Geraets, Wallis Arthur Suchting, Henry Silton Harris. Indianapolis: Hackett, 1991.

———. *Hegel's Phenomenology of Spirit*. Translated by A. V. Miller. Oxford: Oxford University Press, 1977.

———. *Lectures on the History of Philosophy*. Vol. 3, *Medieval and Modern Philosophy*. Translated by Frances H. Simson and E. S. Haldane. Lincoln: University of Nebraska Press, 1995.

———. *Lectures on the Philosophy of World History*. Translated by H. A. Nisbet. Cambridge: Cambridge University Press, 1975.

———. *Science of Logic*. Translated by George di Giovanni. Cambridge: Cambridge University Press, 2010.

———. "The Spirit of Christianity and Its Fate." Translated by Richard Kroner and Thomas Malcom Knox. In *Early Theological Writings*, 182–302. University Park: University of Pennsylvania Press, 2011.

Heidegger, Martin. *Aristotle's Metaphysics Θ 1–3: On the Essence and Actuality of Force*. Translated by Walter Brogan and Peter Warnek. Bloomington: Indiana University Press, 1995.

———. *The Basic Problems of Phenomenology*. Translated by Albert Hofstadter. Bloomington: Indiana University Press, 1988.

———. *Being and Time*. Translated by John Macquarrie and Edward Robinson. New York: Harper and Row, 1962.

———. *Being and Time*. Translated by Joan Stambaugh. Albany: SUNY Press, 1996.

———. *The Fundamental Concepts of Metaphysics: World, Finitude, Solitude*. Translated by William McNeill and Nicholas Walker. Bloomington: Indiana University Press, 2001.

———. *Hegel's Phenomenology of Spirit*. Bloomington: Indiana University Press, 1994.

———. *Heidegger Gesamtausgabe*. Edited by Vittorio Klostermann. Frankfurt: Vittorio Klosterman, 1976.

———. *History of the Concept of Time: Prolegomena*. Bloomington: Indiana University Press, 1992.

———. "Insight into That Which Is: Bremen Lectures 1949." Translated by Andrew J. Mitchell. In *Bremen and Freiburg Lectures: Insight into That Which Is and Basic Principles of Thinking*, 23–44. Bloomington: Indiana University Press, 2012.

———. *Introduction to Metaphysics*. Translated by Gregory Fried and Richard Polt. 2nd ed. New Haven, CT: Yale University Press, 2014.

———. *An Introduction to Metaphysics*. Translated by Ralph Manheim. New Haven, CT: Yale University Press, 1959.

———. "Letter on Humanism." In *Basic Writings*, edited by David Farrell Krell, 213–67. New York: Harper Collins, 1993.

———. *The Metaphysical Foundations of Logic*. Translated by Michael Heim. Bloomington: Indiana University Press, 1984.

———. *On Time and Being*. Translated by Joan Stambaugh. Chicago: University of Chicago Press, 2002.

———. "'. . . Poetically Man Dwells. . . .'" Translated by Albert Hofstadter. In *Poetry, Language, Thought*, 213–29. New York: Harper and Row, 1959.

———. *Ponderings VII–XI: Black Notebooks 1938–1939*. Translated by Richard Rocjewicz. Bloomington: Indiana University Press, 2017.

———. *The Principle of Reason*. Translated by Reginald Lilly. Bloomington: Indiana University Press, 1996.

———. *Wegmarken*. Frankfurt: Klostermann, 1976.

Herzog, Annabel. "Illuminating Inheritance: Benjamin's Influence on Arendt's Political Storytelling." *Philosophy and Social Criticism* 26, no. 5 (2000): 1–27.

Heschel, Abraham J. *The Prophets*. New York: Harper Collins, 2001.

Hirsch, Samson Raphael. *Horeb: A Philosophy of Jewish Laws and Observances*. London: Soncino, 1962.

Hoffmeier, James. *Akhenaten and the Origins of Monotheism*. Oxford: Oxford University Press, 2015.

Hoffmeister, Johannes, ed. *Briefe von und an Hegel*. 5 vols. Hamburg: Felix Meiner, 1952.

Honneth, Axel, and Hans Joas. *Social Action and Human Nature*. Translated by Raymond Meyer. Cambridge: Cambridge University Press, 1988.

Horkheimer, Max. "Materialism and Morality." Translated by G. Frederick Hunter, Matthew S. Kramer, and John Torpey. In *Between Philosophy and Social Science*, 15–49. Cambridge, MA: MIT Press, 1993.

Horkheimer, Max, and Theodor W. Adorno. *Dialectic of Enlightenment, Philosophical Fragments*. Translated by Edmund F. N. Jephcott. Cultural Memory in the Present Series. Edited by Mieke Bal and Hent de Vries. Stanford, CA: Stanford University Press, 2002.

Horowitz, Asher. "'By a Hair's Breadth' Critique, Transcendence and the Ethical in Adorno and Levinas." *Philosophy and Social Criticism* 28, no. 2 (2002): 213–48.

Hughes, Aaron W. *Rethinking Jewish Philosophy: Beyond Particularism and Universalism*. Oxford: Oxford University Press, 2013.

Hulatt, Owen. *Adorno's Theory of Philosophical and Aesthetic Truth*. New York: Columbia University Press, 2016.

Hullot-Kentor, Robert. "The Idea of Natural History." *Telos* 60 (1984): 111–24.

———. "Translation of Theodor W. Adorno's the Idea of Natural History." In *Things Beyond Resemblance*, 252–71. New York: Columbia University Press, 2006.

Husik, Isaac. *A History of Mediaeval Jewish Philosophy*. New York: Harper and Row, 1966.

Hyland, Drew, and John Manoussakis. *Heidegger and the Greeks: Interpretive Essays*. Bloomington: Indiana University Press, 2006.

Hyppolite, Jean. *Studies on Marx and Hegel*. Translated by John O'Neill. New York: Harper, 1969.

Ibn Gabbai, Meir. *Avodat Hakodesh*. Jerusalem: Shivlei Orchot Hachaim, 1992.

Ibn-Sina. *The Physics of the Healing: Books I and II*. Translated by Jon McGinnis. Provo, UT: Brigham Young University Press, 2009.

Ivry, Alfred L. "The *Guide* and Maimonides's Philosophical Sources." In *The Cambridge Companion to Moses Maimonides*, edited by Kenneth Seeskin, 58–82. Cambridge: Cambridge University Press, 2005.

Jacobi, Friedrich Heinrich. *Main Philosophical Writings and the Novel Allwill*. Translated by George di Giovanni. Vol. 18. Montreal: McGill-Queen's University Press, 1995.

Jaeggi, Rahel. *Alienation*. Translated by Alan E. Smith and Frederick Neuhouser. New York: Columbia University Press, 2014.

James, David. *Rousseau and German Idealism*. Cambridge: Cambridge University Press, 2013.

Janack, Marianne. *What We Mean by Experience*. Palo Alto, CA: Stanford University Press, 2012.

Jarvis, Simon. *Adorno: A Critical Introduction*. Cambridge, UK: Polity, 1998.

———. "Adorno, Marx, Materialism." In *The Cambridge Companion to Adorno*, 79–99. Cambridge: Cambridge University Press, 2004.

Jay, Martin. *Marxism and Totality: The Adventures of a Concept from Lukács to Habermas*. Berkeley: University of California Press, 1986.

Kane, Robert. *The Significance of Free Will*. Oxford: Oxford University Press, 1996.

Kant, Immanuel. *Critique of Pure Reason*. Translated by Paul Guyer and Allen W. Wood. Cambridge: Cambridge University Press, 1998.

———. *Critique of the Power of Judgment*. Translated by Paul Guyer and Eric Matthews. Cambridge: Cambridge University Press, 2000.

———. *On History*. Edited by Lewis White Beck. Translated by Lewis White Beck, Robert E. Anchor, and Emil L. Fackenheim. New York: Bobbs-Merrill, 1963.

———. *Philosophical Correspondence, 1759–1799*. Translated by Arnulf Zweig. Chicago: University of Chicago Press, 1967.

Katz, Claire. *Levinas and the Crisis of Humanism*. Bloomington: Indiana University Press, 2012.

———. "Turning toward the Other: Ethics, Fecundity, and the Primacy of Education." In *Totality and Infinity at 50*, edited by Diane Perpich and Scott Davidson, 209–26. Pittsburgh, PA: Duquesne University Press, 2012.

Kavka, Martin. Introduction to *The Cambridge History of Jewish Philosophy: The Modern Era*. Edited by Martin Kavka, Zachary Braiterman, and David Novak, 1–35. Cambridge: Cambridge University Press, 2012.

———. "Is There a Warrant for Levinas's Talmudic Readings?" *Journal of Jewish Thought and Philosophy* 14, nos. 1–2 (2006): 153–73.

Kellner, Menachem. "From Moses to Moses." *Rambam Maimonides Medical Journal* 1, no. 2 (2010): 1–5.

Kelly, George Armstrong. *Idealism, Politics and History: Sources of Hegelian Thought*. Cambridge: Cambridge University Press, 2010.

Kidder, Tracy. *Mountains beyond Mountains*. New York: Random House, 2009.

Kiesewetter, Hubert. *Von Hegel zu Hitler die politische Verwirklichung einer totalitaren Machtstaatstheorie in Deutschland, 1815–1945*. Frankfurt: Lang, 1974.

Kishik, David. *The Book of Shem: On Genesis before Abraham*. Palo Alto, CA: Stanford University Press, 2018.

Korsgaard, Christine M. *Self-Consitution: Agency, Identity, and Integrity*. Oxford: Oxford University Press, 2009.

Kraemer, Joel L. *Maimonides: The Life and World of One of Civilization's Greatest Minds*. New York: Doubleday, 2010.

———. "The Medieval Arabic Enlightenment." In *The Cambridge Companion to Maimonides*, edited by Steven B. Smith, 137–71. Cambridge: Cambridge University Press, 2009.

Kreisel, Howard. "Judah Halevi's Influence on Maimonides: A Preliminary Appraisal." *Maimonidean Studies* 2 (1991): 95–121.

Kripke, Saul. *Wittgenstein on Rules and Private Language*. Cambridge, MA: Harvard University Press, 1982.

Lachterman, David Rapport. "Mathematical Construction, Symbolic Cognition and the Infinite Intellect: Reflections on Maimon and Maimonides." *Journal of the History of Philosophy* 30, no. 4 (1992): 497–522.

Lacoue-Labarthe, Philippe. *Heidegger, Art, and Politics: The Fiction of the Political*. Translated by Chris Turner. London: Blackwell, 1990.

Lara, María Pía. *Narrating Evil: A Postmetaphysical Theory of Reflective Judgment*. New York: Columbia University Press, 2007.

Lazarus-Yaffeh, Hava. "Was Maimonides Influenced by al-Ghazālī?" In *Tehillah Le-Moshe: Biblical and Judaic Studies in Honor of Moshe Greenberg*, edited by Mordechai Cogan, Barry L. Eichler, and Jeffrey H. Tigay, 163–93. Winona Lake, IN: Eisenbrauns, 1997.

Leaman, Oliver. "Maimonides, Imagination and the Objectivity of Prophecy." *Religion* 18, no. 1 (1988): 69–80.

Lear, Jonathan. *Aristotle: The Desire to Understand*. Cambridge: Cambridge University Press, 1988.

Levene, Nancy. *Powers of Distinction: On Religion and Modernity*. Chicago: University of Chicago Press, 2017.

Levinas, Emmanuel. "'Between Two Worlds' (the Way of Franz Rosenzweig)." Translated by Seán Hand. In *Difficult Freedom: Essays on Judaism*, 181–201. Baltimore, MD: Johns Hopkins University Press, 1960.

———. *Beyond the Verse: Talmudic Readings and Lectures*. Translated by Gary D. Mole. London: Continuum, 1994.

———. *Carnets de Captivité: Suivi de Écrits Sur la Captivité; et, Notes Philosophiques Diverses*. Paris: Grasset and Fasquelle, 2009.

———. *Ethics and Infinity*. Translated by Richard A. Cohen. Pittsburgh, PA: Duquesne University Press, 1985.

———. "God and Philosophy." In *Of God Who Comes to Mind*. Translated by Bettina Bergo, 55–78. Stanford, CA: Stanford University Press, 1998.

———. "Hegel and the Jews." Translated by Seán Hand. In *Difficult Freedom: Essays on Judaism*, 235–38. Baltimore, MD: Johns Hopkins University Press, 1960.

———. "Heidegger, Gagarin and Us." In *Difficult Freedom: Essays on Judaism*, 231–34. Baltimore, MD: Johns Hopkins University Press, 1990.

———. "In Memory of Alphonse de Waelhens." Translated by Barbara Harshav and Michael B. Smith. In *Outside the Subject*, 104–16. Stanford, CA: Stanford University Press, 1994.

———. "Interview with Salomon Malka." Translated by Alin Cristian and Bettina Bergo. In *Is It Righteous to Be?: Interviews with Emmanuel Levinas*, edited by Jill Robbins, 93–105. Palo Alto, CA: Stanford University Press, 2001.

———. "Judaism." Translated by Seán Hand. In *Difficult Freedom: Essays on Judaism*, 24–26. Baltimore, MD: Johns Hopkins University Press, 1960.

———. "Judaism and the Present." Translated by Seán Hand. In *Difficult Freedom: Essays on Judaism*, 208–16. Baltimore, MD: Johns Hopkins University Press, 1960.

———. *Of God Who Comes to Mind*. Translated by Bettina Bergo. Stanford, CA: Stanford University Press, 1998.

———. *Otherwise than Being; or, Beyond Essence*. Translated by Alphonso Lingis. Dordrecht, Neth.: Kluwer, 1991.

———. "The Philosopher and Death." Translated by Michael B. Smith. In *Alterity and Transcendence*, 153–69. New York: Columbia University Press, 1999.

———. "Philosophy and the Idea of Infinity." Translated by Alphonso Lingis. In *Collected Philosophical Papers*, 47–61. Dordrecht, Neth.: Martinus Nijhoff, 1987.

———. "Language and Proximity." Translated by Alphonso Lingis. In *Collected Philosophical Papers*, 109–26. Dordrecht, Neth.: Martinus Nijhoff, 1987.

———. "Reality Has Weight." Translated by Alin Cristian and Bettina Bergo. In *Is It Righteous to Be?: Interviews with Emmanuel Levinas*, edited by Jill Robbins, 158–64. Palo Alto, CA: Stanford University Press, 2001.

———. *Totality and Infinity*. Translated by Alphonso Lingis. Dordrecht, Neth.: Kluwer, 1961.

———. "Wholly Otherwise." In *Re-reading Levinas*, edited by Robert Bernasconi and Simon Critchley, 3–11. London: Athlone, 1991.

Levinas, Emmanuel, and Sean Hand. "Reflections on the Philosophy of Hitlerism." *Critical Inquiry* 17, no. 1 (1990): 63–71.

Lewis, David. *On the Plurality of Worlds*. Oxford, UK: Blackwell, 1986.

Lichtenberg, Judith. "Negative Duties, Positive Duties, and the 'New Harms.'" *Ethics* 120, no. 3 (2010): 557–78.

Lobel, Diana. *Between Mysticism and Philosophy: Sufi Language of Religious Experience in Judah ha-Levi's "Kuzari."* Buffalo, NY: SUNY Press, 2000.

Loidolt, Sophie. *Phenomenology of Plurality: Hannah Arendt on Political Intersubjectivity*. London: Routledge, 2017.

Löwith, Karl. *Meaning in History: The Theological Implications of the Philosophy of History*. Chicago: University of Chicago Press, 2011.

Lukács, György. *History and Class Consciousness: Studies in Marxist Dialectics*. Cambridge, MA: MIT Press, 1972.

———. *The Theory of the Novel: A Historico-Philosophical Essay on the Forms of Great Epic Literature*. Translated by Anna Bostock. Cambridge, MA: MIT Press, 1971.

Macdonald, Iain. "Ethics and Authenticity: Conscience and Non-identity in Heidegger and Adorno, with a Glance at Hegel." In Macdonald and Ziarek, *Adorno and Heidegger*, 6–21.

Macdonald, Iain, and Krzysztof Ziarek. *Adorno and Heidegger: Philosophical Questions*. Palo Alto, CA: Stanford University Press, 2008.

Maimonides, Moses. *The Guide of the Perplexed*. 2 vols. Translated by Shlomo Pines. Chicago: University of Chicago Press, 1963.

Manekin, Charles H. "Belief, Certainty, and Divine Attributes in the *Guide of the Perplexed*." *Maimonidean Studies* 1 (1990): 117–41.

Marion, Jean-Luc. *Being Given: Toward a Phenomenology of Givenness*. Palo Alto, CA: Stanford University Press, 2002.

———. *God without Being: Hors-Texte*. Chicago: University of Chicago Press, 1995.

———. *In Excess: Studies of Saturated Phenomena*. New York: Fordham University Press, 2002.

Marmura, Michael. "Ghazali and Demonstrative Science." *Journal of the History of Philosophy* 3, no. 2 (1965): 183–204.

Marx, Karl. *Economic and Philosophical Manuscripts of 1844*. Translated by Martin Milligan. New York: Prometheus, 1978.

———. "The German Ideology, Part I." In *The Marx-Engels Reader*, edited by Robert C. Tucker, 147–200. New York: Norton, 1978.

———. "The Holy Family (Excerpts)." In *Writings of the Young Marx on Philosophy and Society*, edited by David L. Easton and Kurt H. Guddat, 361–87. Indianapolis: Hackett, 1997.

———. *The Marx-Engels Reader*. Edited by Robert C. Tucker. New York: Norton, 1978.

———. "Theses on Feuerbach." In *The Marx-Engels Reader*, edited by Robert C. Tucker, 143–45. New York: Norton, 1978.

Marx, Werner. *Heidegger and the Tradition*. Evanston, IL: Northwestern University Press, 1982.

May, Vivian M. "'Speaking into the Void'? Intersectionality Critiques and Epistemic Backlash." *Hypatia* 29, no. 1 (2014): 94–112.

Maybudi, Rashid al-Din. *The Unveiling of the Mysteries and the Provision of the Pious*. Translated by William Chittick. Louisville, KY: Fons Vitae, 2015.

McCarthy, Richard J. *Freedom and Fulfillment: An Annotated Translation of al-Ghazālī's al-Munqidh Min al-Ḍalāl and Other Relevant Works of al-Ghazālī*. New York: Macmillan, 1980.

McDowell, John. *Mind and World*. Cambridge, MA: Harvard University Press, 1994.

———. "Subjective, Intersubjective, Objective." In *The Engaged Intellect: Philosophical Essays*, 152–59. Cambridge, MA: Harvard University Press, 2009.

McGinn, Marie. "The Real Problem of Others: Cavell, Merleau-Ponty and Wittgenstein on Scepticism about Other Minds." *European Journal of Philosophy* 6, no. 1 (1998): 45–58.

Medina, José. *The Epistemology of Resistance: Gender and Racial Oppression, Epistemic Injustice, and the Social Imagination*. Oxford: Oxford University Press, 2013.

Melamed, Yitzhak Y. "Salomon Maimon et l'échec de la philosophie juive moderne." *Revue Germanique Internationale*, no. 9 (Winter 2009): 175–87.

Mendelssohn, Moses. *Morning Hours: Lectures on God's Existence*. Dordrecht, Neth.: Springer, 2011.

Mensch, James R. *Levinas's Existential Analytic: A Commentary on "Totality and Infinity."* Evanston, IL: Northwestern University Press, 2015.

Mercer, Christia. *Leibniz's Metaphysics: Its Origins and Development*. Cambridge: Cambridge University Press, 2001.

Merleau-Ponty, Maurice. *Phenomenology of Perception*. Translated by Colin Smith. London: Routledge, 2002.

Mignolo, Walter. *The Darker Side of Western Modernity: Global Futures, Decolonial Options*. Durham, NC: Duke University Press, 2011.

Mills, Charles W. *The Racial Contract*. Ithaca, NY: Cornell University Press, 1997.

Mitchell, Andrew J., and Peter Trawny, eds. *Heidegger's Black Notebooks: Responses to Anti-Semitism*. New York: Columbia University Press, 2017.

Moran, Dermot. *Introduction to Phenomenology*. London: Routledge, 2002.

Moran, Richard. *Authority and Estrangement: An Essay on Self-Knowledge*. Princeton, NJ: Princeton University Press, 2001.

Morgan, Michael L. *Beyond Auschwitz: Post-Holocaust Jewish Thought in America*. Oxford: Oxford University Press, 2001.

———. *Discovering Levinas*. Cambridge: Cambridge University Press, 2007.

———. "Emmanuel Levinas as a Philosopher of the Ordinary." In *Totality and Infinity at 50*, edited by Diane Perpich and Scott Davidson, 209–26. Pittsburgh, PA: Duquesne University Press, 2012.

———. "Levinas on God and the Trace of the Other." In *The Oxford Handbook of Emmanuel Levinas*, edited by Michael Morgan, 321–43. Oxford: Oxford University Press, 2019.

Most, Glenn. "Heidegger's Greeks." *Arion* 10, no. 1 (2002): 83–98.

Moyn, Samuel. "Emmanuel Levinas's Talmudic Readings: Between Tradition and Invention." *Prooftexts* 23, no. 3 (2003): 338–64.

———. "Judaism against Paganism: Emmanuel Levinas's Response to Heidegger and Nazism in the 1930s." *History and Memory* 10, no. 1 (1998): 25–58.

Nadler, Steven. *Spinoza and Medieval Jewish Philosophy*. Cambridge: Cambridge University Press, 2014.

Nancy, Jean-Luc. *The Banality of Heidegger*. Translated by Jeff Fort. New York: Fordham University Press, 2017.

Neiman, Susan. *Evil in Modern Thought: An Alternative History of Philosophy*. Princeton, NJ: Princeton University Press, 2002.

Nelson, Eric. *Levinas, Adorno, and the Ethics of the Material Other*. Buffalo, NY: SUNY Press, 2019.

Neuhouser, Frederick. *Foundations of Hegel's Social Theory: Actualizing Freedom*. Cambridge, MA: Harvard University Press, 2003.

———. *Rousseau's Theodicy of Self-Love: Evil, Rationality, and the Drive for Recognition*. Oxford: Oxford University Press, 2008.

Ng, Karen. "Ideology Critique from Hegel and Marx to Critical Theory." *Constellations* 22, no. 3 (2015): 393–404.

Nirenberg, David. *Anti-Judaism: The Western Tradition*. New York: W. W. Norton, 2013.

Norris, Andrew. *Becoming Who We Are: Politics and Practical Philosophy in the Work of Stanley Cavell*. Oxford: Oxford University Press, 2017.

Nuland, Sherwin B. *The Soul of Medicine: Tales from the Bedside*. New York: Kaplan, 2009.

Nuzzo, Angelica. "Reflective Judgment, Determinative Judgment, and the Problem of Particularity." *Washington University Jurisprudence Review* 6, no. 1 (2013): 7–25.

O'Connor, Brian. "Adorno, Heidegger and the Critique of Epistemology." *Philosophy and Social Criticism* 24, no. 4 (1998): 43–62.

———. "Philosophy of History." In *Theodor Adorno: Key Concepts*, edited by Deborah Cook, 179–96. Stocksfield, UK: Acumen, 2008.

O'Connor, Timothy. *Persons and Causes: The Metaphysics of Free Will*. Oxford: Oxford University Press, 2002.

Ormsby, Eric. *Ghazali*. Oxford, UK: Oneworld, 2007.

O'Rourke, James J. *The Problem of Freedom in Marxist Thought*. Dordrecht, Neth.: D. Reidel, 2012.

Overgaard, Søren. "The Problem of Other Minds: Wittgenstein's Phenomenological Perspective." *Phenomenology and the Cognitive Sciences* 5, no. 1 (2006): 53–73.

———. "Rethinking Other Minds: Wittgenstein and Levinas on Expression." *Inquiry* 48, no. 3 (2005): 249–74.

———. *Wittgenstein and Other Minds: Rethinking Subjectivity and Intersubjectivity with Wittgenstein, Levinas, and Husserl*. London: Routledge, 2007.

Parekh, Serena. *Hannah Arendt and the Challenge of Modernity: A Phenomenology of Human Rights*. London: Routledge, 2008.

Patten, Alan. *Hegel's Idea of Freedom*. Oxford: Oxford University Press, 1999.

Peacocke, Christopher R. *Sense and Content: Experience, Thought, and Their Relations*. Oxford, UK: Clarendon, 1983.

Pearson, James. "Distinguishing W. V. Quine and Donald Davidson." *Journal for the History of Analytical Philosophy* 1, no. 1 (2011): 1–22.

Pensky, Max. "Toward a Critical Theory of Death: Adorno on Dying Today." *Adorno Studies* 1, no. 1 (2017): 43–65.

Peperzak, Adriaan. *Beyond: The Philosophy of Emmanuel Levinas*. Evanston, IL: Northwestern University Press, 1997.

———. "Beyond Being." *Research in Phenomenology* 8, no. 1 (1978): 239–61.

———. *To the Other: An Introduction to the Philosophy of Emmanuel Levinas*. West Lafayette, IN: Purdue University Press, 1993.

Perpich, Diane. *The Ethics of Emmanuel Levinas*. Stanford, CA: Stanford University Press, 2008.

Pessin, Sarah. "On Glimpsing the Face of God in Maimonides: Wonder, 'Hylomorphic Apophasis' and the Divine Prayer Shawl." *Tópicos (México)*, no. 42 (2012): 75–105.

Piketty, Thomas. *Capital in the 21st Century*. Cambridge, MA: Harvard University Press, 2014.

Pines, Shlomo. "The Limitations of Human Knowledge according to al-Farabi, ibn Bajja, and Maimonides." In *Studies in Medieval Jewish History and Literature*, edited by Isadore Twersky, 1–82. Cambridge, MA: Harvard University Press, 1979.

Pinkard, Terry. *Does History Make Sense?: Hegel on the Historical Shapes of Justice*. Cambridge, MA: Harvard University Press, 2017.

———. "Innen, Aussen und Lebensformen: Hegel und Wittgenstein." In *Hegels Erbe*, 254–92. Frankfurt: Suhrkamp, 2004.

———. "What Is a Shape of Spirit?" In *The Phenomenology of Spirit: A Critical Guide*, edited by Dean Moyar and Michael Quante, 112–30. Cambridge: Cambridge University Press, 2008.

Pippin, Robert B. *Hegel on Self-Consciousness: Desire and Death in the Phenomenology of Spirit*. Princeton, NJ: Princeton University Press, 2011.

———. *Hegel's Practical Philosophy: Rational Agency as Ethical Life*. Cambridge: Cambridge University Press, 2008.

———. "Natural and Normative." *Daedalus* 138, no. 3 (2009): 35–43.

———. "Naturalness and Mindedness: Hegel's Compatibilism." *European Journal of Philosophy* 7, no. 2 (1999): 194–212.

———. "Necessary Conditions for the Possibility of What Isn't: Heidegger on Failed Meaning." In *The Persistence of Subjectivity*, 57–79. Cambridge: Cambridge University Press, 2005.

———. "On Being Anti-Cartesian: Hegel, Heidegger, Subjectivity, and Sociality." In *Idealism as Modernism: Hegelian Variations*, 375–94. Cambridge: Cambridge University Press, 1997.

———. "What Is the Question for Which Hegel's Theory of Recognition Is the Answer?" *European Journal of Philosophy* 8, no. 2 (2000): 155–72.

Plant, Bob. *Wittgenstein and Levinas: Ethical and Religious Thought*. London: Routledge, 2005.

Popper, Karl. *The Open Society and Its Enemies*. London: Routledge, 2006.

Postone, Moishe. *Time, Labor, and Domination: A Reinterpretation of Marx's Critical Theory*. Cambridge: Cambridge University Press, 1993.

Pritchard, Elizabeth A. "Bilderverbot Meets Body in Theodor W. Adorno's Inverse Theology." *Harvard Theological Review* 95, no. 3 (2002): 291–318.

Putnam, Hilary. *Jewish Philosophy as a Guide to Life: Rosenzweig, Buber, Levinas, Wittgenstein*. Bloomington: Indiana University Press, 2008.

———. "Philosophy as the Education of Grownups: Stanley Cavell and Skepticism." In *Reading Cavell*, edited by Alice Crary and Sanford Shieh, 129–40. London: Routledge, 2006.

———. *Reason, Truth and History*. Cambridge: Cambridge University Press, 1981.

Quine, William Van Orman. *Word and Object*. Cambridge, MA: MIT Press, 1960.

Ramberg, Bjørn. *Donald Davidson: Philosophy of Language*. Basel, Switz.: Wiley-Blackwell, 1991.

———. "Post-ontological Philosophy of Mind: Rorty versus Davidson." In *Rorty and His Critics*, edited by Robert B. Brandom, 351–70. Oxford, UK: Blackwell, 2000.

Rand, Sebastian. "The Importance and Relevance of Hegel's Philosophy of Nature." *Review of Metaphysics* 61, no. 2 (2007): 379–400.

Ravitzky, Aviezer. "Maimonides: Esotericism and Educational Philosophy." In *The Cambridge Companion to Moses Maimonides*, edited by Kenneth Seeskin, 300–324. Cambridge: Cambridge University Press, 2005.

Ravven, Heidi M., and Lenn E. Goodman. *Jewish Themes in Spinoza's Philosophy*. Buffalo, NY: SUNY Press, 2012.

Reines, Alvin J. "Maimonides's True Belief concerning God: A Systematization." In *Maimonides and Philosophy: Papers Presented at the Sixth Jerusalem Philosophical Encounter*, edited by Shlomo Pines and Yirmiyahu Yovel, 24–36. Dordrecht, Neth.: Martinus Nijhoff, 1986.

Rensmann, Lars, and Samir Gandesha. *Arendt and Adorno: Political and Philosophical Investigations*. Palo Alto, CA: Stanford University Press, 2012.

Rhees, Rush. "What Is Language?" In *Wittgenstein and the Possibility of Discourse*, edited by D. Z. Phillips, 21–32. Cambridge: Cambridge University Press, 1998.

Robinson, James T. *Samuel ibn Tibbon's Commentary on Ecclesiastes: The Book of the Soul of Man*. Tübingen, Ger.: Mohr Siebeck, 2007.

Rödl, Sebastian. "The Form of the Will." In *Desire, Practical Reason, and the Good*, edited by Sergio Tenenbaum, 138–60. Oxford: Oxford University Press, 2010.

Rorty, Richard. "Kant vs. Dewey: The Current Situation of Moral Philosophy." In *Philosophy as Cultural Politics: Philosophical Papers*, 4: 184–202. Cambridge: Cambridge University Press, 2007.

———. "Response to Simon Critchley." In *Deconstruction and Pragmatism*, edited by Chantal Mouffe, 41–46. London: Routledge, 1996.

———. "The World Well Lost." In *Consequences of Pragmatism: Essays, 1972–1980*, 1–18. Minneapolis: University of Minnesota Press, 1982.

Rose, Gillian. *The Melancholy Science: An Introduction to the Thought of Theodor W. Adorno*. New York: Columbia University Press, 1978.

Rosenberg, Shalom. "The Concept of Belief in the Thought of Maimonides and His Successors (Hebrew)." *Bar-Ilan Yearbook*, no. 22–23 (1987–1988): 351–89.

———. "The Concept of '*Emunah* in Post-Maimonidean Philosophy." In *Studies in Medieval Jewish Thought and History*, edited by Isadore Twersky, 2: 273–308. Cambridge, MA: Harvard University Press, 1987.

Rosenthal, Franz. *Knowledge Triumphant: The Concept of Knowledge in Medieval Islam*. Leiden, Neth.: Brill, 1970.

Rosenthal, Jerome. "Voltaire's Philosophy of History." *Journal of the History of Ideas* (1955): 151–78.

Rosenzweig, Franz. *The Star of Redemption*. Madison: University of Wisconsin Pres, 2005.

Rousseau, Jean-Jacques. "Discourse on the Origin of Inequality." Translated by Donald A. Cress. In *Basic Political Writings*, edited by Donald A. Cress, 25–81. Indianapolis: Hackett, 1987.

---. "On the Social Contract." Translated by Donald A. Cress. In *Basic Political Writings*, edited by Donald A. Cress, 141–227. Indianapolis: Hackett, 1987.

Rudavsky, Tamar M. *Maimonides*. Oxford, UK: Blackwell, 2009.

Sachs, Carl. "The Acknowledgement of Transcendence: Anti-theodicy in Adorno and Levinas." *Philosophy and Social Criticism* 37, no. 3 (2011): 273–94.

---. *Intentionality and the Myths of the Given: Between Pragmatism and Phenomenology*. London: Routledge, 2016.

Sadler, Ted. *Heidegger and Aristotle: The Question of Being*. London: Athlone, 2000.

Samuelson, Norbert. "On Knowing God: Maimonides, Gersonides, and the Philosophy of Religion." *Judaism* 18, no. 1 (1969): 64–77.

Sartre, Jean-Paul. *Being and Nothingness* Translated by Hazel E. Barnes. New York: Philosophical Library, 1956.

Scholem, Gershom. *Major Trends in Jewish Mysticism*. New York: Schocken, 2011.

---. "Revelation and Tradition as Religious Categories." Translated by Michael A. Meyer. In *The Messianic Idea in Judaism and Other Essays on Jewish Spirituality*, 282–303. New York: Schocken, 2011.

---. "What Is Judaism?" Translated by Jonathan Chipman. In *On the Possibility of Jewish Mysticism in Our Time and Other Essays*, edited by Avraham Shapira, 114–17. Philadelphia: Jewish Publication Society, 1997.

Schwartz, Dov. "Avicenna and Maimonides on Imortality." In *Medieval and Modern Perceptions on Jewish-Muslim Relations*, edited by Ronald Nettler, 185–97. Luxembourg: Psychology Press, 1995.

Schwartz, Regina M. *The Curse of Cain: The Violent Legacy of Monotheism*. Chicago: University of Chicago Press, 1998.

Schwarzschild, Steven. "An Agenda for Jewish Philosophy in the 1980s." In *Studies in Jewish Philosophy*, edited by Norbert Samuelson, 101–25. Lanham, MD: University Press of America, 1987.

Searle, John. *The Construction of Social Reality*. New York: Free Press, 1995.

Seeskin, Kenneth. *Jewish Philosophy in a Secular Age*. Albany, NY: SUNY Press, 1990.

---. "Maimonides' Sense of History." *Jewish History* 18, nos. 2–3 (2004): 129–45.

---. "Metaphysics and Its Transcendence." In *The Cambridge Companion to Moses Maimonides*, edited by Kenneth Seeskin, 82–104. Cambridge: Cambridge University Press, 2005.

Sellars, Wilfrid. *Empiricism and the Philosophy of Mind*. Cambridge, MA: Harvard University Press, 1997.

Shapiro, Marc B. *The Limits of Orthodox Theology: Maimonides' Thirteen Principles Reappraised*. Oxford, UK: Littman Library of Jewish Civilization, 2004.

Sharvit, Gilad, and Karen S. Feldman. *Freud and Monotheism: Moses and the Violent Origins of Religion*. New York: Fordham University Press, 2018.

Sheehan, Thomas. "Heidegger, Aristotle and Phenomenology." *Philosophy Today* 19, no. 2 (1975): 87–94.

Shehadi, Fadlou Albert. *Ghazali's Unique Unknowable God*. Leiden, Neth.: Brill, 1964.

Shuster, Martin. *Autonomy after Auschwitz: Adorno, German Idealism, and Modernity*. Chicago: University of Chicago Press, 2014.

———. "Being as Breath, Vapor as Joy: Using Martin Heidegger to Re-read the Book of Ecclesiastes." *Journal for the Study of the Old Testament* 33, no. 2 (2008): 219–44.

———. "Education for the World: Adorno and Cavell." In *Dissonant Methods: Undoing Discipline in the Humanities Classroom*, edited by Ada Jaarsma and Kit Dobson, 48–64. Edmonton: University of Alberta Press, 2019.

———. "Language and Loneliness: Arendt, Cavell, and Modernity." *International Journal of Philosophical Studies* 20, no. 4 (2012): 473–97.

———. "Levinas and German Idealism: Fichte and Hegel." In *The Oxford Handbook of Emmanuel Levinas*, edited by Michael Morgan, 195–219. Oxford: Oxford University Press, 2019.

———. "Nothing to Know: The Epistemology of Moral Perfectionism in Adorno and Cavell." *Idealistic Studies* 44, no. 1 (2015): 1–29.

———. "Rorty and (the Politics of) Love." *Graduate Faculty Philosophy Journal* 40, no. 1 (2019): 65–78.

Silberbusch, Oshrat. *Adorno's Philosophy of the Nonidentical*. Dordrecht, Neth.: Springer, 2018.

Singer, Peter. "Famine, Affluence, and Morality." *Philosophy and Public Affairs* (1972): 229–43.

Slabodsky, Santiago. *Decolonial Judaism: Triumphal Failures of Barbaric Thinking*. London: Palgrave Macmillan, 2014.

Smith, Adam. *The Wealth of Nations*. New York: Modern Library, 1937.

Smith, Craig. *Adam Smith's Political Philosophy: The Invisible Hand and Spontaneous Order*. London: Routledge, 2006.

Smith, Nick. "Adorno vs. Levinas: Evaluating Points of Contention." *Continental Philosophy Review* 40, no. 3 (2007): 275–306.

Smith, Steven B. *Modernity and Its Discontents: Making and Unmaking the Bourgeois from Machiavelli to Bellow*. New Haven, CT: Yale University Press, 2016.
Soloveitchik, Joseph B. *Halakhic Man*. Translated by Lawrence Kaplan. Philadelphia: Jewish Publication Society, 1983.
Sommer, Marc Nicolas. *Das Konzept einer negativen Dialektik: Adorno und Hegel*. Tübingen, Ger.: Mohr Siebeck, 2016.
Spero, Shubert. "Is the God of Maimonides Truly Unknowable?" *Judaism* 22, no. 1 (1973): 66–78.
———. "Maimonides and the Sense of History." *Tradition* 24, no. 2 (1989): 128–37.
Spinoza, Baruch. *The Letters*. Translated by Samuel Shirley. Indianapolis: Hackett, 1995.
Standish, Paul. "Education for Grown-ups, a Religion for Adults: Scepticism and Alterity in Cavell and Levinas." *Ethics and Education* 2, no. 1 (2007): 73–91.
Stanislawski, Michael. *For Whom Do I Toil?: Judah Leib Gordon and the Crisis of Russian Jewry*. Oxford: Oxford University Press, 1988.
Stauffer, Jill. *Ethical Loneliness: The Injustice of Not Being Heard*. New York: Columbia University Press, 2015.
Stern, Josef. *The Matter and Form of Maimonides' Guide*. Cambridge, MA: Harvard University Press, 2013.
Stewart, Jon. "The Architectonic of Hegel's Phenomenology of Spirit." *Philosophy and Phenomenological Research* 55, no. 4 (1995): 747–76.
Stolz, Fritz. *Einführung in den biblischen Monotheismus*. Darmstadt, Ger.: Wissenschaftliche Buchgeselschaft, 1996.
Strauss, Leo. *Leo Strauss on Maimonides: The Complete Writings*. Edited by Kenneth Hart Green. Chicago: University of Chicago Press, 2013.
Strhan, Anna. *Levinas, Subjectivity, Education: Towards an Ethics of Radical Responsibility*. London: Blackwell, 2012.
Stroebel, Leslie. *View Camera Technique*. Woburn, MA: Focal, 1999.
Stroud, Barry. *Understanding Human Knowledge: Philosophical Essays*. Oxford: Oxford University Press, 2002.
Stroumsa, Guy G. *The Making of the Abrahamic Religions in Late Antiquity*. Oxford: Oxford University Press, 2015.
Stroumsa, Sarah. *Maimonides in His World: Portrait of a Mediterranean Thinker*. Princeton, NJ: Princeton University Press, 2009.
Swinburne, Richard. *The Concept of Miracle*. Dordrecht, Neth.: Springer, 1970.
———. *The Existence of God*. Oxford: Oxford University Press, 2004.

Thiem, Annika. "Adorno's Tears: Textures of Philosophical Emotionality." *MLN* 124, no. 3 (2009): 592–613.

Thoreau, Henry D. *Walden*. Princeton, NJ: Princeton University Press, 1971.

Todd, Sharon. *Learning from the Other: Levinas, Psychoanalysis, and Ethical Possibilities in Education*. Buffalo, NY: SUNY Press, 2003.

Troeltsch, Ernst. *Der Historismus und seine Probleme*. Tübingen, Ger.: J. C. B. Mohr, 1922.

Twersky, Isadore. *Introduction to the Code of Maimonides (Mishneh Torah)*. New Haven, CT: Yale University Press, 1980.

———. "The *Mishneh Torah* of Maimonides." *Proceedings of the Israel Academy of Sciences and Humanities* 5 (1976): 265–95.

Van Ess, Josef. *Die Erkenntnislehre des 'Adudaddin al-Ici: Übersetzung und Kommentar des ersten Buches seiner Mawaqif*. Wiesbaden, Ger.: Franz Steiner, 1966.

Vasey, Craig R. "Emmanuel Levinas: From Intentionality to Proximity." *Philosophy Today* 25, no. 3 (1981): 178–95.

Vital, Haim. *Sha'ar Hagilgulim*. Jerusalem: Yeshivat Kol, 1981.

Weisman, Tama. *Hannah Arendt and Karl Marx: On Totalitarianism and the Tradition of Western Political Thought*. Lanham, MD: Lexington, 2013.

West, Cornel. *Prophetic Fragments: Illuminations of the Crisis in American Religion and Culture*. Grand Rapids, MI: William B. Eerdmans, 1993.

Whitehead, Alfred North. "Process and Reality: An Essay in Cosmology." New York: Free Press, 1978.

Whyman, Tom. "Understanding Adorno on 'Natural-History.'" *International Journal of Philosophical Studies* 24, no. 4 (2016): 452–72.

Wiggins, David. "A Sensible Subjectivism?" In *Foundations of Ethics: An Anthology*, edited by Russ Shafer-Landau and Terence Cuneo, 145–57. Oxford, UK: Wiley-Blackwell, 2007.

Wildt, Andreas. *Die Anthropologie des frühen Marx*. Hagen, Ger.: Kuirs der Fernuniversität, 1987.

Wittgenstein, Ludwig. *On Certainty*. New York: Harper and Row, 1969.

———. *Philosophical Investigations*. Translated by G. E. M. Anscombe. Upper Saddle River, NJ: Prentice Hall, 1958.

———. *Remarks on the Philosophy of Psychology*. 2 vols. Chicago: University of Chicago Press, 1988.

———. *Zettel*. Edited by G. E. M. Anscombe and Georg Henrik von Wright. Translated by G. E. M. Anscombe. Berkeley: University of California Press, 1967.

Wolff, Jonathan. *Why Read Marx Today?* Oxford: Oxford University Press, 2003.

Wolfson, Elliot R. *The Duplicity of Philosophy's Shadow: Heidegger, Nazism, and the Jewish Other*. New York: Columbia University Press, 2018.

———. *Giving Beyond the Gift: Apophasis and the Overcoming of Theomania*. New York: Fordham University Press, 2014.

Wyschogrod, Edith. "God and 'Being's Move' in the Philosophy of Emmanuel Levinas." *Journal of Religion* 62, no. 2 (1982): 145–55.

Wyschogrod, Michael. *The Body of Faith: God and the People of Israel*. New York: Seabury, 1996.

Yeomans, Christopher. *Freedom and Reflection: Hegel and the Logic of Agency*. Oxford: Oxford University Press, 2011.

Yovel, Yirmiyahu. "God's Transcendence and Its Schematization." In *Maimonides and Philosophy: Papers Presented at the Sixth Jerusalem Philosophical Encounter*, edited by Shlomo Pines and Yirmiyahu Yovel, 269–83. Dordrecht, Neth.: Martinus Nijhoff, 1986.

Zahavi, Dan. *Husserl's Phenomenology*. Palo Alto, CA: Stanford University Press, 2003.

———. *The Oxford Handbook of the History of Phenomenology*. Oxford: Oxford University Press, 2018.

Zarader, Marlène. *The Unthought Debt: Heidegger and the Hebraic Heritage*. Translated by Bettina Bergo. Palo Alto, CA: Stanford University Press, 2006.

Zuidevaart, Lambert "Truth and Authentication: Heidegger and Adorno in Reverse." In Macdonald and Ziarek, *Adorno and Heidegger*, 6–22.

INDEX

acknowledgment. *See* Cavell, Stanley, acknowledgment
Adorno, Theodor W.: Auschwitz, 74, 76, 84–85, 97–98, 102, 112; and Cavell, 77; and Kafka, 110–111, 113–114; and Levinas, 107; negation, 76–82, 106–109; negativity, 100–108; materialism, 82–87, 91–100; metaphysics, 87–100, 142–143; moral perfectionism, 78, 148; morality as not being at home in the world, 152–157; new categorical imperative, 76, 84, 89, 108; and Spinoza, 78–81; suffering, 76, 82–87, 105–108, 111–116; theology, 108–111
al-Ghazālī, 19, 32, 36–37, 40–42, 44–46, 54, 58, 66
anachronism: between self and world, 9, 11, 21, 64–65, 114, 119, 155, 204, 206–208; meaning of, 1, 3, 5–6, 9, 11–12, 15–167, 19, 21–24, 64–65, 82, 114, 119, 124, 134, 139, 155, 202, 204, 207–208; non-coincidence with time, 1, 206–208; as phenomenological category, 3, 15, 23
antisemitism, 13–15, 203, 208
apophatic theology. *See* negative theology
Arendt, Hannah, 15, 22, 32, 109–110, 115–116, 121, 136, 143, 159, 182

Aristotle, 19, 32, 35–37, 47, 50, 52–55, 60, 76, 88–96, 100–101
Assman, Jan, 2
Auschwitz, 74, 76, 78, 84–86, 95, 97, 98–99, 102, 105, 112, 122, 124, 127, 132, 155, 182
Avicenna, 47, 53–55

Benjamin, Walter, 17–18, 109–110, 116, 119, 123, 139–141, 143–145, 150–153, 155–156
Bloch, Ernst, 79–80

Camus, Albert, 114
Cavell, Stanley: acknowledgment, 48–49, 184–195; fantasy of inexpressiveness, 178–181; and Levinas, 158–202; scene of instruction, 174; skepticism, in the work of, 193–201; and Wittgenstein, 9, 173, 177, 184–185, 190, 194; word projection, 171
colonialism, 14–15
constellation, 17–18, 31, 110

Davidson, Donald, 160–162, 166–171, 174, 189
Derrida, Jacques, 12, 15, 18, 139, 194–195, 200, 211–212
Descartes, Réne, 95, 164

239

embodiment, 9, 189–190
epistemology, 36, 67, 78, 146, 148, 181
evil, 14, 57, 74, 86, 115–116, 122, 156–157

Fackenheim, Emil, 4
Frankfurt School, the, 17, 85
Freud, Sigmund, 2, 34, 205–206, 208

God, 9–10, 19, 22, 24, 31–35, 41, 46–48, 54–56, 59–61, 63–64, 66, 68–71, 73, 85, 88, 94–95, 112, 115, 122, 155–157, 163, 194, 199, 201, 205–207; and negative theology, 32, 157; and trace, 22, 200
Guide for the Perplexed: concept of certainty in, 34–47; God as first existent in, 47; money changer parable in, 56–58; puzzle in, 33; title of, 19

Hegel, Georg, 81, 101–102, 120, 123–139, 147, 151, 152, 154–156, 179
Heidegger, Martin: and ancient Greeks, 47–48, 50–56; antisemitism of, 203–204; and Aristotle, 32, 47, 50, 52–55; attunement in the work of, 75–76; and certainty of death in the work of, 37–40; and measure, 10
Hirsch, Samson, 22
history: philosophy of history, in Adorno and Benjamin, 139–152; philosophy of history, in Hegel, 127–133; philosophy of history, in Marx, 133–138; universal history, 123–126
Hitlerism, philosophy of, 7, 182

Husserl, Edmund, 3–4, 8, 11, 21, 159, 177, 186

Islam, 5, 12, 18–20, 32, 36–37, 39–41, 44, 46–47, 50, 53–55, 60, 66

Jewish: difference, 2; mysticism, 2, 4–5 (*see also* Kabbalah); philosophy, 17, 22–25, 41, 46, 78. *See also* Judaism
Judaism: as anachronism, 1–9, 11–12, 16–17, 19, 21–24, 204, 206–208; and doubt, 16, 206; as having an essence, 2

Kabbalah, 5, 37, 49
Kafka, Franz, 110–111
Kant, Immanuel, 64, 67–68, 73, 84, 92, 95, 98, 105–106, 112, 120–21, 125, 127–128, 134, 142–143, 145, 168; *Critique of Judgment*, 67–68, 120–121; reflective judgment, 120–121

language: as battering-ram, 176, 190; being a master of, 170–171, 174–175, 197; and disagreement, 167, 170, 175, 179, 183–184; as discourse, 162–165; as infinity, 163–165; as inheritance, 173, 197–198; word projection. *See* Cavell, Stanley, word projection
Leibniz, Gottfried Wilhelm, 47, 49–50
Levinas, Emmanuel: and Cavell, 158–202; face, 177–178, 188, 192–195; Hitlerism, philosophy of, *see* Hitlerism, philosophy of; Other, 165–168, 170, 173–174, 178–180, 182–183, 186–197,

199–200, 205, 208; skepticism, in the work of, 193–201; true temporality, in the work of, 6
Lukács, György, 82–84, 139, 149–150

Maimonides, Moses: death of brother of, 75; and *Guide for the Perplexed*, see *Guide for the Perplexed*; and Islam, 18–19; and *Mishneh Torah*, 19; and phenomenology, 18
Marx, Karl, 45, 77, 82, 98–99, 116, 123–124, 127, 134–139, 144
Merleau-Ponty, Maurice, 3, 9, 187, 189
monotheism, 1–3, 5–6, 12, 205, 207–208
Moses, 59–60, 62–64, 69–70

Nazi, 11, 13–15, 75, 148, 162–163, 182
negative theology, 17, 32, 70, 80, 113, 157; in Adorno, 70–80; Maimonides, 68–69
normativity, 8, 10, 63, 158

ontological. *See* ontology
ontology, 30, 50, 99, 110, 147–148, 170, 183

phenomenology: and appearances, 3–4; and concept of having a world, 4, 57, 68; and Husserl, 3; in Maimonides, 29–73; as religious phenomenology, 31
philosophy of action, 7
philosophy of history. *See* history
Pinkard, Terry, 129–130, 133, 138, 179

Pippin, Robert, 8, 101, 124–125, 128, 147

Quran, the, 36

Rorty, Richard, 62, 77, 160, 162, 168
Rousseau, Jean-Jacques, 57, 126–127, 134

Sartre, Jean-Paul, 3, 102, 178
Scholem, Gershom, 2, 5, 11, 12, 201
Sellars, Wilfrid, 8, 124, 129, 181
skepticism, 22, 42, 49, 114, 169–170, 175–176, 184–186, 193–200, 210
Smith, Adam, 127
spiritual exercises: and Pierre Hadot, 72; in Maimonides, 69–72
Strauss, Leo, 30, 31

Talmud, 6, 11, 20, 22–23, 63, 70
tikun olam, 4
Thoreau, Henry, 30
Torah, 15, 19–20, 60–61, 69–70
tradition: and Judaism, 19; meaning of, 17–18, 19

Voltaire, 125–126

Wittgenstein, Ludwig, 9, 22, 25, 42–43, 114, 130, 170, 172–174, 176–179, 184–185, 187, 190, 194, 197
world: and cognition, 5; feeling "at home" in, 24; and self, 9; and suffering, 24; and wonder, 29–73, 75–76, 114, 119, 193, 206; worldlessness, *see* Heidegger, Martin, antisemitism of

Zohar, the, 4–5

MARTIN SHUSTER is Associate Professor of Philosophy and holds the Professorship of Judaic Studies and Justice at Goucher College in Baltimore, Maryland, where he previously directed the Judaic studies program and where he currently directs the Center for Geographies of Justice. In addition to many articles and book chapters across a range of topics, he is the author of *Autonomy after Auschwitz: Adorno, German Idealism, and Modernity* and *New Television: The Aesthetics and Politics of a Genre* and the coeditor of *Logics of Genocide: The Structures of Violence and the Contemporary World.*

www.ingramcontent.com/pod-product-compliance
Lightning Source LLC
Chambersburg PA
CBHW030105170426
43198CB00009B/502